W9-BHD-970

Studies on the Chinese Economy

General Editors: **Peter Nolan**, Sinyi Professor of Chinese Management, Judge Institute of Management Studies, University of Cambridge, and Fellow of Jesus College, Cambridge, England; and **Dong Fureng**, Professor, Chinese Academy of Social Sciences, Beijing, China

This series analyses issues in China's current economic development, and sheds light upon that process by examining China's economic history. It contains a wide range of books on the Chinese economy, past and present, and includes not only studies written by leading Western authorities but also translations of the most important works on the Chinese economy produced within China. It intends to make a major contribution towards understanding this immensely important part of the world economy.

Titles include:

Thomas Chan, Noel Tracy and Zhu Wenhui
CHINA'S EXPORT MIRACLE

Xu Dixin and Wu Chengming (*editors*)
CHINESE CAPITALISM, 1522–1840

Christopher Findlay and Andrew Watson (*editors*)
FOOD SECURITY AND ECONOMIC REFORM

Samuel P. S. Ho and Y. Y. Kueh
SUSTAINABLE ECONOMIC DEVELOPMENT IN SOUTH CHINA

Kali P. Kalirajan and Yanrui Wu (*editors*)
PRODUCTIVITY AND GROWTH IN CHINESE AGRICULTURE

Bozhong Li
AGRICULTURAL DEVELOPMENT IN JIANGNAN, 1620–1850

Alfred H. Y. Lin
THE RURAL ECONOMY OF GUANGDONG, 1870–1937

Dic Lo
MARKET AND INSTITUTIONAL REGULATION IN CHINESE INDUSTRIALIZATION

Jun Ma
THE CHINESE ECONOMY IN THE 1990s

Guo Rongxing
HOW THE CHINESE ECONOMY WORKS

Sally Sargeson
REWORKING CHINA'S PROLETARIAT

Ng Sek Hong and Malcolm Warner
CHINA'S TRADE UNIONS AND MANAGEMENT

Michael Twohey
AUTHORITY AND WELFARE IN CHINA

Wang Xiao-qiang
CHINA'S PRICE AND ENTERPRISE REFORM

Xiaoping Xu
CHINA'S FINANCIAL SYSTEM UNDER TRANSITION

Yanni Yan
INTERNATIONAL JOINT VENTURES IN CHINA

Wei-Wei Zhang
TRANSFORMING CHINA

Xiao-guang Zhang
CHINA'S TRADE PATTERNS AND INTERNATIONAL COMPARATIVE
ADVANTAGE

Studies on the Chinese Economy
Series Standing Order ISBN 0–333–71502–0
(*outside North America only*)

You can receive future titles in this series as they are published by placing a standing order.
Please contact your bookseller or, in case of difficulty, write to us at the address below with
your name and address, the title of the series and the ISBN quoted above.

Customer Services Department, Macmillan Distribution Ltd, Houndmills, Basingstoke,
Hampshire RG21 6XS, England

The Chinese Economy in the 1990s

Jun Ma
Economist
International Monetary Fund
Washington, DC

palgrave

Published by
PALGRAVE
Houndmills, Basingstoke, Hampshire RG21 6XS and
175 Fifth Avenue, New York, N. Y. 10010
Companies and representatives throughout the world

PALGRAVE is the new global academic imprint of
St. Martin's Press LLC Scholarly and Reference Division and
Palgrave Publishers Ltd (formerly Macmillan Press Ltd).

Outside North America
ISBN 0–333–75134–5

Inside North America
ISBN 0–312–22556–3

This book is printed on paper suitable for recycling and
made from fully managed and sustained forest sources.

A catalogue record for this book is available
from the British Library.

Library of Congress Cataloging-in-Publication Data
Ma, Jun, 1964–
The Chinese economy in the 1990s / Jun Ma.
    p. cm — (Studies on the Chinese economy)
    Includes bibliographical references and index.
    ISBN 0–312–22556–3 (cloth)
1. China—Economic conditions—1976– I. Title. II. Series.
HC427.92.M323   1999
330.951'059—dc21
                                                        99–23358
                                                        CIP

10   9   8   7   6   5   4   3   2
09   08   07   06   05   04   03   02   01

Printed and bound in Great Britain by
Antony Rowe Ltd, Chippenham, Wiltshire

To Ching and Albert

Contents

List of Tables

Acknowledgements

This book is based on about a dozen papers and notes that I wrote or co-authored with colleagues over the past few years for many journals, conferences, and research projects, as well as my lecture notes for teaching the course on Chinese Economy at George Washington University. During the course of these studies, I benefited from a vast number of people in the US and in China. On many policy issues, discussions with economists from the World Bank and the International Monetary Fund were especially useful. Among others, these colleagues include Rajiv Lall, Hyung-ki Kim, Anjali Kumar, Tamar Manuelyan Atinc, Anwar Shah, Heng-fu Zou, Bert Hofman, Harry Broadman, Albert Keidel, Kangbin Zheng, Yang Wang, Xiaofeng Hua, David Robinson, John Norregaard, Thomas Richardson, Michael Bell, Hoe Ee Khor, Hong Zheng, Jianming Qi, and Xiaolei Wang. Thanks are also due to Renhong Wu of the Centre for Strategic International Studies, Ying Liu of George Washington University, and George J. Viksnins and Stephanie Stanco of Georgetown University. Comments from conference and seminar participants at Georgetown University, Rutgers University, University of Minnesota, University of Chicago, the annual meetings of the Chinese Economist Society (North America), the monthly seminars ofthe Chinese Professional Forum (Washington, DC), the 1994 and 1995 annual meetings of the American Economist Association, and the 1995 annual meeting of the Association for Asian Studies also helped me develop and sharpen my arguments.

I also thank my friends in China, from whom I obtained much raw material and was informed about the current thinking of Chinese researchers and policy-makers. These people include Lu Baifu from the Development Research Centre of the State Council, Zhang Tong, Wong Weixing, and Yu Zhihua of the Ministry of Finance, Jiang Wangjin from the People's Bank of China, Guo Shuqing, Liu He, and Xu Lin from the State Planning Commission, Shen Hong from the Chinese Academy of Social Science, Wang Zhan from Shanghai Economic Research Centre Yu Li from Northeastern University of Finance and Economics, Jiang Jingfa from Jianxi University of Finance and Economics, Lu Deming from Fudan University Economic Research Center, Yi Zhengqiu from Guangdong System Reform Commission, Xu Jingan from Shenzhen System Reform Commission, Zhang Wei from Shanghai

Wangguo Brokerage, Nie Ming from Bank of China, and Deng Xi from the Agricultural Bank.

I thank Macmillan for its continued interest in my work – it published my first English book on *Intergovernmental Relations and Economic Management in China* in 1997, and now publishes my second book in English. I enjoyed working with the publishing editors in the production of this book. Special thanks to Sunder Katwala, Eleanor Birne, and Keith Povey, who oversaw the production process.

Portions of some chapters in this book appear in my articles for the *Journal of Contemporary China, World Development* and *Asian Economic Journal*. Two chapters of this book are based on papers co-authored with Dr Li Yu of Northeastern University of Finance and Economics of China, and Dr Kenneth Xu of CitiBank. My thanks to the Carfax Publishing Ltd, Elsevier Science Ltd, East Asian Economic Association, and Drs Yu and Xu for permissions to use these materials.

I owe a special debt to my wife, my parents and parents-in-law. My wife, Ching Chung, was very understanding about my inability to spend a great deal of time with our baby Albert during the writing of this book. Her constant encouragement and support, as well as those of my parents and parents-in-law, have been one of the most valuable inputs to this book. I should also thank our baby Albert for not turning off my computer once everyday.

Finally, I shall claim that I am the only person responsible for any remaining errors of this book. The views expressed in the book are mine and should not be attributed to the World Bank or the International Monetary Fund.

JUN MA

List of Abbreviations

BOC	Bank of China
BOCM	Bank of Communications
CBC	Construction Bank of China
CEE	Central and Eastern European
CITC	Consolidated Industrial and Commercial Tax
CITIC	China International Trust and Investment Corporation
CJV	Contractual Joint Venture
COE	Collectively Owned Enterprise
COV	Coefficient of Variation
CSRC	Chinese Securities Regulatory Commission
EJV	Equity Joint Venture
ETDZ	Economic and Technological Development Zones
FEAC	Foreign Exchange Adjustment Centres
FBIS	Federal Bureau of Information Services
FERT	Foreign Economic Relations and Trade
FDI	Foreign Direct Investment
FOV	Solely Foreign-owned Venture
FSU	Former Soviet Union
FTC	Foreign Trade Corporation
GDP	Gross Domestic Product
GNP	Gross National Product
ICBC	Industrial and Commercial Bank of China
IMF	International Monetary Fund
MOF	Ministry of Finance
MOFERT	Ministry of Foreign Economic Relations and Trade
MOFTEC	Ministry of Foreign Trade and Economic Cooperation
NBFI	Non-bank Financial Institutions
NFA	Net Foreign Assets
NTS	National Tax Services
NYSE	New York Stock Exchange
OLS	Ordinary Least Square
OTC	Over the Counter
PBC	People's Bank of China
RCC	Rural Credit Cooperatives
SAIC	State Administration of Industry and Commerce
SAMB	State Assests Management Bureau

SCSPC   State Council Securities Policy Committee
SD   Standard Deviation
SETC   State Economic and Trade Commission
SEZ   Special Economic Zone
SHSE   Shanghai Securities Exchange
SOE   State-owned Enterprise
SPC   State Planning Commission
SRC   State Economic System Reform Commission
SZSE   Shenzhen Securities Exchange
TFP   Total Factor Productivity
TIC   Trust and Investment Corporations
TVE   Township and Village Enterprise
UCC   Urban Credit Cooperatives
VAT   Value Added Tax

1
Introduction and Overview

This book presents a comprehensive overview and some economic analyses of China's economic reform experiences, particularly those since the late 1980s. It covers many institutional details in key aspects of the Chinese economy, including fiscal and monetary management, financial sector development, state-owned enterprise reform, international trade, foreign investment, decentralization and regional development. It is argued in the book that while China has achieved a spectacular growth record over the past 20 years, and its reform efforts have successfully laid the foundation of a market-based economic management system, the country continues to face major challenges in sustaining its growth performance. Based on a close examination of the reform policies adopted by the Chinese government, the book attempts to identify the institutional barriers to the effective implementation of these policies and to draw implications from other countries' experiences for China's future reform. This book will be of interest to scholars and students who study the Chinese economy.

What does this book contribute to the vast literature on the Chinese economy? First, while many books published over the past decade provide a historical overview of the Chinese economy, very few are recent enough to address reform experiences in the 1990s. China is experiencing rapid changes in all aspects of its economic system, and almost all books become outdated within a few years of their publication. This book attempts to provide students and researchers who study the Chinese economy with updated information within a systematic framework. Many reform measures initiated in the 1990s are discussed in detail, such as the tax assignment system, indirect monetary instruments, prudential regulations governing the banking system, stock markets, the shareholding experiment, the modern enterprise system, and various aspects of trade, foreign investment and regional development.

Secondly, this book combines both the perspectives of insiders and outsiders in examining the Chinese economy. As a former researcher with China's Development Research Centre of the State Council, I tend to look at issues in light of the institutional constraints faced by policy-makers. On the other hand, with formal training in western economics in the United States and years of work experience with the World Bank and the International Monetary Fund, I have become familiar with the analytical approaches used by western economists. I believe that combining the two different perspectives has helped the book generate insights that are both academically interesting and operationally realistic.

The next three sections of this chapter present a general overview of the Chinese economy, mainly written for readers who are not familiar with this subject. The first section offers a brief description of China's economic structure and growth performance, as compared with those of other countries. The second section looks at several key factors and policies that have contributed to China's economic performance over the past 20 years. The third section discusses the main challenges that China faces in sustaining its economic development in the future.

Growth Performance and Changes in Economic Structure[1]

From 1978 to 1997, China maintained an annual average Gross Domestic Product (GDP) growth rate of 10 per cent, higher than those of any other country in the world during the same period. Between 1992 and 1997, China's performance was even more impressive, with its annual average rate of GDP growth reaching 11 per cent (see Table 1.1). These achievements have been considered a miracle by many observers, especially in comparison with other former socialist countries that experienced significant economic downturns during the early and mid-1990s.[2,3]

As a result of rapid economic growth, the average income of the Chinese people also rose significantly. From 1978 to 1997, the real income of urban residents grew at an annual average rate of 6 per cent, and that of rural residents at an annual average rate of 8 per cent.[4] The growth of peasants' income drastically reduced China's officially measured poor population, which declined from 33 per cent in 1978 (World Bank, 1992) to around 4 per cent in 1997 (Li, 1998). In 1996, the government announced in its Ninth Five Year Plan that it would 'basically eliminate poverty by Year 2000'.[5]

Table 1.1   China: basic indicators, 1978–97

Year	Nominal GDP (yuan bn)	GDP index (1978=100)	Per capita GDP (yuan)	Percentage change of retail price index	Population (m)	Index of rural per capita income (1978=100)	Index of urban per capita income (1978=100)
1978	362.4	100.0	376.5	–	962.6	100.0	100.0
1980	451.8	116.0	457.7	6.0	987.1	138.1	127.0
1985	896.4	192.9	846.9	8.8	1 058.5	261.2	161.6
1986	1 020.2	210.0	949.0	6.0	1 075.1	267.9	182.5
1987	1 196.3	234.3	1 094.5	7.3	1 093.0	278.4	185.6
1988	1 492.8	260.7	1 344.6	18.5	1 110.3	289.6	187.9
1989	1 690.9	271.3	1 500.3	17.8	1 127.0	285.8	181.7
1990	1 854.8	281.7	1 622.3	2.1	1 143.3	300.7	197.8
1991	2 161.8	307.6	1 866.5	2.9	1 158.2	317.8	209.5
1992	2 663.8	351.4	2 273.4	5.4	1 171.7	328.1	228.3
1993	3 463.4	398.8	2 922.3	13.2	1 185.2	338.6	251.6
1994	4 675.9	449.3	3 901.5	21.7	1 198.5	355.5	273.7
1995	5 847.8	496.5	4 828.1	14.8	1 211.2	375.4	287.2
1996	6 779.5	544.2	5 539.3	6.0	1 223.9	409.2	296.7
1997	7 477.2	562.0	6 048.5	0.8	1 236.2	428.0	306.8

Sources: State Statistical Bureau, 1996, 1997a; Chen, 1998; Li, 1998.

China's rapid economic growth was accompanied by important changes in the sectoral composition of the economy. In 1978, agriculture, industry and construction, and services accounted for 28 per cent, 48 per cent, and 24 per cent of GDP, respectively. The past 19 years witnessed a significant decline in the importance of the agricultural sector and a corresponding increase in the significance of the service sector in the national economy. In 1997, the value added produced by these three sectors accounted for 20 per cent, 50 per cent, and 30 per cent of GDP, respectively (see Table 1.2). As a consequence of the shift from agricultural to nonagricultural activities, agricultural labour as a percentage of total employment dropped from over 70 per cent in 1978 to around 50 per cent in 1996. The growth of nonagricultural activities was most noteworthy in rural China, with the output of Township and Village Enterprises (TVEs) growing at an annual average real rate of over 20 per cent between 1978 and 1996. In terms of employment, those employed by TVEs accounted for 28 per cent of the total rural labour force in 1996, up from 9 per cent in 1978. In 1996, income generated from nonagricultural sources accounted for almost 40 per cent of total net income of China's rural population.

Table 1.2   China: composition of GDP and employment by sector, 1978–97 (%)

Year	Value added			Employment		
	Agriculture	Industry and construction	Services	Agriculture	Industry and construction	Services
1978	28.1	48.2	23.7	70.5	17.4	12.1
1980	30.1	48.5	21.4	68.7	18.3	13.0
1985	28.4	43.1	28.5	62.4	20.9	16.7
1986	27.1	44.0	28.9	60.9	21.9	17.2
1987	26.8	43.9	29.3	59.9	22.3	17.8
1988	25.7	44.1	30.2	59.3	22.4	18.3
1989	25.0	43.0	32.0	60.0	21.7	18.3
1990	27.0	41.6	31.3	60.1	21.4	18.5
1991	24.5	42.1	33.4	59.7	21.4	18.9
1992	21.8	43.9	34.3	58.5	21.7	19.8
1993	19.9	47.4	32.7	56.4	22.4	21.2
1994	20.2	47.8	31.9	54.3	22.7	23.0
1995	20.5	48.8	30.7	52.2	23.0	24.8
1996	20.5	49.6	29.9	50.5	23.5	26.0
1997	19.4	50.4	29.8	–	–	–

Sources: State Statistical Bureau, 1997a; Chen, 1998.

Key Factors Contributing to China's Growth Performance

The Chinese economy is an enormously complex system and its performance has been affected by numerous factors. In comparing the performance of China with those of Central and Eastern European (CEE) and former Soviet Union (FSU) countries, some observers emphasized the importance of such favourable initial conditions as China being an agriculture-based economy, having less stringent state control over economic activities, having a generally stable political environment, and being able to attract foreign investment from a large number of wealthy overseas Chinese (e.g. Sachs and Woo, 1994; World Bank, 1996c) at the onset of its reform. While some (but not all) of these arguments explain why CEE and FSU countries were not able to adopt the Chinese reform approach in general, they do not tell us why China could significantly enhance its growth performance since it adopted the market-oriented reform in 1978, compared to the period before 1978.[6] Clearly, the fundamental policy changes at the end of the 1970s, along with the continued reform efforts made by the government at both the central and local levels throughout the reform period, played an unequivocal role in stimulating and sustaining China's economic development over the past 20 years. Below we look at the five most important policy changes:

Decentralization   Decentralization has taken the form of delegating fiscal and administrative powers by the central government to the provincial and lower level governments. For example, in 1980, the central government decided to allow local governments to collect certain revenues and retain a substantial part of the proceeds. The significance of the decentralization effort was evidenced by the fact that, in 1997, the central government controlled only 27 per cent of total government expenditure, compared with 51 per cent in 1978 (see Chapter 2). Over the past two decades, the central government also relinquished substantial power in other aspects of economic management, including authorizing local governments to approve large investment projects, transferring many formerly centrally administered state-owned enterprises (SOEs) to localities, and allowing localities to play a more important role in setting local industrial policies and using resources from financial institutions (see Chapters 8 and 9). Despite their side effects (Ma, 1997), these decentralization efforts greatly stimulated the local authorities' enthusiasm and provided them with substantial resources in promoting local economic development. Benefiting from the central government's general strategy of 'experimenting with new policies first at the local level', many important policy innovations that proved successful nationwide indeed originated from localities.

Marketization and growth of the non-state sector   In the pre-reform era, the government controlled almost every aspect of the SOEs' operations, including production planning, price setting, product distribution, purchases of energy and raw materials, and wage and employment policies. A major achievement of the reform programme in the 1980s and early 1990s was the transformation of a government-run state enterprise sector to one that granted SOE managers substantial autonomy in their day-to-day management. For example, in the early 1980s, more than 80 per cent of commodity prices were controlled by the state, while in the mid-1990s this ratio declined to less than 10 per cent. Along with price liberalization, most SOEs, especially small and medium SOEs, have been authorized to make decisions in the planning of production and investment, marketing of products, and purchase of inputs. Reforms in the financial sector and labour market also provided SOEs with more flexibility in obtaining financing from various sources (such as bank credit, and the issuance of stocks and bonds) and in employing their labour force on market terms.

Another, and probably more important reason for the decline in the significance of government control over microeconomic activities is the rapid growth of nonstate-owned enterprises – including collectively owned enterprises, privately owned enterprises, foreign-invested enterprises, and shareholding enterprises – that generally enjoy more management autonomy than SOEs. From 1978 to 1997, the share of SOEs in total industrial output declined from 78 per cent to 27 per cent (see Chapter 6). In the agricultural sector, the adoption of the family responsibility system in the late 1970s and early 1980s turned virtually all collective farms into household-run businesses, although the government today still controls a portion of the marketing of grain, edible oil, and cotton through the official procurement system.[7] A similar trend of nonstate sector development was evident in the retail sector, as the share of retail sales by state-owned units accounted for only 27 per cent in 1996, down from 67 per cent in 1978. These developments fundamentally changed the main sources of China's economic growth from investment-driven SOEs under government planning in the pre-reform era to entrepreneurial initiatives in an environment of intense competition. Chapter 9 of this book presents a statistical analysis which, using provincial level data, shows that a higher level of non-state sector activities relative to those of the state sector is typically associated with a higher rate of economic growth.[8]

Commitment to maintaining macroeconomic stability   From 1978 to 1997, China maintained an annual average inflation rate, measured by the retail price index, of 7 per cent, despite a few short episodes of higher inflation at around 20 per cent per year (1987–8 and 1993–5). It is most noteworthy that such a stability has been achieved in the context of liberalizing more than 90 per cent of previously state-controlled prices. In other transition countries, price liberalization typically led to a large one-off increase in the price level and many of these countries suffered from chronic inflationary spirals.[9] The result of China's soft landing programme during 1996–7 was particularly impressive: the average inflation rate was brought down to less than 4 per cent from 15 per cent in 1995, but GDP growth remained at an average annual rate of over 9 per cent.

China's macroeconomic performance over the past two decades reflected the central government's strong commitment to maintaining price stability, and its successful strategy of gradual price liberalization. The government has been very cautious in determining the pace of price decontrol, with a clear tolerance limit on the inflation that price reforms would generate. The government tended to favour a slow down, and even a temporary reversal, in the liberalization of prices, exchange rates, and interest rates, when macroeconomic stability was deemed to be threatened. In addition, the government has consistently adopted the strategy of dual-track system in many areas,[10] which allowed market mechanisms to gradually develop and market prices to gradually expand their coverage in total transactions. The government has also been cautious in selecting opportunities for price and other reforms, thereby minimizing the inflationary effect of these reforms.

China's generally favourable macroeconomic situation has permitted a very high savings rate of 35 to 40 per cent in most of the reform period, compared with an average of 18 per cent in other low- and middle-income countries (World Bank, 1996c). As the role of government budget in mobilizing investment resources declined significantly, the banking system and securities market became more efficient channels through which household savings were turned into investment (see Chapters 4 and 5). China's appropriately tight macroeconomic policies also contributed to confidence in the domestic currency. With a very high level of international reserves (US$140 billion at the end of 1997), and the government's prudent attitude towards foreign exchange reform, China was one of the least affected Asian countries by the region's financial crisis in 1997 and 1998.

Opening to trade and foreign investment   Today, China is much more open than 20 years ago in terms of trade and foreign investment. In 1978, China was largely a closed economy, with a trade-to-GDP ratio of 9 per cent. By 1997, this figure reached 36 per cent (see Chapter 7). From 1986 to 1997, the total actual foreign investment in China amounted to US$326 billion. Foreign investment has risen rapidly since 1993, and, in 1997, actual foreign investment reached US$62 billion. Since 1994, China has continued to be the largest recipient of foreign direct investment (FDI) in the developing world; its annual inflow has been only next to that of the United States.

Openness to trade and investment has contributed to China's economic growth in several ways. First, the export sector is now an important part of the national economy. In 1997, the growth of the value added produced by the export sector accounted for about 11 per cent of GDP growth. Secondly, reduced protection of the domestic market forced domestic firms to face competition from the rest of the world, resulting in significant pressures for improving productivity and product quality. Thirdly, the large amount of capital inflow not only provided China with the much-needed investment for growth but also brought in advanced technologies and managerial skills. Indeed, evidence from many sectors (e.g. electronics and automobiles) has shown that forming joint ventures with foreign investors is the single most effective way to catch up with developed countries within a relatively short period of time.

Challenges to China's Future Development

While China has achieved an outstanding growth record over the past two decades, the importance of several contributing factors to this performance has gradually declined. For example, decentralization and marketization as sources of greater incentives for local governments and enterprises would no longer be the top explanatory variables for continued growth in the next decade or two, as several aspects of the Chinese system have already been over-decentralized and government control over enterprise activities is no longer the main deterrent to private sector development. In the meantime, China faces significant pressures from neighbouring countries' sharp currency devaluations and increasing challenges due to chronic SOE losses, the resultant heavy fiscal and quasi-fiscal burden, systemic risks in the banking sector, large regional disparity and rising income inequality, and difficulties in effective protection of the environment. Failure to address any of these issues may lead to a slow down of China's economic growth and even expose the government to serious political risks. This section briefly discuss these issues; other chapters of this book will look into many of these questions in greater detail.

Asian financial crisis   The Asian financial crisis broke out in Thailand in mid-1997 and spread rapidly to other Asian economies, hitting particularly hard Indonesia and Korea. Unable to resist large speculative attacks on their currencies, these countries experienced massive capital outflows and sharp currency devaluation, with the resultant economic contractions, rising unemployment, and social unrest. In mid-1998, the Japanese yen also suffered from serious downward pressures. From 30 June 1997 to 30 June 1998, the Thai baht depreciated by 36 per cent, the Korean won by 35 per cent, the Indonesia ruphia by 84 per cent, and the Japanese yen by 19 per cent (International Monetary Fund, 1998). By maintaining a stable exchange rate at 8.3 yuan per US dollar, the Chinese yuan experienced a significant real appreciation against these Asian currencies, and the competitiveness of its exports in Asian and other markets declined considerably. In addition, the widespread recession in other Asian countries also contributed to the sharp fall in the growth of external demand for China's products. In 1998, China's exports grew by only 0.5 per cent, compared with a 21 per cent increase in 1997. China's deteriorating export performance contributed to the slowing of GDP growth from 8.8 per cent in 1997 to 7 per cent in the first half of 1998. The Chinese government responded to these pressures by re-introducing certain tax incentives for exports and foreign investment, and by lowering interest rates and increasing investment in infrastructure projects to stimulate domestic demand. These measures will, to some extent, mitigate the problems caused by weak external demand, but if the Asian crisis continues to unfold and last, China's medium-term growth target will have to be revised downward.

SOE problem   Currently, more than 40 per cent of SOEs are operating at a loss (see Chapter 6). These enterprises currently employ about 40 million workers. The government is now pursuing a strategy of establishing a 'modern enterprise system' through corporatizing large SOEs and selling off shares of small and medium SOEs. The hope is that the large SOEs will improve their financial performance while most of them remain solely owned by the state, and that many small and medium SOEs will be revitalized by introducing the shareholding system. There are serious questions, however, as to whether the incentive system of large SOEs would change sufficiently simply due to corporatization, and whether the 'insider control' problem in many shareholding enterprises could be effectively addressed. If not, many reformed SOEs will continue to suffer from losses and remain a source of macroeconomic instability.

Rising unemployment   Unofficial estimates suggest that by including those 'waiting for work' (Xia Gang Zhi Gong) from SOEs, the actual average unemployment rate in major cities could be close to 10 per cent in early 1998, significantly higher than the level a few years ago. If all loss-making SOEs are closed or sold off in the near term, total unemployment could be well above the absorptive capacity of the existing social safety net. Reports on protests by retrenched workers in many Chinese cities have become more frequent recently (*New World Times*, 1998), and these social pressures can easily become arguments for slowing down the planned SOE reform. The sluggish domestic demand, weak export performance, and lack of labour market flexibility further exacerbate the unemployment situation.

Systemic risks in the banking system   Currently, nonperforming loans are estimated to be 20 to 30 per cent of the total loan portfolio of the banking system. This is considered largely due to imprudent lending practices and government-directed credits to inefficient SOEs (see Chapter 3). In the meantime, many state-owned commercial banks fail to meet the minimum capital adequacy requirement stipulated by the Commercial Bank Law. Although the implicit deposit guarantee from the government for major state-owned commercial banks has so far prevented widespread panic and bank runs, the risks facing the banking system have significantly increased as the majority of bank funds are now from households rather than SOEs or government institutions that are subject to government control. The government was fully aware of this problem and, in early 1998, announced the plan to recapitalize major banks through issuing Y270 billion in treasury bills, to improve commercial banks' independence and to strengthen bank supervision. The fate of this plan, however, depends heavily upon the success of the SOE reform programme; otherwise such government bail-outs may need to be repeated in the future.

Weak revenue performance   Despite the partial success of the 1994 tax reform, the revenue-to-GDP ratio remains at a very low level of around 12 per cent (see Chapter 2). With a tight budget constraint – most budgetary revenues are spent on wages and benefits of government employees, and purchase of goods and services for existing operations – the government's fiscal resources are inadequate for the provision of such basic public services as infrastructure, health care, education, and social safety net, and for addressing the issue of increasingly large regional disparities. The government's weak revenue performance has become an important reason for the problem of numerous non-transparent charges and levies imposed by local government agencies, many of which are recorded outside the budget and constitute sources of corruption. In addition, the government's inability to provide sufficient financing from the budget for key projects results in excessive pressures on the banking sector for extending policy loans both by policy banks and commercial banks – a fact that is contradictory to the goal of commercializing the banking system. Looking ahead, China also faces several long-term fiscal problems, including the large contingent liabilities for recapitalizing banks and accrued public enterprise pensions.

Regional disparities and income inequality   In 1996, per capita GDP in Shanghai was Y22 275 (US$2680), 11 times that of Guizhou's Y2093 (US$252).[11] The already large disparities also tended to worsen, as the coastal provinces grew at a higher rate than the inland areas. From 1978 to 1996, the annual average real GDP growth rate of the coastal areas was 11.3 per cent, compared to the rates of 9.6 per cent and 9.4 per cent for the middle and western areas, respectively.[12] During the same period, inequality across income groups also rose significantly. From 1981 to 1993, the ratio of per capita income of the top 20 per cent to that of the bottom 20 per cent in urban areas increased from 2.29:1 to 2.87:1, and the absolute difference between these two groups increased from Y432 to Y2,526 (Li and Deng, 1996). The deteriorating distribution of income reflected increased market opportunities for the more educated and skilled labour force, reduced government control over wage setting, growing difficulties in SOE operations and the associated layoffs, and a decline in pension and other welfare benefits for socially disadvantaged groups in real terms.

Environmental degradation   From 1981 to 1990, China's deforestation rate was 0.7 per cent of total forest area per year, compared with 0.1 per cent in the United States, 0 per cent in Australia, and −0.4 per cent in Germany (World Bank, 1996). CO_2 emission in China was about 11 per cent of the world total in 1989, and by 1994 it rose to 14 per cent (Hu, 1997).[13] In the meantime, water quality has deteriorated significantly over the past decades in most major cities and industrialized rural areas. China is facing a serious dilemma in decision-making on environmental issues: should it make massive investments today in environmental projects and in the relocation of polluting plants to save the environment for sustainable development in the long-run? Such investments would inevitably crowd out many profitable projects in the short-run, and neither entrepreneurs nor local authorities would have enough incentives to do this.

Organization of this Book

The rest of this book is organized as follows. Chapter 2 reviews China's fiscal reforms over the past two decades, with a focus on recent developments. It points out that the past 18 years' fiscal reform replaced the traditional revenue remittance system with a tax system which resembles the western system in many ways; allowed enterprises to compete on a more equal footing; reduced the scope of government involvement in the production sector; and decentralized the fiscal management system by granting the localities greater flexibility in collecting revenues and making expenditure decisions. Nevertheless, issues in the areas of central–local fiscal relations, fiscal capacity to control regional disparity, and management of extra-budgetary and off-budgetary funds remain to be addressed.

Chapter 3 turns to a discussion on monetary reform. During the past two decades, China established a two-tier financial system consisting of the central bank and many commercial banks and non-bank financial institutions. The central bank has increasingly used indirect policy instruments to conduct macroeconomic management and, for the first time in history, successfully achieved a soft landing of an overheated economy in 1996–7. This chapter argues that, despite these achievements, China's monetary reform is far from complete. The central bank's ability to use indirect policy instruments such as open market operations is still limited; interest rate decontrol is still on the agenda; commercial banks are still overburdened by the large volume of non-performing loans; and many prudential regulations are not yet fully in place.

Chapter 4 looks at the recent development of banking sector reform and, in particular, the policy measures designed to introduce a framework of prudential regulations. As China moves gradually towards liberalization of the banking sector by commercializing state banks and introducing more competition to the sector, it also gives attention to the establishment of bank regulations that will prevent instability in the financial sector. The Commercial Bank Law, effective on 1 July 1995, was a milestone of China's bank regulation. This chapter points out several institutional problems inherent in the Chinese system that pose serious challenges to the effective implementation of the promulgated bank regulations. These problems include: (1) the large amount of non-performing loans extended to SOEs and the continued political pressure to protect SOE employment which prevent the banks from effectively reducing their share of risky assets; (2) the strong influence of local governments which curtails banks' flexibility in determining the structure of their assets; and (3) the rules on loan classification and loan loss provisioning, which continue to distort banks' balance sheets and thus compromise the quality of bank supervision.

The development of the stock markets is another important element of China's reform in the financial system. Chapter 5 presents an overview of the development of the two Chinese stock markets, with the focus on their operational mechanism and regulatory framework. After giving a brief history of the Shanghai and Shenzhen stock markets, the chapter provides some detailed accounts of the primary and secondary markets and a discussion of the present regulatory framework. It is concluded in this chapter that although the growth of these stock markets has been impressive, they are still primitive and inherit many elements of the central planning system. Major issues that remain to be addressed include, among others, the nontransferability of state shares, excessive government intervention, incompleteness of regulations, and market segmentation.

Chapter 6 reviews China's recent experience in introducing the shareholding system to and corporatization of SOEs and the ensuing corporate governance issues. It first discusses the problems arising from the experiment with the shareholding system and the 'modern enterprise system', and then proposes a new framework for China's state enterprise reform in which SOEs are classified into three categories according to the types of their products/services and associated market structures: government enterprises, public corporations (special public legal entities), and joint stock companies. It is argued that the 'modern enterprise system', which fails to distinguish these three types of SOEs, unrealistically requires all SOEs to separate commercial and government functions, and attempts to apply the Company Law uniformly to all SOEs. A realistic reform strategy for China is to design different policies, legal frameworks, and corporate governance structures for different types of SOEs.

Chapter 7 gives an overview of China's foreign trade development, and identifies the policies that have promoted China's trade performance. These policies included mainly decentralization of the trade management system, the regional targeting policy, and the sectoral targeting policy. The targeting policies used instruments such as tax breaks, foreign exchange retention privileges, government provision of cheap materials and credits, and duty-free imports. As a part of China's regional targeting policy, the strategy of combining openness toward foreign investment with export orientation in the special economic zones and open coastal cities has been particularly successful. Among the targeted regions, Guangdong Province has been a model for developing a foreign investment-based and export-led development strategy.

Chapter 8 looks at China's regional policy differentials during the past 18 years and draws implications from recent developments. The regions discussed are the four special economic zones (SEZs), Hainan, 14 open coastal cities, Pudong, and inland provinces. The performances of these regions under their special policies are also analysed. It is pointed out that, as the windows opening to the outside world, the SEZs have succeeded in improving China's trade status and greatly increased China's use of foreign investment and technology. More importantly, the gradually developed market-oriented ownership structure and indirect macroeconomic management system in the SEZs have proved to be efficient and are being replicated elsewhere in China. As the open door policy is extended to many inland and border provinces, it is likely that the role of tax incentives in the newly opened areas will be less important than that experienced by the SEZs in the early 1980s, and the relative attractiveness of an area to foreign investment will rely more on other factors, such as infrastructure, government efficiency, administrative restrictions and the supply of skilled labour.

Before 1979, the provinces' development patterns and their growth performances largely depended on the central government's arrangement, which was strongly influenced by its politically driven strategy. Since the late 1970s, the process of decentralization created a situation in which each province's development was more directly linked with the province's own resource endowment and economic policy than as a result of nationwide policies. Under the decentralized system, each province has its own power, to a large extent, to decide the locality's fiscal, credit, investment, and trade policies. A province's development strategy, its attitude toward and capability to use reform policies, together with its relationship with the centre, jointly determines its economic performance. Chapter 9 attempts to identify the main factors that influenced the provinces' growth performances during the decentralization process. This process is illustrated by the changes in the provinces' fiscal relations with the central government, ownership structure of the industrial sector, openness to trade, and utilization of foreign investment. Based on a descriptive analysis of the decentralized economic structure, this chapter develops a simple regression model to quantify the importance of various institutional determinants of the provinces' growth performances.

While this book has covered some of the most important issues in the Chinese economy, it is obviously not intended to be exhaustive. Topics such as agricultural development, urbanization, income distribution, environmental protection, nonbank financial institutions and bond markets also deserve discussions if my time permits. However, if I were to wait until I have studied all these subjects, this book would probably never be published.

2
Fiscal Reform

Fiscal reform has been one of China's most important areas of reform since 1978. Over the past 20 years or so, fiscal reform has largely replaced the traditional revenue remittance system with a tax system that resembles the western system in many ways; allowed enterprises to compete on a more equal footing; reduced the scope of government involvement in the productive sector, allowing the government to focus more on the delivery of public goods and services; decentralized the fiscal management system by granting the localities greater flexibility in collecting revenues and making expenditure decisions. This chapter provides a brief overview of the evolution of the fiscal reform since the late 1970s, with an emphasis on developments since 1990. Remaining fiscal problems are also discussed in this chapter.

Tax Reform

Enterprise Taxation before 1994

Before 1978, fiscal policy played a very limited role in macroeconomic management. Its main function was to allocate budgetary resources to sectors and enterprises in order to fulfil the state-set production plan. The state-owned enterprises (SOEs) remitted almost all their profits to the government, and received investments from the government through the budgetary channel. The government raised revenue through profit remittances from SOEs; there were no personal or enterprise income taxes and, thus, no tax policy.

In 1979, the government introduced the profit retention system, under which SOEs were allowed to retain a portion of their profits. The chief objective of this reform was to provide incentives for enterprises to increase profits. However, the system was not standardized, as each SOE had to negotiate its revenue retention rate with its supervisory government agency (e.g. a line ministry or an industrial bureau). Moreover, the government frequently revised retention rates according to the actual profits of the SOEs, thereby penalizing those of high performance. In 1983–4, the profit retention system was replaced by a system in which all SOEs paid standard income taxes according to the tax law. At the same time, the depreciation funds of SOEs were separated from the government budget and placed under enterprise control.

The uniform enterprise income tax system introduced in 1983–4 was criticized for creating an unequal distribution of retained profits across enterprises. Complaints were heard from SOEs with a large number of retirees, those receiving little capital investment from the state, and those subject to government price controls. In 1987–8, the SOE income tax system was replaced by the 'contract responsibility system', under which SOEs remitted a certain amount or percentage of their profits (including taxes and non-tax profit remittances) to the government based on individually negotiated contracts. Many scholars correctly pointed out that the contract responsibility system closely resembled the profit retention system applied during 1970–84 in the sense that the profit-sharing schemes under both regimes were based on ad hoc, one-to-one negotiations.

According to the government, the contract responsibility system had three objectives. The first objective was to further increase the SOEs' autonomy. According to the contracts, the government would not intervene in the daily operations of firms that fulfilled their contracts. The second objective was to encourage SOEs to maximize profits. Theoretically, firms under the contract system had an incentive to reduce costs and increase productivity, because the higher their profits, the more money they could retain. The third objective was to stabilize government revenue since the base amounts of SOEs' remittances were fixed in the contracts.

In addition to profit remittance under the contract system, SOEs were subject to the 'income adjustment tax', some special levies on profits,[1] and a number of turnover taxes.[2] The income adjustment tax was designed to reduce the gap in per capita after-tax profits across enterprises by correcting the profit differentials created by initial conditions and government policies (e.g. initial state investment in the firm, location, and degree of price controls). By design, the rate of the adjustment tax negotiated between each SOE and the government was highly discretionary and differentiated. Not surprisingly, enterprises bargained energetically with their line ministries to obtain favourable terms on this tax (Tseng *et al.*, 1994).

Contrary to government expectations, the contract responsibility system did not lead to a substantial increase in SOE profit (see Chapter 6); rather, the government revenue-to-GDP ratio continued to decline. The main problem was that enterprises were not held responsible for their financial losses, while they could gain substantially when their profits increased. In other words, the risks and benefits faced by the SOEs were asymmetrical. Although the contracts stipulated that the contracted level of profit remittance to the government should be guaranteed, in reality, when a firm suffered losses, the government had to re-negotiate the amount of contracted revenue remittance, increase subsidies, or offer special credits. Under such a soft-budget constraint, enterprises did not have enough incentive to improve financial performance; bargaining with the government for a lower remittance quota or a low-interest loan often proved more effective in raising an enterprise's profit than striving to improve productivity. Moreover, given substantial autonomy under the contract system, the managers of SOEs tend to act in the interest of the employees. Short-term behaviour such as increasing wages and bonuses at the expense of the firms' long-term development were pervasive.[3]

Another major problem of the enterprise tax system before 1994 was that different types of enterprises were taxed at different rates. For example, profits of large and medium SOEs were taxed at the notional rate of 55 per cent; collectively owned enterprises were taxed according to a progressive rate structure; and foreign-invested companies were taxed at 33 per cent, except in SEZs and coastal open cities. In addition, there were numerous conditions under which an enterprise could be exempted from taxation or enjoy reduced tax rates.

Tax Reform in 1994

There were three major problems with the tax system before 1994: (1) it failed to provide incentives for enterprises to increase their tax bases. Together with several other factors discussed later in this chapter, this contributed to the decline in the revenue-to-GDP ratio from about 31 per cent in 1978 to 13 per cent in 1993 (see Table 2.1); (2) tax burdens were distributed unequally across enterprises based on the form of ownership; and (3) there were as many as 37 taxes, many of which overlapped and sometimes contradicted each other. To address these problems, the government launched a major tax reform in 1994. The main changes introduced in the 1994 tax reform were as follows:

Table 2.1   China: budgetary revenue, expenditure and deficit (Ybn), 1978–97

	GDP	Revenue	Expenditure	Surplus	Revenue-to-GDP ratio	Expenditure-to-GDP ratio	Deficit-to-GDP ratio
					(%)	(%)	(%)
1978	362.4	113.2	111.1	2.1	31.2	30.7	−0.6
1979	403.8	114.6	128.2	−13.5	28.4	31.7	3.4
1980	451.8	116.0	122.9	−6.9	25.7	27.2	1.5
1981	486.2	117.6	113.8	3.7	24.2	23.4	−0.8
1982	529.5	121.2	123.0	−1.8	22.9	23.2	0.3
1983	593.5	136.7	141.0	−4.3	23.0	23.8	0.7
1984	717.1	164.3	170.1	−5.8	22.9	23.7	0.8
1985	896.4	200.5	200.4	0.0	22.4	22.4	0.0
1986	1 020.2	212.2	220.5	−8.3	20.8	21.6	0.8
1987	1 196.3	219.9	226.2	−6.3	18.4	18.9	0.5
1988	1 492.8	235.7	249.1	−13.4	15.8	16.7	0.9
1989	1 690.9	266.5	282.4	−15.9	15.8	16.7	0.9
1990	1 854.8	293.7	308.4	−14.7	15.8	16.6	0.8
1991	2 161.8	315.0	338.7	−23.7	14.6	15.7	1.1
1992	2 663.8	348.3	374.2	−25.9	13.1	14.0	1.0
1993	3 463.4	434.9	464.2	−29.3	12.6	13.4	0.8
1994	4 675.9	521.8	579.3	−57.4	11.2	12.4	1.2
1995	5 847.8	624.2	682.4	−58.2	10.7	11.7	1.0
1996	6 779.5	740.8	793.8	−53.0	10.9	11.7	0.8
1997	7 477.2	864.2	919.7	−55.5	11.6	12.3	0.7

Sources: State Statistical Bureau, 1996, 1997; Chen, 1998; and author's calculations.

1. Turnover Taxes

The previous system of turnover taxes included a value-added tax (VAT), product tax, and business tax. The 1994 reform substantially broadened the coverage of the VAT, which is now applied to all manufacturing, wholesale, and retail enterprises, regardless of whether they are domestic, foreign-owned, or joint venture enterprises. For most products the VAT rate is 17 per cent, a rate higher than those applied before. The VAT is now the single largest source of government revenue, accounting for 42 per cent of total budgetary revenue in 1995 (see Table 2.2). A business tax of 3 to 5 per cent is applied to services other than retail and whole-sale businesses (such as entertainment, food, insurance, financial, and transport services) and to real estate sales. The 1994 reform also introduced a consumption tax, which applies to a small number of consumer goods (such as alcoholic and tobacco products). When the new tax system was introduced, the product tax and the industry and commerce tax assessed on foreign-invested enterprises were abolished.

Table 2.2   China: sources of government budgetary revenue, 1995

	Total amount (Ybn)	Share in total revenue (%)
1. Taxes	573.74	91.9
Value Added Tax on Domestic Goods and Services	260.23	41.7
Consumption Tax on Domestic Goods	54.15	8.7
VAT and Consumption Tax on Imported Goods and Services	38.29	6.1
Business Tax	86.56	13.9
Income Tax on SOEs	71.47	11.4
Income Tax on COEs	11.9	1.9
Customs Duties	29.18	4.7
Resource Tax	5.5	0.9
Agricultural Tax	24.36	3.9
Tax Rebates to Exporting Companies	−54.98	−8.8
2. Subsidies to SOEs	−32.77	−5.2
3. State Budget Adjustment Fund	3.49	0.6
4. Education Surcharges	8.34	1.3
5. Other Non-tax Revenues	29.38	4.7
6. Special Levies for Capital Projects	41.64	6.7
Total Revenue	624.22	100.0

Source: Editorial Board of Fiscal Yearbook of China, 1996, pp. 463–4.

2. *Enterprise Income Tax*

The tax reform cut income tax rates for large and medium-sized SOEs from 55 per cent to a uniform 33 per cent.[4] This rate now applies to all types of enterprises, regardless of ownership. The 33 per cent flat rate includes a 30 per cent national tax and a 3 per cent local surcharge. The latter is designed to be flexibly applied by local governments. At the same time, the income adjustment tax and mandatory contributions to several funds formerly levied on SOEs (including 'the state energy and transportation construction fund') were abolished.

3. *Personal Income Tax*

The 'personal income adjustment tax', which applied to individuals, and the 'tax on private businesses in urban and rural areas', which applied to privately owned businesses, were replaced in 1994 with the 'personal income tax'. The monthly deductible of the personal income tax remains 800 Yuan, as it was in the 'personal income adjustment tax'. A uniform personal income tax is now applied to Chinese and foreigners, but additional deductions are allowed for foreigners. A progressive rate from 5 to

45 per cent is applied to income from wages and salaries. A progressive rate from 5 to 35 per cent is applied to income from business activities of private manufacturers and merchants and to subcontracting and rental income. A 20 per cent flat rate is applied to income from publications, remuneration for services, patents and copyrights, interest and dividends, rental and transfer of assets, and other sources.

Composition of Budgetary Revenue

The 1994 reform led to some important changes in the composition of the government's budgetary revenue, most notably due to the increase in the VAT as a percentage of total revenue. Table 2.2 shows the shares of major revenue sources in 1995. The main revenue categories are:

1 *Taxes on domestic goods and services (the VAT, consumption tax, and business tax)*   These three taxes accounted for 70 per cent of total budgetary revenue in 1995. The VAT on domestic goods and services alone accounted for about 42 per cent. The business tax, accounting for 14 per cent of total budgetary revenue, was the second single largest revenue source. The significance of these taxes in total budgetary revenue has increased steadily over the past decade, and the 1994 tax reform further improved their position. In terms of the share of taxes on domestic goods and services in total budgetary revenue, China has surpassed the levels of most other countries.

2 *Taxes on enterprise profits*   Revenue from the enterprise income tax from state- and collectively owned enterprises accounted for about 13 per cent of total budgetary revenue in 1995. The importance of the enterprise income tax in total budgetary revenue has dropped significantly over the past decade, partly because of changes in tax structure (such as the introduction of various turnover taxes before the profit tax is levied) and partly because of the decline in SOEs' profitability. The share of the enterprise income tax in total budgetary revenue is now comparable to the average share in developing countries.

3 *Taxes on international trade*   Custom duties accounted for less than 5 per cent of China's total budgetary revenue in 1995. This percentage is close to the developed countries' average of 3 per cent, and much lower than developing countries' average of 29 per cent (Burgess and Stern, 1993).

4 *Non-tax revenue*   Non-tax revenue used to be a major revenue source in the pre-reform period because it included profit remittances from SOEs and depreciation funds. It became less important after 1984,

when profit remittances were converted to taxes. Currently, nontax revenue includes profit remittances from a small number of SOEs, the education surcharge, as well as various fees, user charges, and fines. Nontax revenue accounted for about 13 per cent of total budgetary revenue in 1995.

Expenditure Management

Before 1978, China's government budgetary expenditure accounted for nearly one-third of the national GDP. From 1978 to 1996, budgetary expenditure as a percentage of GDP declined from 31 per cent to about 12 per cent (see Table 2.1). The obvious reason for this decline was that budgetary revenue as a percentage of GDP declined in parallel. A number of factors have contributed to the decline. First, during the first few years of reform (1979–83), the government deliberately transferred part of its revenue to enterprises by allowing them to retain some of their profits. This reform was designed to increase the enterprises' management autonomy as well as their incentive to increase revenue. Secondly, the financial performance of SOEs has deteriorated since the mid-1980s. Since 1986, the government started running deficits and gradually recognized the need to increase its revenue base. However, the poor financial performance of the state sector failed to contribute to the government budgetary increase. Some scholars have attributed the decline in profit rates of SOEs to the 'de-monopolization process' (Naughton, 1992), while others have argued that the contract responsibility system discouraged SOEs from increasing revenue. Thirdly, the nature of central–local fiscal relations acted as a disincentive to local tax efforts, and contributed to the decline in revenue-to-GDP ratio. This point is illustrated in detail in Ma (1997a).

The composition of budgetary expenditure has also changed significantly over the past 18 years (see Table 2.3). In 1978, in a reflection of the highly centralized revenue collection system, almost all investments in SOEs came from the state budget. The government was heavily involved in the productive sector: 40 per cent of government expenditure was capital construction. Total budgetary allocation to economic construction (the sum of expenditures on capital construction, enterprise circulating funds, technical upgrading, geological prospecting, and agricultural development) accounted for more than 60 per cent of total government expenditure. On the other hand, social expenditures, such as those on education, health and social welfare, accounted for only 12 per cent. Between 1978 and 1996, the composition of expenditure

Table 2.3   China: government budgetary expenditure by use, 1978 and 1996 (Ybn)

	1978		1996	
	Amount	%	Amount	%
Total	112.2	100.0	793.8	100.0
Capital Construction	45.2	40.3	90.7	11.4
Circulating Funds	6.7	5.9	4.3	0.5
Technical Upgrading, etc.	6.3	5.6	52.3	6.6
Geological Prospecting	2.0	1.8	6.9	0.9
Administration of Industry and Commerce	1.8	1.6	12.0	1.5
Agriculture	7.7	6.9	51.0	6.4
Cultural, Education, Science and Health	11.3	10.0	170.4	21.5
Pension and Social Welfare	1.8	1.6	12.8	1.6
Defence	16.8	15.0	72.0	9.1
Government Administration	4.9	4.4	104.1	13.1
Price Subsidies	1.1	1.0	45.4	5.7
Debt Repayment			131.2	16.5

Source: State Statistical Bureau, 1997a, p. 241.

underwent several significant changes. First, the proportion of investment in production projects declined sharply, reflecting the declining role of the government in the production of private goods. The share of capital construction in total government expenditure fell from 40 per cent in 1978 to only 11 per cent in 1996, while the share of budgetary allocation to economic construction (as defined above) declined from 60 per cent in 1978 to 26 per cent in 1996. Secondly, social expenditure on education, health, and welfare increased from 12 per cent of total government expenditure in 1978 to 23 per cent in 1996. Thirdly, administrative expenses, price subsidies, and debt repayment increased quickly during this period. The sum of administrative expenses in industry and commerce, as well as general government administrative expenses, increased from 6 per cent of total expenditure in 1978 to 15 per cent in 1996. Price subsidies increased from one per cent in 1978 to 6 per cent in 1996. Debt service (interest and principal payments) was not listed as an expenditure item in 1978, while it accounted for 17 per cent of total government outlay in 1996.

These structural changes reflected the deepening of various aspects of the economic reforms. The declining role of government expenditure in economic construction mirrors the rapidly declining importance of SOEs in total output: from 1978 to 1996, the share of SOEs' output in total industrial output fell from about 80 per cent to only 28 per cent. The increase in social expenditure has been consistent with the shift in government focus from direct involvement in production activities to the provision of public goods and services, as well as the government's increasing concern over deteriorating terms of income distribution. Issuing debt was not a policy option in the late 1980s; in 1994, debt financing of fiscal deficits was written into the Budget Law.

Central–Local Fiscal Relations

Before 1980, China's fiscal system was characterized by centralized revenue collection and centralized fiscal transfers, i.e. most taxes and profits were remitted to the central government and then transferred back to the provinces according to expenditure needs approved by the center. Since the early 1980s, the central–provincial fiscal relation has gone through three major phases.[5] In 1980, the highly centralized system was changed into a revenue-sharing system in which the central and provincial governments each began to 'eat in separate kitchens'. This system, called the contract responsibility system, emulated a similar system adopted in rural areas in the late 1970s.[6] There were three basic types of revenue under the reformed system: central revenues (those revenues that accrue to the centre), local revenues (those accrue to the localities), and shared revenues (shared between the centre and localities). During the 1980–4 period, about 80 per cent of the shared revenues were remitted to the central government and 20 per cent were retained by local governments. Almost all revenues, except a few minor central revenues, were collected by the local finance bureaux. The bases and rates of all taxes, whether central, local, or shared, were determined by national legislation or the central government.

Although some localities became more enthusiastic about collecting revenues during the 1980–4 period, the uniform sharing formula created surpluses in wealthy provinces and deficits in poor provinces. In 1985, the State Council redesigned the revenue-sharing arrangements by varying schedules based on localities' budget balances in the previous years. The central government allowed financially weak regions to retain more revenues, while it continued to maintain a tight grip over those regions, including Shanghai, Beijing, Tianjin, Liaoning, Jiangsu, and Zhejiang, that were the most important sources of central revenue. Revenues from these regions generally grew more slowly than the national average since the high share of remittance dampened local enthusiasm for expanding the tax bases. To mitigate this effect, in 1988, the State Council decided to adopt a new system that introduced six types of central–provincial revenue-sharing methods, each applied to a number of provinces (Agarwala, 1992).

The 1988 fiscal contract system further increased the revenue share retained by localities, particularly those that were major contributors to the central government's revenue. However, the contracts were not strictly adhered to and were revised repeatedly for some regions. In 1991, when the 1988–90 system was supposed to expire, the central government was unable to negotiate satisfactory replacements; as a result, the 1988–90 system was extended until the end of 1993, with limited modifications on revenue-sharing ratios and quotas.

Since 1979, both the total budgetary revenue as a percentage of GDP and the share of central government budgetary revenue in total budgetary revenue have declined rapidly. From 1979 to 1993, the ratio of total budgetary revenue to GDP declined from 28 per cent to about 13 per cent; the central government's share (after revenue-sharing) declined from 51 per cent to 28 per cent (see Table 2.1). Since the late 1980s, the central government has been increasingly concerned with the potential political and economic consequences of the weakening of its fiscal power, and has repeatedly expressed its intention to increase both the revenue-to-GDP ratio and the ratio of central government budgetary revenue to total budgetary revenue. Although this proposal was written into the Eighth Five Year Plan (1991–5), the decline of these two ratios continued between 1990 and 1993.

In an attempt to raise these two ratios as well as to strengthen the central government's ability to use tax and expenditure policy instruments, the central government decided in late 1993 to replace the fiscal contract system with the tax assignment system, which re-defined the central, local, and shared revenue sources. Under the new system, the central taxes mainly include: customs duties; a consumption tax collected by customs; a value added tax (VAT) and income tax on centrally owned state enterprises; turnover taxes on railway, banks, and insurance companies; and income taxes on financial institutions authorized by the headquarters of People's Bank of China (PBC). The local taxes mainly include the business tax (except for turnover taxes on banks, railways, and insurance companies), income tax on locally owned state enterprises, and personal income tax. The shared taxes include the VAT, securities trading tax, and natural resources tax. Revenue from the VAT is divided with 75 per cent going to the central government and 25 per cent to local governments. The securities trading tax, currently collected only in Shanghai and Shenzhen in the form of a stamp duty, is divided 50:50

between the central and local coffers. Proceeds of the natural resources tax are largely kept by local governments for the time being.

Along with the changes in the division of revenue sources, a major effort was made by the central government to establish its own revenue collection bodies. In 1994 and 1995, the centre set up national tax services (NTSs) in all provinces to collect central revenues and shared revenues. These NTSs are organized on the basis of the divisions in charge of collecting central and shared taxes under the old tax bureaux. After the reorganization, these divisions became the NTSs, and divisions that were previously in charge of local taxes became Local Tax Services. The State Bureau of General Taxation, the central headquarters of the NTSs, is empowered to supervise local NTSs, appoint their directors, and provide funding for their operations.

The immediate impact of the tax assignment system on the division of revenue sources between the central and local governments was rather drastic. The percentage of total budgetary revenue collected by the central government jumped from 22 per cent in 1993 to 56 per cent in 1994 (see Table 2.4). While many changes in the tax system contributed to the increase in the share of central government revenue, the most important one was that the centre is now in charge of collecting the VAT, a local responsibility under the fiscal contract system. In 1994, this tax alone accounted for about 42 per cent of total government revenue.

While the tax assignment system has introduced more transparency and stability to the revenue-sharing system, many elements of the old system remain. As a compromise with many provinces that opposed the reform in 1993, the centre agreed that this reform would be carried out in a progressive way over the span of a few years. The centre promised to return part of the shared revenues to ensure that each province would retain no less revenue than it did in 1993. The retained revenue of a province in 1993 would be used as the basis for calculating the amount of shared revenues to be returned from the central government to local governments after 1994.[7] The centre would increase its share of total government revenue only from the increase in the shared revenues, mainly the VAT. To win the support of local governments, the centre also promised to allow the tax exemptions approved by provincial level governments to continue for a few years and not to shift new expenditure responsibilities to localities.

The experience of implementing the tax assignment system over the past three years has not been fully satisfactory. The biggest challenge faced by the central government is the unexpected decline in the share of central government revenue after the one-off increase in 1994.[8] From 1994 to 1996, the share of central government budgetary revenue in total budgetary revenue fell steadily from about 56 per cent to less than 50 per cent (see Table 2.4). A number of factors have contributed to this decline. First, the bases for many local revenues (e.g. the business tax and personal income tax) increased at much higher rates than those of central revenues. For example, in 1995 proceeds from the personal income tax increased by 80 per cent and those from the business tax increased by 28 per cent, compared with the 11 per cent growth of central revenue. The increase in business tax revenue partly reflects the stronger-than-before incentive of many local governments to promote the service sector, as the proceeds of this tax became 100 per cent local since 1994. A related explanation is that while local revenues from nonstate-owned

Table 2.4   China: central–local fiscal status, 1979–96

	Revenue		Expenditure	
	Central (%)	*Local (%)*	*Central (%)*	*Local (%)*
1979	20.2	79.8	51.1	48.9
1980	24.5	75.5	54.3	45.7
1981	26.5	73.5	55.0	45.0
1982	28.6	71.4	53.0	47.0
1983	35.8	64.1	53.9	46.1
1984	40.5	59.5	52.5	47.5
1985	38.4	61.6	39.7	60.3
1986	36.7	63.3	37.9	62.1
1987	33.5	66.5	37.4	62.6
1988	32.9	67.1	33.9	66.1
1989	30.9	69.1	31.5	68.5
1990	33.8	66.2	32.6	67.4
1991	29.8	70.2	32.2	67.8
1992	28.1	71.9	31.3	68.7
1993	22.0	78.0	28.3	71.7
1994	55.7	44.3	30.3	69.7
1995	52.2	47.8	29.2	70.8
1996	49.5	50.5	27.1	72.9

Note: Revenue does not include (exclude) fiscal transfers from (to) the centre.
Expenditure equals revenue plus fiscal transfers from the centre to the province, and minus fiscal transfers from the province to the centre.
Source: Calculated using data from State Statistical Bureau, 1997a.

units have become increasingly important, central revenues continue to rely primarily on state-owned enterprises, the least dynamic sector in the economy. Secondly, the separation of central and local tax administration greatly stimulated the enthusiasm of local governments to collect revenues. In many provinces, local tax services are better equipped and their employees are better paid compared with the NTSs. Thirdly, while officially the NTSs are independent from local authorities, their operations rely on local agencies for many services (such as water, electricity, gas, child care, education of employees' children). In case of conflict of interests, the NTSs often find it difficult to insist on the priority of the collection of central taxes.

Improving the intergovernmental fiscal transfer system was another stated objective of the 1994 fiscal reform, but progress in this area has been limited. Currently, the Chinese transfer system consists of four types of transfers (grants). The first type of transfer is based on the old contract system prevailing during 1988–93. Since 1994, local governments have continued to remit revenues to or receive transfers from the centre according to their fiscal contracts in effect in 1993. The second type of transfer is the 'returned revenue' from the centre according to a calculation that ensures each locality retains no less than what it had in 1993. These two types of transfer account for more than two-thirds of total central government transfers, but they suffer from at least two major flaws. First, they were not designed to address the increasingly important regional disparity issue; rather, they were largely designed to recognize the vested interests of the localities. Secondly, the criteria based on which these transfers are determined are rather ad hoc; that is, these transfer mechanisms lack scientific measurements of fiscal capacities and fiscal needs. This can easily lead to an unjustified distribution pattern and encourage bargaining on the part of localities.

The third type of transfer includes various specific purpose grants, such as those for price subsidies, education projects, environmental projects, disaster relief, and poverty alleviation. The fourth type of transfer, introduced in 1996, was referred to by the Ministry of Finance as the 'transitional fiscal transfer program'. It aims to reduce regional disparities in the level of public services and bases the assessment of local fiscal capacities and needs on objective variables. In 1996, the size of the new programme was only 0.5 per cent of total central government revenue and the programme was applied to just 18 provinces and autonomous regions (Zhang, 1996). In 1997, this programme was slightly modified in its calculation of local fiscal capacities and needs, and its size was expanded to around 1 per cent of total central government revenue.

Social Security Reform

In recent years, social security reform has become an increasingly pressing issue on the government's agenda. Although China's population is still young relative to that of most developed countries – the proportion of the population at or above age 65 is 7 per cent in China compared with 15 per cent in Japan and 14 per cent in the US – the Chinese government has taken the view that long-term sustainability of the social security system requires immediate reform.

Until recently only urban employees of government agencies or SOEs were offered public pension benefits. The majority of the population in the rural areas was not covered by the public pension system, with a few exceptions in the rich countryside where local governments offer pension benefits to the elderly. Pensions for government employees were paid from the government budget. A retiree of a typical SOE received pensions from his/her enterprise, which ran a pay-as-you-go pension scheme with the firm's own revenue. The risks of such a small-scale pension system were high, particularly when many SOEs began to operate at a loss over the past few years. Many SOEs could simply no longer afford to pay their retirees the promised full pension benefits. Moreover, the distribution of the pension burden across enterprises was extremely uneven: many old SOEs were heavily burdened by their large number of retirees (some SOEs had more retirees than current workers), while others (mainly new firms) had very few or no retirees. The recent pension reform therefore started by pooling the risks of the SOE pension system.

After several years of experiment in various regions and enterprises, in March 1995 the State Council issued 'The Directive on Further Reform of the Enterprise Pension System'. The objective of this directive was to establish a multi-pillar pension system involving funds contributed by the state, employers, and individuals. This system consists of three elements: a basic public pension funded on a pay-as-you-go basis, a fully funded pension financed by mandatory contributions, and voluntary personal savings. The basic pension and the fully funded pension schemes are funded by contributions from enterprises and employees; the size of the contribution could range from 10 to 20 per cent of the employees' total wages, depending on the region. Of this 10–20 per cent, employees contribute about 2–5 per cent, and the rest of the premiums are borne by the enterprises.

By the end of 1995, 43 major cities had been included in the reform plan, and 13 provinces, autonomous regions, and cities directly under the State Council had formulated their reform plan. By the third quarter of 1995, about 87 million workers and 21 million retirees had participated in the mandatory pension system, and nearly 5 million workers had participated in supplementary and personal retirement savings programs (Liu, 1996). A recent report on the current public pension schemes covering enterprise employees (Yan, 1996) estimates that, on average, the total pension and unemployment insurance contributions from enterprises and employees amount to 23 per cent of employees' wages. Of this amount, about 20 per cent is from enterprises and 3 per cent from individuals. The basic pension and funded pension schemes are managed by social insurance departments of the provincial level governments (supervised by the Ministry of Labour and directly under the provincial bureaux of labour), which make pension payments to retired employees. The funded pension scheme invests in government bonds and bank deposits[9] and the benefit levels will be linked to personal contributions.

Reform of the pension system in the rural areas has progressed relatively slowly, starting with some experiments in 1991. The recently promulgated 'Plan for a Rural Pension System' suggests that the rural pension system will rely primarily on personal contributions, and will be supplemented by subsidies from local governments and support by government policies. The main constraint that the rural pension system faces is that the government cannot afford to contribute any significant amount to a pension system in rural China covering some 1 billion people. The pension systems established in rural areas are thus all 'self-sufficient', and the development level depends very much on the income level of the region and the fiscal resources of the grassroots level (such county, township and village) governments. By 1995, about 1400 counties (out of 2300 counties in the country) established their pension systems of various sizes (Liu, 1996).

The strategy that the Chinese government has adopted in reforming its social security system is to establish a public pension pillar providing only minimum levels of old age security. The partially funded nature of this system will enable the government to avoid the old-age crisis being experienced by many industrialized countries. The Singapore model of treating old age social security as mainly a financial sector issue (with mandatory contributions and market-based operations) is attractive to Chinese policy makers. It seems that the Chinese government is making a serious attempt not to overburden fiscal authorities with a huge public pension system.

Remaining Problems

China's fiscal reforms in the 1990s have made impressive progress towards broadening tax bases, increasing social expenditures, standardizing central–local fiscal relations, and establishing a sustainable pension system. However, in most of these areas, reforms have been partial in nature. A long list of problems remain to be addressed. This section briefly discusses a few issues that are, or should be, among the top concerns of the fiscal authorities.

1   The tax system remains weak, as reflected by the declining budgetary revenue-to-GDP ratio. This ratio declined from 31.2 per cent in 1978 to 12.6 per cent in 1993, and further to 10.9 per cent in 1996. Despite a modest increase in this ratio to 11.6 per cent in 1997, it has not reached the desired level envisaged by the 1994 reform plan. Important factors responsible for the weak revenue performance in recent years include the low profitability of state-owned enterprises, which still account for about 60 per cent of total government revenue, and the slow progress in improving revenue collection from the nonstate sector.

2   The share of central government budgetary revenue in total budgetary revenue has continued to decline since the 1994 tax reform. The 1994 reform did, to some extent, strengthen the central government's ability to use tax and expenditure policies by recentralizing some taxing powers from the localities. The share of central government budgetary revenue in total budgetary revenue increased from 22 per cent in 1993 to 56 per cent in 1994. However, since 1994, the growth rate of central revenues has been significantly lower than that of local revenues. As a result, in 1995 and 1996, the centre's share in total budgetary revenue further declined to 52 per cent and 50 per cent, respectively. The centre's original objective of increasing the centre's share to 60 per cent is unlikely to be achieved.

3   As a result of the tight budgetary situation, the central government has not been able to set up a sizeable equalization transfer programme for redistribution purposes. As pointed out by some scholars (Hu, 1995), China's regional disparity in income level and fiscal capacity is one of the largest in the world. However, its fiscal transfer system has played almost no role in equalization, with most transfers determined on the basis of vested interests and political influences (Ma, 1997a).

4   A large part of government revenue is not included in the formal budgetary system. These include extra-budgetary funds and off-budgetary funds.[10] It is estimated that while the government budgetary

revenue accounts for only 11–12 per cent of GDP, the size of extra-budgetary and off-budgetary revenues is similar to that level, making the consolidated government revenue-to-GDP ratio close to 25 per cent of GDP.[11] Under the fiscal contract system before 1994, many localities and line departments found various ways to shift budgetary revenues to these funds in order to avoid revenue sharing with the central government. After the tax reform of 1994, localities and line departments continue to use extra-budgetary and off-budgetary funds as a way to avoid central government (or higher level government) restrictions on the use of funds. The consequence of almost half of the public sector revenue wandering outside the budgetary system is that the fiscal authority has limited control over the allocation of resources, particularly when budgetary expenditures are largely 'entitlements' with little flexibility. The redistributive role of fiscal allocation is thus seriously constrained by the government's inability to control extra-budgetary and off-budgetary funds.

To address these issues, the government should consider the following actions: (1) strengthening national tax services at the provincial and local levels – lines of authority of central and local tax services, including the priority of central over local tax collections, should be clearly established; (2) further broadening tax bases, particularly the VAT, and eliminating unnecessary tax exemptions; (3) setting up a consolidated public sector accounting system that includes budgetary, extra-budgetary and certain off-budgetary revenues and expenditures in order to effectively conduct macroeconomic control; and (4) continuing the reform of the state enterprise sector and further reducing the government's involvement in the productive sector. This will ease the pressure for nonproductive subsidies to SOEs and allow more flexibility for budgetary allocation to social services.

The Japanese Experience and the Reform of China's Central–Local Fiscal Relations

While it is impossible to find two identical systems of intergovernmental relations in the world, theoretically one can identify two extreme models. The first is the so-called separation model, in which divisions of fiscal powers and expenditure responsibilities between levels of government are clearly defined through national legislation and cannot be easily altered by the central government or by any of its agencies. Although no country adopts a 'pure' separation model, the American and Canadian systems appear to be close to this model. The second model, which

I refer to as the 'ad hoc model', is one in which the central government (not the legislature) has complete discretion in defining the division of fiscal powers and responsibilities between levels of government. Like many other formerly centrally planned economies, China operates a system that has many elements of the 'ad hoc model'.

Interestingly, the Japanese system represents an intermediate case between the separation model and the ad hoc model. Although Japan is a unitary country, it has adopted many elements of the separation model. For example, in Japan, the national legislature determines the division of tax bases and expenditure responsibilities, as well as the formula for intergovernmental transfers. At the same time, in a number of areas, the Japanese system allows the central government to exercise its discretionary powers. These include delegated functions, central government approval on new local taxes and local bond issuances, a personal dispatching system, etc. The following table describes in detail the differences among the three models – the separation model, the Japanese model, and the ad hoc model – in four aspects.[12]

Table 2.5   A comparison of three models of central–local relations

	The separation model	*The Japanese model*	*The ad hoc model*
Division of revenue sources	Complete separation of central and local tax bases. Local tax bases and rates are determined by local legislation. The centre has no power to influence local tax matters. Conditions: capital and population mobility; mechanisms to ensure local government accountability.	Division of tax bases is determined through national legislation. Local taxes are set by the Local Tax Law. But local authorities can introduce new local taxes (discretionary taxes), subject to the approval from the Ministry of Home Affairs. The centre allows the localities to vary the rates of some local taxes within certain ranges. Local assemblies decide fees and user charges.	The central government (not the National Congress) decides the division of taxing powers between the levels of government. Local tax bases and rates are set by the centre.
Division of expenditure responsibilities	Clear separation of central and local functions. The centre cannot issue	The broad division of expenditure responsibilities is defined by the	The centre has the discretion to redefine the expenditure

	unfunded mandates to localities. The centre can be involved in local projects through specific purpose grants. Conditions: modest regional disparity and strong local government capacity	Local Finance Law. The centre uses agency delegated functions and specific purpose grants to influence local spending.	responsibilities of local governments. There are many unfunded mandates. Changes in expenditure responsibilities are often announced in the form of a Ministry of Finance circular.
Local borrowing	Local council or government decides whether and how much to borrow. However, if the local government is not able to repay debts, the centre has no obligation to bail it out. Conditions: a developed capital market; local government accountability; central government commitment to the 'no bail out' policy.	A law defines the limit on local borrowing. Localities can borrow freely up to the limit; for borrowing above the limit, approval from the Ministry of Home Affairs is required.	The central government decides on a discretionary basis whether and how much the localities can borrow.
Intergovernmental transfer	Formula for distributing general purpose transfer is determined by the national legislation. Each specific purpose transfer programme is created by national legislation.	The total amount of transfer and the formula for distributing general purpose transfer is determined by national legislation. The Ministry of Home Affairs works out the details (modification coefficients, etc.) of the general purpose transfer. Each specific purpose transfer programme is created by national legislation; the distribution is at the line ministries' discretion.	No formula for grant distribution. Distribution is at the centre's discretion.

Accepting the political constraint that a federal system is not feasible in China's foreseeable future, the reform of intergovernmental fiscal relations cannot simply copy the separation model. The experience from Japan indicates that it is possible to construct a model that ensures a relatively high degree of local autonomy and preserves stability in a unitary political system. To address the problems associated with China's discretionary system (such as the negative impact on local tax effort, lack of stability and transparency, ineffectiveness of intergovernmental transfer in addressing regional disparities, etc.), the Japanese model can serve as a very useful reference. Specifically, future reforms in China should properly combine the rule-based elements (legal definition of local tax bases and local expenditure responsibilities, a formula-based transfer system, a legal limit to local borrowing, etc.) and the effective instruments for central government intervention (such as the control over major local tax rates, approval of local bond issuance, coordination mechanisms provided by the Ministry of Home Affairs, the personnel-dispatching system, etc.). The rest of this section details some implications of the Japanese experience for the ongoing reform of intergovernmental fiscal relations in China.

Division of Taxing Powers

Under the separation model, the assignment of taxing powers to different levels of government is determined through national legislation. The US Constitution allows access of state and local governments to virtually any tax bases except customs duties. In Canada, the Constitution grants provincial and local governments the right to levy any taxes other than custom duties and indirect taxes (however, the Supreme Court ruled that sales tax is a form of direct tax).[13] In these countries, the rates of state and local taxes are determined by legislation at the respective levels. Thus, the subnational authorities have full control over the taxes assigned to them, and the national government has no influence on either the bases or the rates of these taxes. This system allows the subnational governments to choose diverse levels of taxation in response to the diverse needs of their citizens. One important argument for this arrangement is that the mobility of tax bases (population and capital) restrains the subnational governments from over-taxing businesses and residents in their own jurisdictions; in other words, granting subnational governments substantial taxing power would not lead to excessive taxation.

Under the ad hoc model, the division of taxing powers is determined by the central government, rather than through national legislation.

This allows the central government to frequently change the rules in its own interest. Without a commitment to a stable division of powers, the subnational governments tend to react strategically to expected policy changes, thereby leading to very unpredictable outcomes (including reduced local tax efforts as well as frequent and intense bargaining over the assignment of revenue sources). In China, the bases and rates of major local taxes are determined by the centre, but the localities may choose to vary their tax efforts in order to adjust the effective tax rates and tax bases. Since an effective enforcement of unified local tax rates and bases is difficult, as evidenced by past experience under the fiscal contract system, the centre's nominal control over local tax rates and bases only weakens the system's transparency, predictability and stability.

Between the separation model, in which localities have the right to determine local tax rates and tax bases, and the ad hoc model, in which local governments act only as tax collectors of centrally determined local taxes, the Japanese model provides a somewhat intermediate case that reconciles the need for central government control and local autonomy. Under the Japanese system, national tax laws set fixed tax rates for a number of local taxes, and provide ranges within which some other local taxes can float. Local governments and local assemblies are given the authority to propose new taxes and most of these proposals are approved by the centre. The major advantages of such an arrangement are as follows: (1) by keeping uniform rates of certain local taxes and maintaining the right to approve new taxes, the centre can avoid or mitigate the problems of excessive taxation by some 'leviathan' local governments or inadequate taxation due to regional tax competition; and (2) the localities are given some flexibility to choose tax rates and bases according to their local conditions, including income levels, the preferences of the local residents, and resource endowments.

Compared with the separation model, the Japanese model of division of taxing powers appears to be more appropriate for China for at least three reasons. First, the vast regional disparity in China requires that the central government maintain effective control over enough fiscal resources for redistribution purposes. Granting localities unlimited taxing powers may reduce the centre's ability to perform its redistribution functions. Secondly, China does not have the kind of mobility of tax bases (e.g. labour and capital) seen in the US, thus Tiebout's 'voting with your feet' doctrine does not provide an effective mechanism for controlling the leviathan behaviour of local governments. Moreover, as direct election is still far from reality at the local (provincial and county) level, and citizen participation in local public administration is still limited, the tendency for local governments to impose excessive levies must be controlled by alternative mechanisms. Thirdly, although letting localities choose tax rates according to local conditions may improve welfare, this benefit is often considered secondary by politicians in low-income countries, where the common demand for basic services such as education, health, and access to clean water and roads dominates most local governments' agendas.

Division of Expenditure Responsibilities

Under the separation model, the assignment of expenditure responsibilities is determined by national legislation and cannot be altered at the discretion of the central government. Generally speaking, the central government has no legal right to issue unfunded mandates to local governments. It can influence local spending through grants (particularly matching grants), but the extent to which such instruments are used is limited. Although in reality no country makes a black-and-white distinction between central and local responsibilities, the degree of intervention by the central governments in local affairs is generally lower in the US and Canada than in most unitary countries. The most important feature of the separation model is that it guarantees that localities have the maximum autonomy in choosing the levels and kinds of local services according to the needs of their citizens. It protects local governments from arbitrary burden-sharing requirements that might otherwise have been imposed by the central bureaucracy.

Under the ad hoc model, the central government decides the responsibilities of the localities. In other words, the centre has the authority to issue unfunded mandates to localities. For example, the Chinese central government often uses 'decentralization' as a policy instrument to transfer budgetary pressures to lower level governments. The problems of such a model include reduced tax effort, excessive bargaining, and lack of accountability of local governments to their constituents.

The Japanese system differs from the ad hoc model in that the division of most expenditure responsibilities are delineated in laws and regulations (such as the Local Finance Law and regulations promulgated by various ministries). It also differs from the separation model in that the centre spends large sums of money to influence the level and structure of local spending. In the early 1990s, specific purpose grants alone (of which most were matching grants) were about one-third of local own-source revenues (excluding the local allocation tax and the local transfer tax). Assuming the average matching rate is one-third, about two-thirds of local own-source revenues were spent on cost-sharing projects with the central government. The extensive use of matching grants in Japan has allowed the central government to enforce minimum standards and ensure quality of most public services across the country.

A complete separation of central and local functions is not feasible in China for a number of reasons. First, a high degree of local autonomy needs to be accompanied by a substantial local administrative capacity, for example, to identify, evaluate, and implement public projects. Such a capacity is still quite limited in most parts of China, particularly in poor regions. Secondly, China ranks among the countries with the largest regional disparities in the world. Addressing this issue requires substantial involvement by the central government to fund and set standards for basic public services. A fully autonomous local government system may only exacerbate regional disparities in the level and quality of public services. In conclusion, compared to the separation model, the Japanese model provides a more realistic solution to China's problem. Specifically, China needs both elements of the Japanese system: a legal division of expenditure responsibilities that will ensure system stability, and some central government-funded mandates that can help poor localities reach the minimum level and quality of services.

Intergovernmental Fiscal Transfer

On intergovernmental fiscal transfers, the separation model and the Japanese model do not differ significantly. Under both models, all major intergovernmental transfer programmes are created by national legislation. For example, Japan's Local Allocation Tax, the major equalization transfer programme, is governed by the Local Allocation Tax Law. This law stipulates that the Local Allocation Tax should be based on a standard formula; the final authority to approve the distribution formula (including unit costs of various local expenditure items) lies with the Diet (the National Assembly); and the Ministry of Home Affairs is responsible for the operation of the transfer system and for determining the modification coefficients. A simplified formula of the Japanese Local Allocation Tax is as follows:

$$\text{Transfer} = \text{Basic Fiscal Needs} - \text{Basic Fiscal Capacity}$$

that is, the transfer to a locality depends on its basic fiscal needs and basic fiscal capacity. Basic fiscal capacity is measured by multiplying the locality's tax bases by the national standard tax rates. The assessment of basic fiscal needs is very complicated. The first step is to divide the aggregate fiscal needs into several categories, such as education, welfare, police, road construction, etc. The second step is to estimate the fiscal need in each category using the following formula:

Fiscal need = measurement unit × unit cost × modification coefficient

where the measurement unit reflects the size of the beneficiaries, unit cost reflects the standard cost per measurement unit, and modification coefficient reflects the extraordinary needs or cost differentials across regions. For example, the measurement unit for primary education is the number of students or teachers, unit cost is the national standard per student cost, and modification coefficients reflect population density, temperature, teachers' salary, type of school, etc. (Ma, 1994). This legal framework ensures that no single locality can effectively influence the distribution of the Local Allocation Tax in favour of itself without affecting many other localities. The fact that the Ministry of Home Affairs does not have the final authority to approve the formula and unit costs is an important mechanism to deter any attempt to manipulate distribution. In the meantime, a certain degree of flexibility is given to the Ministry of Home Affairs, as it has the authority to determine the modification coefficients, which marginally affect the distribution of the Local Allocation Tax. As for specific-purpose grants, the administration has more flexibility in determining the recipients. The Diet creates these grant programmes, but the distribution methods (including the matching rates) are mostly governed by administrative ordinances.

Under the ad hoc model, the size and distribution methods of intergovernmental fiscal transfers are all determined by the central government. Before 1994, China addressed the problems of vertical and horizontal fiscal imbalances through a combination of upward revenue-sharing schemes and central government transfers. Currently, China's unconditional transfers are largely based on the 1993 distribution pattern, which was in turn based on one-to-one negotiations between the centre and localities. In other words, the current system retains many discretionary features of the old contract system. In addition, there is no generally applicable formula for specific purpose grants, and the decisions made were subject to intense negotiations and local government lobbying. It is reported that nearly every specific purpose grant made by the central government was backed by some senior leaders' 'notes' written on behalf of a recipient region (Ma, 1997a).

China should move towards a formula-based general-purpose transfer system and replace a major part of the current specific-purpose transfer system with a matching grant system. The resources for equalization transfer (e.g. a certain percentage of the centre's total revenue) should be guaranteed by an intergovernmental transfer law. This law should also designate a central government agency to be responsible for the operation of the system. The key elements of the transfer formula should be approved by the National People's Congress, while the technical details can be left to the designated agency. This law should also stipulate that provincial and lower-level governments are obliged to provide necessary data to the designated agency for calculation of grant distribution, and local officials who manipulate such statistics should be subject to administrative and even legal penalties.

Local Borrowing

In many countries, local borrowing is an important source for financing long-term development projects such as roads, bridges, and telecommunication facilities. Local borrowing for such projects is justified on the ground that the benefits of these projects often last for decades and that the costs of these projects should be borne mainly by future taxpayers, who are the beneficiaries of such projects. Under the separation model, the central government does not restrict local government borrowing, and bears no responsibility for the consequences. A typical example is the United States, where the federal government sets no limit on state and local borrowing. For this model to work, a number of conditions should exist: (1) a relatively developed capital market that is able to evaluate the risk of the proposed local bond issuance. With such a market, localities with poor financial management records are unlikely to sell their bonds at favourable rates; (2) mechanisms that can hold local authorities accountable for their borrowing activities to the residents (examples include: direct local election of chief executives, strong local councils, free media, independent auditing of local government financial activities, etc.), thus limiting the possibility of excessive borrowing; and (3) the central government's credible commitment to a 'no bail out' policy. If the borrowing governments could not repay debts due to over-borrowing or mismanagement of borrowed funds, they should have no choice but to declare bankruptcy (e.g. in the case of Orange County, California in 1993).

Under the ad hoc model, the central government decides whether and how much each locality could borrow on a case-by-case basis. In China, local governments are in principle not allowed to borrow from either banks or through issuing debts. Each year only small amounts of quota are allocated to provinces by the PBC (the central bank) for locally owned state enterprises to issue development or corporate bonds.

The allocation of such quotas is not based on transparent criteria. The restriction on local borrowing limits the local governments' capacity to improve infrastructure and, in cases where capital expenditures are financed by tax revenues, forces the current generations to bear the costs of the projects that have long-lasting benefits.

The Japanese system of local government borrowing is somewhere in between the separation and the ad hoc models. In Japan, local borrowing is allowed to the extent that the local governments have the capacity to repay the debts and the use of borrowed funds is permitted for capital projects. According to Article 5 of Japan's Local Finance Law, expenditures eligible for local bonds include: (1) expenditures relating to local government enterprises, such as transportation, gas supply, and water supply; (2) investments and loans; (3) repayment of previous bonds; (4) emergency measures, restoration work, and relief measures in times of disaster; (5) construction of public facilities and facilities for official use; and (6) other expenditures prescribed by specific laws as eligible for local bonds. When issuing bonds, a local government must include in its annual budget such items as the purpose of the issue, planned interest rates, and conditions of repayment. These items must be approved by the local government assembly. In addition, prefectures and designated cities must obtain permission for issuing local bonds from the Minister of Home Affairs. Municipalities must obtain permission from the prefectural governors.

Japan's Ministry of Home Affairs bases bond–permit approval on what is called the bond–charge ratio. This bond–charge ratio is the amount of general revenue spent on debt service to total general revenue represented by the average of the past three fiscal years. Where the bond–charge ratio is between 20 and 30 per cent, the issuance of local bonds for general works projects without central government subsidies and bonds for recreation, sports, and social-welfare projects are not permitted. Where the bond–charge ratio is 30 per cent or over, bonds are not approved except for natural disaster restoration, local public enterprise expenses, and a few other specific expenditures.

Which model of local borrowing is more appropriate for China? My view is that China needs a system that allows the local governments to borrow while keeping adequate macroeconomic control. It is clear from past experience that macroeconomic stability must be a high priority of the central government in designing rules for local borrowing. China's rudimentary capital market does not impose on borrowers the types of constraints imposed by the US capital market, and the lack of transparency in the local budget process creates opportunities for local governments to borrow excessively. Therefore, the central authority must set limits on local borrowing in order to prevent a local debt crisis. On the other hand, China should allow localities with healthy fiscal conditions to borrow funds in order to finance long-term capital projects for development purposes. In brief, China needs a Japanese-style system that has the following characteristics: (1) well defined uses of borrowed funds; (2) clearly defined, formula-based limits of local borrowing; and (3) an approval procedure that is transparent and predictable.

Conclusions

Most of the important elements of China's central–local fiscal relations are not determined through national legislation; rather, they are determined at the discretion of the central government. This system leads to frequent policy changes, excessive bargaining between levels of government, various incentive problems (e.g. reduced local tax effort), and increased regional disparities. Given the political constraint that a federal structure is not feasible in China's foreseeable future, the Japanese model of central–local relations, which relies upon a legal division of fiscal powers and responsibilities while retaining effective instruments for the central government to conduct macroeconomic control, provides a more interesting reference for China than the pure 'separation model', which emphasizes the sovereignty of local authorities. Future reforms in China should appropriately combine the rule-based elements (e.g. a legal division of tax bases and expenditure responsibilities, and a formula-based transfer system) and the instruments for central government interventions (such as the control over major local tax rates, control over local borrowing, a personnel dispatching system, etc.).

3
Monetary Reform

Introduction

Parallel to fiscal reforms, China's monetary reforms started in the early 1980s, and picked up speed in the early 1990s. During the past two decades of monetary reform, China has converted the People's Bank of China (PBC) into a central bank that formulates and implements monetary policies; established a state banking system that consists of four major specialized banks, three policy banks, and many commercial banks; created a large number of nonbank financial institutions that conduct trust and investment services, securities underwriting and transactions, and insurance business. Over the past few years, the central bank has increasingly used indirect policy instruments to conduct macroeconomic management and, for the first time in history, successfully achieved soft landing of an overheated economy in 1994–5 by reducing the inflation rate (measured by the retail price index) from 22 per cent in 1994 to 6 per cent in 1996 and 1 per cent in 1997 while keeping the economy growing at an annual average rate of 11 per cent.

Nevertheless, China's monetary reform is far from complete. The central bank's ability to use indirect policy instruments such as open market operations is still limited; interest rate decontrol is still on the agenda; commercial banks are still overburdened by a large volume of nonperforming loans made to state-owned enterprises; and enforcement of prudential regulations is yet to be strengthened. This chapter will review the progress of China's monetary reforms since the early 1980s, with an emphasis on developments in the 1990s, and point out a number of outstanding issues that need to be addressed by reforms in the coming years.

Monetary Management before 1994

Before 1983, most investments in fixed assets were direct transfers or grants from the government budget. In 1983, direct grants were replaced with interest-bearing loans to agriculture, construction, and production enterprises in an attempt to solve the soft-budget problem of state enterprises. As fiscal investment declined rapidly relative to Gross National Product (GNP) over the past decades, the importance of the banking system in enterprise financing increased accordingly. From 1978 to 1993, the share of budgetary financing in the country's total investment in capital construction and technical upgrading and transformation declined from 58 per cent to 4 per cent, while the share of bank loans in total fixed investment increased from a negligible amount to 23 per cent (State Statistical Bureau, 1997a). As the banking system gradually became a primary channel for financing investments, the importance of regulating bank activities in macroeconomic management increased accordingly.

Various specialized banks were created or re-established during the 1980s. The Agriculture Bank, the Construction Bank, and the Bank of China were separated from the operations of the PBC. Each of these institutions was to provide service to a designated sector of the economy. By 1993, China's financial system was dominated by the following specialized banks and nonbank institutions: (1) the Agriculture Bank; (2) the Bank of China; (3) the Construction Bank; (4) the Industrial and Commercial Bank; (5) Rural Credit Cooperatives; (6) Urban Credit Cooperatives; (7) the Bank of Communications; (8) the China International Trust and Investment Corporation (CITIC); (9) Guangda Finance Corporation; and (10) the People's Insurance Company.

Officially, the PBC's role was to formulate and implement monetary policies. However, since the PBC was only a ministry-level body under the State Council, all major monetary policies, including the credit plan and the cash issuance plan, were subject to approval by the State Council. The responsibility of the central bank was therefore to carry out the central government's monetary policy and make sure all the financial institutions follow the financial rules of the government.

Until the end of 1997, the credit plan was the central bank's single most important instrument of monetary control. The credit plan determined the credit ceiling for each specialized bank and each of its local branches; a credit ceiling defined the maximum amount of loans each specialized bank and each of its local branches could extend within a year. The specialized banks used the funds they controlled (the deposits they obtained, their own capital, plus the amount of money they were allowed to borrow from the central bank according to the credit plan) to make loans. Although the central bank also formulated a cash issuance plan every year parallel to the credit plan, the cash supply was in effect endogenous as long as the total credit supply was determined. In particular, the demand for cash came largely from wage payments and agricultural procurement. The former had to do with how much money was lent through the banking system, and the latter was a 'hard' demand, and neither was at the central bank's discretion.

In addition to the credit plan, the central bank had used a number of other policy instruments. These included:

Reserve ratios   The specialized banks kept a certain proportion of deposits with the central bank in the form of required reserves. The central bank might change the reserve ratio as an instrument of monetary policy. In 1985, the required reserve ratio was 10 per cent. The ratio was raised to 13 per cent in 1988. In 1992 an additional excess reserve ratio of 7 per cent was applied, bringing the total effective reserve ratio to 20 per cent. However, the reserve ratios were not effective because specialized banks had generally held excess reserves. In most cases, the binding constraint that the specialized banks faced was the credit plan.

Interest rate adjustments   The central bank strictly controlled interest rates for deposits and lending in all specialized banks. The rates were uniform across banks, and varied according to types of projects. In accordance with industrial policy, lending to agricultural, infrastructure and energy sectors were in general subject to low rates. The central bank occasionally adjusted the official interest rates as an instrument of demand control. However, the effectiveness of this instrument was limited since the official interest rates were often negative and borrowing by SOEs was often insensitive to interest rates.

Lending to specialized banks   The central bank extended credit to specialized banks that experienced temporary liquidity problems. The lending rate for such credit was occasionally used as an instrument of monetary control.

Monetary Reform during 1994–96

In late 1993, in an attempt to establish a well-functioning monetary control system, the central government announced a comprehensive reform plan to begin in 1994. The main aspects of this reform plan were as follows:

The central bank and its functions It was stated in the reform plan that the central bank's main function was to formulate and implement monetary policy. 'The primary objective of monetary policy is to maintain the stability of the value of the currency, and on that basis, to support the growth of the economy' (FBIS, 1993). Other functions of the central bank would include enforcing strict supervision over financial institutions, conducting clearance, and issuing banknotes.

The central bank's relations with specialized banks and other commercial banks According to the plan, the authority to formulate monetary policies must be concentrated in the hands of the PBC head office. To strengthen the central bank's hand in this task, powers previously given to PBC branches to control funds were taken back to the bank's headquarters to lessen the interference of local governments in the making and implementation of monetary policy. In particular, a system consisting of only six regional PBC branches was planned to be established to replace the old system in which each PBC branch was located in an individual province. The heads of the regional PBC branches were to be directly appointed by the PBC headquarters without consulting the provincial governments.

Instruments to conduct monetary policies The PBC was to gradually use more indirect means to control the money supply, such as open market operations, discount rates, reserve ratios, and operations in the foreign exchange market. The application of the mandatory credit plan was to be gradually phased out. The PBC would also regulate interbank lending.

Deficit financing In the new system, deficit financing would mainly rely on issuing bonds, while direct central bank lending to the budget would be prohibited. This reform was referred to as 'increasing the central bank's independence'.

Policy lending and commercial lending The four specialized banks were to be transformed into commercial banks that aim at profit-making and be responsible for their losses. Competition among the commercial banks was encouraged by letting the specialized banks conduct business formerly outside their designated scope. Investment and securities' firms would be separated from the commercial banks.

Under this plan, the policy lending functions of the Agricultural Bank, the Bank of China, the Construction Bank, and the Bank of Industry and Commerce were separated from these banks and formed the basis of three newly established policy banks. The main task of the three policy banks – the State Development Bank, the Import–Export Bank, and the Agricultural Development Bank – was to grant policy loans (typically subsidized and directed loans) to selected projects in accordance with the industrial policy. The main sources of funds of these policy banks include PBC credit, postal savings, and issuance of bonds. In the meantime several other banks were turned into joint stock banks, and the urban and rural credit cooperatives were transformed into cooperative banks.

Interbank lending   The maximum length of maturity allowed for interbank loans was shortened from three months to three days.

In March 1995, the 'Law of the People's Bank of China' (the PBC Law) was passed by the National People's Congress. The legislation formalized many of the measures initiated in the 1994 monetary reform. The key provisions of this law are:

1. The functions of the PBC should include formulating and implementing monetary policies, issuing currency, regulating financial institutions, maintaining the payment and clearing system, and holding and managing foreign exchange reserves.

2. The PBC should formulate and implement monetary policies under the leadership of the State Council; the Governor of the PBC should be nominated by the Premier of the State Council and appointed by the National People's Congress.

3. The PBC should use the following policy instruments to conduct monetary policies: reserve ratio, central bank base rate, rediscounting, lending to commercial banks, open market operations, trading of foreign exchange, and other instruments prescribed by the State Council.

4. The PBC should approve the establishment of new financial institutions and regulate their activities.

5. All expenditures of the PBC should be included in the state budget system.

Since the 1994 monetary reform and the subsequent passage of the PBC Law, the PBC has increased its autonomy with respect to other government agencies and made more extensive use of a range of intermediate monetary instruments. In 1994, the PBC stopped direct lending to the Ministry of Finance (MOF). However, the reform plan of reorganizing PBC branches at the regional level was not implemented until 1998 due to strong objections from provincial authorities that had vested interests in influencing PBC branches.

Between 1994 and 1997, while the credit plan was still the major policy instrument, other instruments, including open market operations, PBC refinance facility, and interest rate adjustments, had gradually gained importance. In 1995 and 1996, the PBC issued a series of short-term central bank bills to facilitate its open market operations. In January 1996, the PBC lifted the control over interest rates in the interbank market. Since then, official deposit and lending interest rates were adjusted more frequently and tended to reflect, to a certain degree, interest rate changes in the interbank markets. In the meantime, PBC lending to commercial and policy banks began to play an important role in liquidity management. When banks' liquidity was considered high, PBC loans were recalled, and vice versa. Reserve ratio adjustments, however, continued to be an insignificant instrument mainly because almost all banks held large amounts of excess reserves.

Monetary Reform since 1997

The authorities took three significant steps in reforming the monetary management system in late 1997 and early 1998. The timing of these measures was clearly influenced by the authorities' increased concern about the financial risks that China's banking system might be exposed to in the wake of the financial crisis in other Asian countries.

The first step, announced in late 1997 and to begin in 1998, was the implementation of the long delayed plan of reorganizing the central bank's branch system. Under the old system where each PBC branch was located in one province, PBC branches were often used by provincial leaders as means to prevail on the central bank for higher credit ceilings or upward revisions of credit ceilings. Some provincial authorities even purposely underinvest in central government's priority projects in order to gain bargaining power for additional credits from the PBC.[1] After the reform, the PBC will no longer maintain branches in each province; rather, it will only has branches at the regional level, with each region covering several provinces. This reform will ensure that the PBC operates independently from interventions of local authorities, which are typically more concerned about their growth performance than macroeconomic stability. By removing the close links between PBC branches and provincial authorities, the central bank will gain more flexibility in determining and implementing prudent monetary policies. It was envisaged by the PBC, however, the process of implementing this reform might take several years, and PBC branches at the provincial level would be retained at least in 1998 (Dai, 1998).

The second major reform, effective 1 January 1998, was to phase out the credit plan (which consisted of credit ceilings imposed on commercial banks) as a way of monetary control. At least three factors contributed to the government's decision to introduce this historical change at the end of 1997. First, since 1994 China began to face large and persistent current account surpluses and capital inflows, which created upward pressures for the Chinese Yuan. To maintain a relatively stable exchange rate, the PBC had to intervene frequently in the foreign exchange market – mostly in the form of purchasing foreign exchange – thereby significantly increasing the PBC's net foreign assets (NFA). Consequently, the PBC's net domestic assets as a percentage of reserve money declined from 88 per cent at end-1993 to 64 per cent at end-1996. Similarly, net domestic assets of the banking system as a percentage of broad money declined from 93 per cent at end-1993 to 87 per cent at end-1996 (International Monetary Fund, 1998). In the meantime, the coverage of the credit plan became much narrower as the share of state-owned banks in total domestic credit declined rapidly from 78 per cent in 1990 to 51 per cent in 1996 (Wang, 1998). In other words, the relevance of the credit plan to the control of monetary aggregates is no longer significant.

Secondly, the PBC's liquidity management became more complicated than before: when the PBC's NFA increased due to its purchase of foreign exchange, it had to sterilize the increase in NFA by restraining domestic credit (e.g. a reduction in PBC lending to commercial banks) in order to achieve its target for money supply.[2] The frequency of the PBC's foreign exchange interventions and the ensuing sterilization made the implementation of any rigid annual credit plan virtually impossible.

Thirdly, over the past few years the PBC had consciously invested in the development of various indirect policy instruments, including the accumulation of short-term T-bills, more frequent operations in the T-bill markets, and more flexible applications of the refinance facility and interest rate adjustments. The experience gained during these years in managing liquidity with indirect monetary instruments proved sufficient for a complete transition from the credit plan to indirect policy instruments at the end of 1997.

The third major reform, announced in March and to be implemented in late 1998, was that the government planned to issue Y270 billion of treasury bonds to recapitalize the four major state-owned commercial banks, including China Agriculture Bank, Industry and Commerce Bank of China, the Construction Bank of China, and the Bank of China. The immediate objective was to assist these banks, which accounted for 90 per cent of the entire banking system's assets in 1997, to meet the PBC's minimum capital adequacy ratio of 8 per cent. Currently, the major state-owned banks are overburdened by large amounts of non-performing loans – estimated at 20–30 per cent of total loan portfolios (Zhang and Zhong, 1997) – and some even face solvency problems. The government feared that without large-scale recapitalization, there would be a potential risk of banking crisis if the public lost confidence in the ailing banks. The bond financed government bail-out package was considered a non-inflationary way to address this potential risk. Nevertheless, simply injecting money to insolvent banks may not be sufficient to ensure banks to return to profitability and sustained solvency. In particular, establishing an arm's- length relationship between the government and state-owned enterprises on the one hand, and commercial banks on the other hand, will be the key to avoiding repeated government bail-out.[3]

China's Inflation Experience in the 1990s

Between 1979 and 1997, the Chinese economy experienced four expansions and four contractions in terms of GNP growth. Variation in production growth was significant: the peak of GNP growth rates during the 1979–96 period reached 14.5 per cent in 1988 while the trough was about 4 per cent in 1989. At the same time, the magnitude of price changes was large compared to those in many other countries. In 1983, the increase in the retail price index was only 1.5 per cent; in 1988, this price index went up to 18.7 per cent; the index declined to 2.1 per cent in 1990, and surged again to 21.7 per cent in 1994. The past two years' macroeconomic experience has been more favourable, however, than other years of the post-reform era. In 1996 and 1997, GDP grew by 9.7 per cent and 8.8 per cent, respectively, while the retail price index only increased by 6.0 per cent and 1.1 per cent, respectively (see Table 3.1). This section provides an brief overview of the main explanations of China monetary cycles and discuss the relevance of different mechanisms suggested by the literature on China's macroeconomic situation in the 1990s.

Many articles have analyzed China's money supply and inflation. Chow (1987) applies the quantity theory of money to China and finds that the ratio of money supply to real output is an important variable in explaining the price level. Feltenstein and Ziba (1987) estimate a money supply function and argue that the change in money supply (broad money) can be explained by changes in wage payments, agricultural procurement payments, and government deficits. Feltenstein and Ha (1989) estimate the repressed inflation and liquidity overhang. Woo

Table 3.1   China: selected macroeconomic indicators, 1978–97 (Yuan bn)

Year	GDP (current price)	GDP index (1978 = 100)	Percentage change of retail price index	Currency in circulation	M1	Quasi-money	M2	Foreign exchang reserves (US$bn)
1978	362.4	100.0			58.0	30.9	89.0	
1979	403.8	107.6	2.0		92.1	40.6	132.8	0.8
1980	451.8	116.0	6.0		114.9	52.2	167.1	−1.3
1981	486.2	122.1	2.4		134.5	63.3	197.8	2.7
1982	529.5	133.1	1.9		148.8	77.7	226.6	7.0
1983	593.5	147.6	1.5		174.9	96.4	271.3	8.9
1984	717.1	170.0	2.8		244.9	114.9	359.9	8.2
1985	896.4	192.9	8.8	98.8	301.7	185.8	487.5	2.6
1986	1 020.2	210.0	6.0	121.8	385.9	249.0	634.9	2.1
1987	1 196.3	234.3	7.3	145.5	457.4	338.3	795.7	2.9
1988	1 492.8	260.7	18.5	213.3	548.7	411.5	960.2	3.4
1989	1 690.9	271.3	17.8	234.2	583.4	555.9	1 139.3	5.6
1990	1 854.8	281.7	2.1	264.4	701.0	767.2	1 468.2	11.1
1991	2 161.8	307.6	2.9	317.8	898.8	961.1	1 859.9	21.7
1992	2 663.8	351.4	5.4	433.6	1 171.4	1 261.3	2 432.7	19.4
1993	3 463.4	398.8	13.2	586.5	1 424.4	1 583.2	3 007.6	21.2
1994	4 675.9	449.3	21.7	728.9	2 055.6	2 637.7	4 693.3	51.6
1995	5 847.8	496.5	14.8	788.5	2 401.0	3 676.9	6 077.9	73.6
1996	6 779.5	544.2	6.0	880.2	2 851.5	4 758.0	7 609.5	105.3
1997	7 477.2	562.0	0.8	1 017.8	3 482.6	5 617.4	9 100.0	139.9

Notes: M1 = the sum of currency outside banks and demand deposits other than those of the central government. Quasi-money = time, savings and foreign currency deposits of resident sectors other than the central government. M2 = M1 plus quasi-money.
Sources: Editorial Department of Fiscal Yearbook of China, 1995; State Statistical Bureau, 1996, 1997a; Chen, 1998; Dai, 1998.

et al. (1993) argue that increasing government subsidies to loss-making SOEs is responsible for increasing the deficit and macroeconomic instability. Garnaut and Ma (1993) and Cardoso and Yusuf (1994) provide some descriptive analyses based on the recent experience of Chinese inflation. While these studies confirm that an excessive money supply would create inflation and that the source of the money supply could be decomposed into a number of factors, they do not answer the question of why the central government could not or was not willing to control the money supply at a level that yielded stable prices.

A number of recent studies point out several different institutional causes of inflation. The main views are summarized below:

1. *Monetization of deficits.* The World Bank (1995b) argues that, when lumping budgetary deficits and implicit deficits (subsidies to SOEs through policy loans), the actual deficit-to-GDP was as high as 7–10 per cent in the early 1990s. It suggests that the financial losses incurred by SOEs and the resulting monetization of budgetary and implicit deficits by the central bank was a main cause of China's inflation.

2. *Disintermediation crisis.* Naughton (1995) argues that obvious disintermediation crises occurred in both 1988 and 1992–3. By disintermediation, he refers to the situation in which depositors opt out of (withdraw their deposits from) the banking system and shift to durable or other financial instruments that won't depreciate with the currency, in the expectation of high inflation. He supports his argument by noting that the growth rate of savings deposits in 1988 dropped to about 25 per cent from 40 per cent in 1987, and the growth rate in 1993 was only 27 per cent compared with 30 per cent in 1991. He claims that such disintermediation crises put 'the banking system into a severe credit squeeze, because suddenly the deposit base drops'. He further concludes that the substantial increase in PBC lending to commercial banks in 1993, which increased the level of base money, was a response to the disintermediation crisis (to inject additional liquidity to the banking system). If one reads the statistics carefully, however, it is easy to see that the 'disintermediation' explanation is inconsistent with the data Naughton presents: the absolute level of savings deposits in both 1988 and 1993 actually increased by 25 per cent or more, rather than dropped.

3. *Frictional inflation.* Some Chinese scholars propose that inflation arises during periods of reform for 'frictional' reasons (see, for example, Fan, 1989). During China's decades of central planning, the structure of production was mainly determined by the planners' demand for producer and investment goods. Reforms in the 1980s led to a rapid increase in consumer demand, while a greater proportion of national income was put in the hands of consumers. Demand for consumer goods rises faster than the supply, as the adjustment of the production structure takes time. The lag between the change in demand and that in supply results in 'frictional inflation'. Again, this theory does not tell us why the central bank simply accommodates the high demand for money. In addition, the Chinese-language literature largely remains at the descriptive and institutional stage, mainly due to the lack of effective modelling tools.

4. *The two-track system.* Sicular (1990) proposes that inflation can arise due to inherent contradictions between plan and market. Her

model uses China's grain market as an example of the two-track system, under which the government requires farmers to sell certain quantities of their grain output to the state at below-market planned prices and then the government sells the grain at a low, ration price to urban consumers. The model shows that market opportunities (i.e. the difference between the market price and the planned price) encourage plan evasion and cause a shortfall in planned deliveries. This forces the government to either raise the planned procurement price or purchase more from the free market. Both measures imply increased government subsidies, which, assuming that subsidies are covered by money printing, generates inflation.

While increased government subsidies in the process of grain procurement have surely contributed to increasing the government deficit and to the resulting inflationary pressure, it is not clear how significant this mechanism is to the overall price change. First, an increase in price subsidies may or may not increase government deficits proportionally, depending on the overall budgetary arrangement. Secondly, government deficits in China are not totally financed by borrowing from the central bank. In the early 1990s more than 70 per cent of the deficits were financed by government debts. A simple ordinary least square (OLS) regression of government borrowing from the central bank on price subsidies yields an R^2 of only 0.28, indicating little explanatory power of the dependent variable.[4] Thirdly, one cannot assume that one yuan of government borrowing from the central bank means that the central bank creates an additional yuan of base money. To what extent government borrowing from the central bank is financed by money creation depends on the changes in all other items in the central bank's balance sheet. In addition, the accommodative policies of the government (e.g. raising procurement prices or increasing subsidies to urban consumers) are assumed in the model; it does not explain why the government chooses to follow these practices.

5. *Enterprise–government game.* Wang (1991) bases his theory on decentralized resource control at the enterprise level. His model assumes that each firm maximizes its output, and the government maximizes total output of all firms. The firms allocate their own resources between fixed capital investment and circulating funds, while the government only provides the circulating funds to the firms. To compete for resources from the government, the firms allocate less than the optimal amount of resources to fixed capital investment. The prisoner's dilemma game among firms leads to a lower level of total output than the optimum. To achieve a high level of output, the govern-

ment decides to print money to provide more circulating funds to the firms, thus creating inflation.

6. *Central–local credit game.* Ma (1996a) presents a game theoretic model which shows how China's inflation over the past decade can be a consequence of the decentralized financial system. Under the decentralized system a game is played between local authorities (local banks) and the central authority (the central bank), that results in an equilibrium with inflation. The model assumes that each region has an objective of maximizing local output value, and that credit expansion is the primary means of achieving this goal. However, the signals the region uses to choose investment projects are distorted because of price controls in certain sectors. Unlike the regions, the central government values different projects using shadow prices, and cares about growth as well as low inflation. Knowing that the centre values certain key (essential) projects, however, the region purposely under-invests in these projects, and creates pressures on the centre to grant a higher credit ceiling. The model shows that after the region has allocated the initial credit ceiling, the central bank has the *ex post* incentive to revise the ceiling upward. The central bank's pre-announced credit plan is not credible and the equilibrium yields a higher inflation rate and a lower welfare level than if the centre could commit to a fixed credit ceiling.

Evidence from 1992–3 tends to substantiate the story of investment distortion between different types of projects. The famous story of 'white notes' is the best example of how local governments distort the investment structure in order to force the central bank to increase the credit ceiling. Over the first few years of the 1990s, many provinces reported to the central bank that they had used up all their credit allowance and had no money to purchase grain. They had to issue 'white notes' – IOUs – to the farmers, creating strong resentment among the farmers. To redeem the IOUs, the centre was forced to offer additional credit to these regions (Li and Jiang, 1993). In the first quarter of 1993 alone, the local branches of the specialized banks lent a net of 100 billion yuan to nonbank financial institutions for operations including acquisition of real estate assets and purchase of securities (World Bank, 1994a), while leaving many essential projects in the central government priority list underfinanced. This became one of the primary reasons for the dismissal of the central bank governor, Li Guixian, in June 1993.

7. *Increase in foreign exchange reserves.* Naughton (1995) and a recent World Bank report (World Bank, 1996a) suggest that in 1994 and 1995, a major factor behind the increase in money supply was the increase in foreign exchange reserves. By the end of 1994, foreign exchange reserves

reached US$51.6 billion, up from US$30.4 billion at the end of 1993 and US$19.4 billion in 1992. By the end of 1996, China's foreign exchange reserves reached US$108 billion, the highest level in history, and the second highest in the world. The main reason for the increase in foreign exchange reserves was the large foreign capital inflow. In 1994, 1995, and 1996 China's actual foreign capital inflow reached US$33 billion, US$38 billion, and US$41 billion respectively, the largest capital inflow in the developing world. In order to keep the competitiveness of the export sector,[5] the central bank had to purchase foreign exchange to stabilize the exchange rate. According to the World Bank (1996a), the increase in foreign reserves contributed 70 per cent of reserve money growth in 1994 and 60 per cent in 1995. A similar analysis I conducted shows that in 1996 the contribution of increase in foreign reserves to reserve money growth was close to 50 per cent.

It is interesting to note that the significance of many causes of inflation discussed above has declined over the last few years as the central bank determined to implement the soft landing programme. In particular, the PBC's direct lending to the budget was terminated, the public retained confidence in the banking sector, the banking system's quasifiscal subsidies to the agriculture sector was substantially reduced, and excess capacity of the enterprise sector has grown rapidly. From 1995 to 1997, notwithstanding the large increase in foreign exchange reserves, inflation has been brought down due to the following actions of the central bank, in addition to the termination of direct central bank credit to finance budget deficit: (1) conducting sterilization policies to offset the expansionary effect of its intervention in the foreign exchange market; (2) increasing commercial banks' foreign exchange reserves; (3) recovering loans made to commercial banks and nonbank financial institutions; (4) prohibiting PBC branches from making loans to local banks and nonbank financial institutions; (5) reducing special credits; and (6) opening RMB special deposits to mop up liquidity from the economy.

Another interesting phenomenon in recent years is that, broad money has consistently grown at a much higher rate than the combined growth rates of GDP and inflation. The fact that inflation declined despite the high growth in broad money suggests a continued decline in broad money velocity. This, in turn, reflects the increase in money demand due to a sharp decline in the inflation rate. However, such a trend may not last in the long run as it is a typical phenomenon during periods of disinflation (as in the case of 1994–6 in China). China's inflation rate dropped to its trough in 1998 and one therefore should not expect a continued large increase in money demand.

Future Reforms

The monetary reform since 1994 addressed a number of important drawbacks in the old system which weakened the central bank's control over the money supply. In particular, the prohibition of the MOF's borrowing from the central bank, the phasing-out of the credit plan and increased application of indirect policy instruments, the centralization of personnel management of the PBC branches and specialized banks, and the separation of policy lending from commercial lending are all steps in the right direction. These measures have reduced the possibility of direct monetization of fiscal deficits, reduced local pressures on the central bank for excessive credit supply, and increased the central bank's flexibility in liquidity management.

However, many of these reforms are partial in nature and should be continued and deepened in order to fully achieve their ultimate objectives. Although the MOF no longer borrows directly from the PBC, the state banks continue to perform a significant fiscal role as they are obliged to provide liquidity to SOEs.[6] Despite the creation of three new policy banks, the specialized banks have not been fully commercialized, as they continue to be burdened with policy lending mandates. This section discusses three problems that are to be addressed by future reforms in the years to come: central bank independence, interest rate decontrol, and financing of policy banks.

Central bank independence. The central bank is still under the strict control of the State Council. For various political reasons, the State Council may be more 'radical', compared with a truly independent central bank, in the sense that it tends to favour rapid economic growth and job creation rather than inflation control. Under the current system, the central bank is therefore not likely to enforce a more prudent money supply if the State Council cannot resist demands for rescuing SOEs, maintaining political stability, or solving bottleneck problems in industrial structure. Without a mechanism for commitment to a prudent monetary policy, excessive money growth may recur in other forms under the new system.

Despite the pressures from local governments and/or enterprises, a conservative central bank is less likely to be tempted to lend excessively to commercial banks. This suggests that the central bank should be independent from the central as well as the local governments. A number of cross-country studies have presented empirical evidence suggesting that a more independent central bank is usually associated with a lower inflation rate (Alesina and Summers, 1993). A separate paper (Ma, 1996a) shows that the Chinese central bank's inability to honour a pre-announced low inflation policy (as evidenced by repeated upward revisions of credit ceilings during high inflation periods) is in part a result of the fact that it has the same objective as the government. I therefore recommend that, as a medium-term reform objective, China place the central bank under the NPC, and grant the central bank independence in the sense that: its decisions are not reviewed by other bodies except the NPC or its standing committee; its governor is appointed for extended periods and cannot be removed without cause; it does not have to seek approval for its budget; and it is not subject to external audits.

Interest rate decontrol   The last few years have seen an upsurge of illegal lending and corruption scandals within the state banking system. At the same time the PBC controls official lending rates, the commercial banks – formerly specialized banks – are encouraged to operate based on market principles: selecting low risk and high yield projects. A large number of loss-making SOEs thus find it increasingly difficult to obtain loans from the state-owned banks. These SOEs are forced to resort to personal connections, bribery, and pressures from local governments to obtain loans at official rates. Banks, on the other hand, lend directly to these SOEs only (1) when pressures from the government (on behalf of the SOEs) are sufficiently strong; and (2) when loan officers receive bribes (cash or in-kind) from the borrowers. Another common practice, which allows banks to legally circumvent the interest rate control, is to lend to non-bank financial institutions (NBFIs) which are subject to a looser interest rate control. The NBFIs then re-lend the funds at higher rates and share the profits with the banks.

The main purpose of the government's control over lending rates is to subsidize the state-owned enterprises. The past few years' experience suggests, however, that this objective has been largely unmet. From time to time, the central government seemed determined to stop illegal lending at rates higher than the official rates and to penalize bribery-taking bank officers. However, the persistence of such behaviours suggests that the long-term solution to the problem of 'dual rate system' will have to be interest rate decontrol. In the presence of interest rate control, there are always incentives for commercial banks to divert funds from the banking system to black market lending. Since a large number of SOEs effectively receive loans at market rates (due to the high transaction costs involved in borrowing from state banks), the continuation of interest rate control is no longer justified. Moreover, the asymmetric treatment of banks and NBFIs further reduces the effectiveness of interest rate control. I believe that the time for a general interest rate decontrol – with certain exceptions to protect a small number of key SOEs – is basically ripe. Such a reform can generate immediate benefits in terms of fairness and transparency in the bank lending process, and will eliminate the root of widespread corruption. Other benefits of liberalizing interest rates include a higher investment rate and more competition among banks that would help improve efficiency.

Financing of policy banks   The separation of policy lending from commercial lending will help eliminate the commercial banks' (formerly specialized banks) practice of bargaining with the central bank for expanded credit quotas, but financing the policy lending projects will still be a big problem. The central government, when it formulated the 1994 reform plan, expected that the funding sources of the policy banks would include the central government's budgetary allocation, social insurance funds, postal deposits, and investment funds. The experience of the past three years turned out to be very different. The central government has invested almost no fiscal resources due to its tight budgetary situation and, as China is just beginning to establish a formal pension system, social insurance funds are not yet available for project investment. The three policy banks have financed most of their lending projects by issuing bonds and borrowing from the PBC. In the case of the Agriculture Development Bank, financing has been provided mainly by the PBC. While this may be the only option for the moment, PBC financing of policy loans should not continue in the long run as it contradicts the central bank's goal of maintaining price stability. By definition, the fiscal authority should support policy lending in the form of interest rate subsidies or direct subsidies to the banks.

4
Banking Reform: From Administrative Control to a Regulatory Framework

Introduction

Along with the decentralization and market-oriented reforms in other aspects of the economy, China's banking system has also changed dramatically since 1979. Various specialized banks were created or re-established and became the main channels of enterprise finance. Nonbank financial institutions began to operate and compete with state banks for savings and loans. Foreign banks have recently been allowed to operate in China, although their scope is restricted. The central government is moving towards establishing a western-style monetary management system with indirect measures playing the key roles. It has planned or implemented the elimination of various forms of administrative controls, including credit ceilings, interest rate control, and restrictions over cross-bank competition, either in the short or medium term. These reforms are expected to contribute significantly to a more efficient allocation of financial resources.

However, liberalization of the banking system does not automatically ensure the stability of the financial system, which is crucial to the stability of the overall economic environment. The relaxation on banking control in China created serious macroeconomic problems in 1992–3 when many banks and their affiliated nonbank financial institutions poured resources into imprudent activities, such as speculation in the real estate and stock markets. The increasing share of nonperforming loans in banks' total outstanding loans and the increasing share of household deposits in banks' total liabilities also posed serious pressure for the banks to reconsider the quality of their assets and the liquidity risks involved. A system of prudential and protective regulations to ensure the soundness of the banking system is therefore urgently necessitated.

This chapter discusses the recent developments of China's bank regulations and the associated problems that need to be considered and resolved, with reference to other countries' experiences. The focus of the chapter is on the regulations imposed on commercial banks, since those on the central bank are quite different. The second section briefly describes the development of the Chinese banking system over the past 20 or so years. The third section, the centre of this chapter, looks at the process of China's deregulation and the recent developments in establishing a regulatory framework. Several problems that hinder the effective implementation of bank regulations are identified. The last section offers some conclusions.

Institutional Changes of China's Banking System

Before the founding of the People's Republic of China in 1949, the Chinese banking system included the central bank, three commercial banks – the Bank of Communications, the Agricultural Bank, and the Bank of China – and numerous small independent banks and financial institutions. In 1949 the three major commercial banks were merged or linked into the central bank, which dominated and provided almost all the banking services in China until 1978.

After 1978, as a part of the economic reform programme turning the highly centralized management system into a more decentralized and liberalized one, the Agricultural Bank, the Construction Bank and the Bank of China were separated from the operations of the central bank. The separation of the banking business was based on the belief that a more decentralized system would operate more efficiently. Each of these institutions was intended to provide service to a designated sector in the economy. This approach prevented competition among the banking institutions and required the prospective customers – the peasants, the industrial enterprises, and the trade or foreign-invested companies – to deal with a single institution.

China's banking system now comprises a wide variety of banks. Under the PBC (the central bank), the major commercial banks and nonbank institutions are:
1. Agricultural Bank of China
2. Bank of China
3. Construction Bank of China
4. Industrial and Commercial Bank of China
5. Bank of Communications
6. State Development Bank

7. Import–Export Bank
8. Agricultural Development Bank
9. Rural Credit Cooperatives
10. Urban Credit Cooperatives
11. Smaller regional banks

The PBC is the central bank of China with three sets of branches according to administrative division. Until 1998, it had branches at the provincial level, in prefectures and cities under provincial governments, and more than 2,000 sub-branches at the county level. The PBC is a body at the ministerial level on a par with the MOF. The PBC is in charge of drawing up and implementing monetary and exchange policies; supervising banks, nonbank financial institutions and insurance companies; and examining and approving the establishment, merger and dissolution of financial institutions (Xie, 1995).

The Agricultural Bank of China (ABC) was first established in 1955, closed in 1957, reopened from 1963 to 1965, and re-established in 1979. Its main responsibilities are to receive deposits, extend loans to agricultural and rural industrial projects, and provide settlement services for rural industrial and commercial enterprises. Recently, it was allowed to engage in deposits and loans denominated in foreign exchange and international settlement. It has branches in every province, municipality and county.

The Construction Bank of China (CBC) operated from 1954 to 1966. It was absorbed into the PBC for 13 years and then reconstituted in 1979. It manages government grants for fixed-asset investments and extends loans to fixed-asset investments. Like the Agricultural Bank, the PCBC has branches in every province, municipality and county. There are 38 000 branches together with business offices.

The Industrial and Commercial Bank of China (ICBC) was separated from the central bank in 1984. It is now the biggest commercial bank, with branches in every province, municipality and county. It receives most of its deposits from urban and rural individuals, provides working capital and settlements for urban industrial and commercial enterprises, and processes deposits and loans denominated in foreign exchange and international settlements.

The Bank of China (BOC) was organized in 1908 and served as China's central bank for 40 years. It operated with a joint public/private ownership dominated by the State. Since 1949 BOC has primarily focused on deposits and loans of foreign exchange and international settlements.[1] It has branches in every province and municipality, and in almost every county, and operates a global correspondent and branch network. By the end of 1992, the BOC had 494 overseas branches in 18 countries and regions.

The Bank of Communications (BOCOM) was re-established in 1986 after 38 years of inactivity on China's mainland.[2] It is a shareholding bank, with the major shareholders being the central and local governments. The scope of business for the BOCOM is not limited to a single line of commerce, and the institution has offered financial services throughout the world. As a universal bank, BOCOM had competitive advantages over the four major specialized banks with mandated single functions until the mid-1990s.

As part of 1994's monetary reform, commercial lending and policy lending in the state banking sector were separated. The four specialized banks have been transformed into commercial banks, which operate with reduced government policy-lending mandates. Three policy-lending banks – the State Development Bank, the Agricultural Development Bank, and the Import–Export Bank – were set up to grant policy loans to selected projects in the agricultural, infrastructure, and import–export sectors, respectively. The sources of funds of these policy banks mainly include proceeds from issuing bonds, pension funds, postal savings and PBC loans.

Since the late 1980s, many new commercial banks have been established and located in provinces or the SEZs. Examples include Guangdong Development Bank, the Bank of China Merchants (Shekou), Shenzhen Development Bank, and Pudong Development Bank. In the meantime, a large number of nonbank financial institutions, including trust and investment corporations, securities firms, insurance companies, and, recently, investment banks and investment funds, have emerged at the local level (Kumar *et al.*, 1997). By the end of 1997, 170 foreign banks and nonbank financial institutions had opened operational branches and offices in China (Xu and Qian, 1998). Foreign bank branches are allowed to conduct foreign currency business in China and, by April 1997, nine foreign banks were granted the permission to engage in RMB business in the Pudong New Area on a trial basis.[3] A number of private banks (Siren Qianzhuang) also operate in China. The private banks typically pay higher interest rates on deposits than the major financial institutions, and they charge higher loan rates than the major banks. Although these private banks are not officially sanctioned by the government, they would not continue to operate without tacit approval of the state.

As the institutional structure of the banking system evolved, the importance of the banking system in the country's finances increased dramatically. Before 1983, the highly centralized planning system in China operated mainly by collecting revenue from state enterprises and allocating investment through budgetary grants. The banking system served a very limited purpose in the economy. It provided the credit needed by enterprises to implement plans for physical output and provided and monitored cash used principally to cover labour costs and purchases of agricultural products. Investments in fixed assets in state-owned enterprises were all direct transfers or grants from the government budget. In 1983, as a major economic reform, direct grants were replaced with interest-bearing loans to agricultural, construction, and industrial enterprises in an attempt to solve the soft-budget problem of state enterprises. Over the past 15 years, the importance of budgetary allocation in total investment declined rapidly, and the banking system gradually became the primary channel through which investments are financed and the central authority exercises macroeconomic control. As a result, efficient resource allocation became more closely linked to the performance of the banking sector.

China's banking system expanded rapidly during the reform period. Since 1985, most of the specialized banks have opened branches in all major cities and counties. From the end of 1985 to the end of 1996, the number of branches of state banks rose from 60 785 to 168 101 and the number of employees increased from 973 355 to 2 098 336. During the same period, total deposits increased from Y427 billion to Y6860 billion, while total loans increased from Y591 billion to Y6116 billion. At the end of 1996, outstanding loans from the banking system were 6.6 times the government's budgetary expenditure in 1996, reflecting the rapidly increasing role of the banking system in the economy.

From Liberalization to a Regulatory Framework

Despite the establishment of many commercial banks and nonbank financial institutions and the rapidly increasing magnitude of their operations, the entire banking system was under strict government control until recently. Many of the loans from the commercial banks were more like public transfer payments than the traditional interest-bearing bank loans observed in western countries. Compared to the liberalization in the commodities' market, which freed more than 90 per cent of industrial commodities from government control, the progress of financial reform lagged behind. The major elements of government control are discussed below.

The credit plan   Until the end of 1997, the main instrument the PBC used to control the money supply was the credit plan, which defined credit ceilings for all major commercial banks and policy banks and their local branches as well as for the long-term loans of nonbank financial institutions. Under the credit ceilings, credit allocation was subject to government control at various levels. The central government designated certain amounts of credit to key projects listed in its annual investment plan. Provincial and county governments also imposed their preferences on local branches of commercial banks in their allocation of credit.

The scope of bank activities   The sectors to which each specialized bank could lend were regulated by the PBC. To ensure the monopoly position of the specialized banks, the central bank prevented specialized banks from engaging in businesses in areas other than those designated, and nonbank financial institutions from engaging in deposit and lending businesses. As a result, although the number of commercial banks increased rapidly, the whole banking system still lacked competition.

Interest rate control   Due to concerns such as controlling costs for SOEs (an increase in such costs may reduce the profitability of these firms and be translated into an increase in output prices), the central bank maintained control on interest rates for both deposits and loans. The PBC also set differentials between preferential and other interest rates for priority state-supported projects. In addition, it set a margin between the upper and lower limits of interest rates for rural and urban credit cooperatives.

Restriction over nonstate-owned banks   To protect the profitability of the state banks and to ensure the state's control over the use of financial resources, the government banned private banks and prevented foreign banks from engaging in RMB business until recently.[4] Since almost all banks are owned by the state, the system has produced serious incentive problems as the banks are not responsible for losses but can gain from ventures if they make profits. These controls have also stifled competition and inhibited innovation.

The Trend of Liberalization in Recent Years

An increase in the magnitude of the banking sector cannot replace the liberalization of the banking system, which would foster competition among banks, reduce costs of intermediation, and facilitate a more efficient allocation of credit. By recognizing the costs of direct controls in the banking sector, the government has, in recent years, initiated a number of liberalization programmes in an attempt to shift to a system of indirect monetary control. Chief among these reforms was the elimination of the credit plan (see Chapter 3). Other reform measures have also been or will be implemented in the future, including the relaxation of control over the scope of bank business and interest rate decontrol.

Shenzhen, the testing ground of China's economic reform, has experimented with many of these reforms over the past decade. It abolished the credit plan and introduced the assets–liability and risk management programme as the main instrument for regulating banks. In 1994, on a nation-wide scale, the credit ceilings on financial institutions other than specialized banks were eliminated and replaced by regulations regarding assets–liability and risk management. At the end of 1997, this reform was extended to all commercial banks in China.

Shenzhen also eliminated the restriction on industrial sectors or types of lending. Originally, specialized banks were only allowed to lend to designated clients in certain fields (e.g. the Agricultural Bank to lend to agricultural projects, the Construction Bank to lend to basic construction projects, the Industrial and Commerce Bank to provide working capital, the Bank of China to conduct business in foreign currency, etc.). After the reform, all banks can freely compete with others to lend to any clients. This reform has also been extended to other parts of China. Consequently, formerly specialized banks increasingly engage in businesses that were not in their original domains. For example, all major commercial banks now conduct foreign exchange transactions, and can lend to nearly all sectors of the economy. In addition, many regional banks and joint venture banks have been approved in recent years, and are allowed to operate in a wide range of areas.

Although proposals regarding interest rate decontrol have been made for many years, limited progress has been achieved. Nevertheless, in recent years, the central bank has more frequently used interest rate adjustments as an instrument to manage aggregate demand and to differentiate priorities of investment projects. In January 1996, the PBC lifted its control over interest rates on the interbank market.

An important side-effect of the relaxation of administrative controls has been the increasing risk of instability in the banking sector. Since 1992, when the control over banks' involvement in securities business was relaxed, all specialized banks and most of their major branches set up their own nonbank financial institutions, such as trust and investment corporations (TICs), finance companies, and securities firms, to engage in imprudent or even fraudulent operations. Through their affiliated entities, these specialized banks diverted funds earmarked for agriculture and other key projects into speculation in the stock market and real estate market. When the monetary control was tightened in late 1993, many of these operations lost money and led to a large amount of nonperforming loans in the banking system. By the end of 1997, about 90 per cent of the TICs in China were effectively insolvent.[5]

Towards a Regulatory Framework

Experience from industrial and newly industrialized countries suggests that most of the administrative controls prevailing in China should eventually be eliminated if the financial market is to play the role of efficiently allocating financial resources, aiding the pricing of assets, and helping the management of risks. However, financial market decontrol itself will lead to chaos if financial regulations are not properly installed at the same time.

The basic justification for bank regulation lies in the critical role of commercial banking in the economy. Banks' demand deposits are the primary component of the money supply, and a country's money transactions often take the form of exchanges of bank deposits. Disruption of this basic system can disrupt the entire economy. In addition to playing the role of the payment system, commercial banks also invest a large percentage of deposits in illiquid assets, or relatively long-term investments. That is, what is not needed to maintain reserves can be invested in higher-yielding, less liquid assets. For this investment function to work well, depositors must have confidence that their money is safe, and the failure of one bank should not precipitate massive deposit withdrawals, or runs, at other institutions. Bank regulation is intended to monitor the risk of failure in the system as a whole, to guard against a domino effect when one institution fails (Johnson, 1993).

When China's banking sector is opened to competition from regional commercial banks, shareholding banks, private banks, and foreign banks in the future, many banks are no longer be guaranteed by the government. Consequently, there is a need for prudential and protective regulations. Two major changes in China's state banks' balance sheet over the past 15 years have increased the urgency of the introduction of these regulations. First, on the assets side, doubtful and bad loans increased rapidly and accounted for about 20 to 30 per cent of the total outstanding loans in recent years (Zhang *et al.*, 1997). This indicates a decline in the quality and an increase in the risk of bank assets. The increasing amount of nonperforming debt is a result of the chronic decline of SOEs' financial performance – from 1978 to 1996, the ratio of profit to total output in SOEs declined from 24 per cent to 10 per cent (State Statistical Bureau, 1997a). Secondly, on the liabilities side, the proportion of household deposits in banks' total liabilities increased sharply from 8 per cent in 1978 to near 50 per cent in 1996 (State Statistical Bureau, 1997a). This change can be largely explained by the relaxation of government control over enterprise wages and bonuses, as well as policies that led to a rapid increase in peasants' income. Previously, bank liabilities were mainly composed of enterprise deposits and government deposits that could be effectively controlled by the credit plan or fiscal policy. As the share of household deposits in total liabilities increased, any small change in households' saving behaviour might lead to a major change in banks' liabilities that could not be easily controlled by the government. In other words, the liquidity risk of bank liabilities is much higher today than in the early period of reform.

As China gradually moved towards liberalization of the banking sector by commercializing state banks and introducing more competition among banks, it paid attention to the establishment of financial regulations that would prevent instability in the financial sector. The Commercial Bank Law passed in 1995 was a milestone of China's bank regulation.[6] It indicates that when the Chinese government planned to quit as a player in the game, it began to set the rules of the game.

In many western countries, prudential regulations that apply to banks include clear rules on criteria for entry, capital adequacy standards, asset diversification, limits on loans to insiders, external audits, enforcement powers, and failure resolution mechanisms. Criteria for entry typically cover the minimum capital requirement, the qualifications of management, the development of reasonable business plans and projects, and the financial strength of the proposed owners. Capital adequacy standards ideally include risk-based capital–assets ratios that take into account the riskiness of different assets, both on and off the balance sheet. In many countries, prudent regulations also include a clear definition of the different components of capital and they impose limits on the distribution of dividends if minimum standards are not met. The guidelines formulated by the Basle Committee of Bank Supervisors are based on developed countries' experiences, but are increasingly adopted by developing countries (Polizatto, 1992). China's Commercial Bank Law has taken into account many of the elements suggested by the Basle Agreement, while treating some in the context of transition. Following is a discussion of several major aspects of China's bank regulations, as stated in the Commercial Bank Law and other related documents (NPC, 1995).

The capital adequacy standard   The capital adequacy standard was first adopted in Shenzhen. This system requires banks to have sufficient capital and uses the capital adequacy ratio to restrict liabilities. In 1994, this system was introduced to all nonbank financial institutions in China. Since the promulgation of the Commercial Bank Law, all commercial banks have been required to maintain their ratio of capital to risk-adjusted assets at 8 per cent. Nearly three years after the promulgation of the Law, however, none of the four former specialized banks has met this requirement. In early 1998, the government announced that it would issue special bonds in the amount of 270 billion yuan to recapitalize four major state commercial banks – ABC, ICBC, CBC, and BOC – to enable them to meet the capital adequacy ratio.

Other asset–liability ratios   The Commercial Bank Law also requires that all commercial banks control their total loans at or below 75 per cent of total deposits. However, over the past few years, the PBC has followed more flexible guidelines on this requirement: for specialized banks, the growth of credit loans were limited to less than 75 per cent of the average growth of deposits during every 10-day period; for other commercial banks, credit loans were not permitted to exceed 75 per cent of deposits; for urban credit cooperatives (UCCs), credit loans were not permitted to exceed 70 per cent of total loans; and for rural credit cooperatives (RCCs), credit loans were not permitted to exceed 75 per cent of total loans. For nonbank financial institutions, there was also a requirement relating to the percentage of loan *vis-à-vis* deposits: trust loans (investments) were not to exceed 20 times their total capital, and trust loans from their own resources were not to exceed 75 per cent of their deposits (Xie, 1995). In addition to PBC restrictions the loan–deposit ratio, the Commercial Bank Law also requires that a commercial bank maintain the ratio of liquid assets to liquid liabilities at no less than 25 per cent and limit lending to any single borrower to 10 per cent of its capital.[7]

Criteria for entry   The Commercial Bank Law sets the minimum capital requirements for banks and nonbank financial institutions. These requirements are as follows: (1) the minimum paid-in capital of a national bank is 1 billion yuan; (2) the minimum paid-in capital of an urban cooperative bank is 100 million yuan; and (3) the minimum paid-in capital of a rural cooperative bank is 50 million yuan. The PBC has the authority to adjust the minimum capital requirements, but they must not be lower than those stipulated by the Commercial Bank Law.

Separation of banking from nonbanking activities   The 1992–3 financial chaos, which was due to many banks' engaging in investment in the securities market, led to the recent regulation requiring all banks to divest themselves of investment banking and securities trading affiliates. The Commercial Bank Law stipulates that commercial banks are not allowed to engage in securities trading and underwriting, and should not invest in nonbank financial enterprises and productive enterprises.

Some scholars have questioned why China should pursue the separation of commercial banking from investment banking, when over the past two decades the financial regulations in developed countries have moved toward favouring universal banking.[8] It has also been argued that, in reality, in most countries, ownership and management of financial and nonfinancial firms have always been linked – possibly because it improves communication and economizes on managerial skills. A strict separation of functions may limit abuse, but it may also slow the process of development. This arguement is supported by the fact that in the cases of both Germany and Japan, close ties between their respective financial and nonfinancial firms have contributed to the development of their product sectors.[9] It has been recognized that in the German and Japanese cases, interlocking ownership and control allowed lenders to monitor borrowers' activities more effectively, thus allowing banks to take financial risks that would be unacceptable if post-lending controls were not well developed (Aoki and Qian, 1995; Xu and Wang, 1997). Some scholars therefore proposed that a debt–equity swap would allow banks to turn themselves from creditors to shareholders of the SOEs, thereby substantially increasing the banks' powers and incentives to closely monitor the firms' management.

However, there are strong arguments against the above proposal, and these counter-arguments seem to have played roles in shaping the current Chinese Commercial Bank Law. In developing countries like China, the question of universal banking is closely linked with the development of effective prudential and supervisory mechanisms. Universal banking relies to a large extent on functional and conduct regulation, creating a greater need for collecting and analysing detailed information, and for taking prompt corrective actions where required. In the past, universal banking has produced negative results in several developing countries, though in large part these may have been encouraged by the laxity of supervision and/or the availability of heavily subsidized credits that provided strong incentives for excessive borrowing and for abusing the system (Vittas, 1992). In addition to the fact that universal institutions are more difficult to supervise effectively, allowing universal banking might exacerbate the dominant position of large banks. The experience of developed countries shows that securities markets develop faster in countries where banks' activities are limited to short-term commercial finance and less rapidly in countries with universal banking. In countries allowing universal banking a broad array of financial products appears less likely to develop. Therefore, China's decision to segregate commercial banking from investment banking activities at this stage is likely to be appropriate.

Despite the promulgation of the Commercial Bank Law and the ensuing divestiture of nonbank financial institutions by banks over the past few years, some banks continued to invest their funds in the stock markets, exposing themselves to high risks. These illegal investments were often channelled through loans to banks' subsidiaries, nonbank financial institutions, nonfinancial enterprises, or through individuals. In some cases, speculation by banks also resulted in a high volatility of stock prices. In June 1997, the PBC issued the 'Circular on Prohibiting Bank Funds from Flowing to the Stock Market' (PBC, 1997). This circular required all banks to close their stock accounts (whether in the names of their subsidiaries or individuals) within 10 days, further limited the use of interbank borrowing by nonbank financial institutions, and prohibited stock exchanges from offering overdraft facilities. In the same month, the PBC announced that the chief executive officers of several commercial banks were dismissed for their involvement in illegal operations in the stock markets.[10]

Challenges to the Effective Implementation of Bank Regulations

The fundamental difficulties in implementing prudential regulations in China do not lie in technical design or experience; rather, the historical legacy left by the large state sector and the tradition of government intervention in banking activities poses the major challenge to the effectiveness of bank regulations. This section takes up three issues.

Loss-making state-owned enterprises This problem is not encountered in western countries where most of the bank regulations originated. China currently has more than 400,000 state-owned enterprises, one-third of which are operating at a loss. A large number of SOEs are heavily indebted: in one city in Liaoning Province, the average debt–assets ratio was about 90 per cent in 1997.[11] Many SOEs rely almost exclusively on the state banking system for circulating funds, and some SOEs even rely on bank credit for paying their employees' wages. Banks find it almost impossible to recover loans extended to loss-making SOEs for several different reasons. Despite the government's announcement of speeding up SOE reform in 1997, many medium and large SOEs are still not allowed to go bankrupt for political reasons. In other cases, some SOEs have adopted the strategy of separating the old enterprise into two entities: one takes over most of the liabilities to the banks and nonperforming assets and then declares bankruptcy; another takes over the good assets and is turned into a new company that inherits no obligation to repay bank loans. Because the current regulation requires that the proceeds from liquidation must first be used to settle unemployed workers, banks typically receive little or nothing from liquidation proceeds (Gao, 1998).

The reason behind the reluctance of the government to allow a large number of bankruptcy cases is the lack of a well-functioning social safety net, including the unemployment insurance system. Many SOEs have the strong belief that 'there is no need to repay bank loans if we don't have the money, as we are state-owned, and banks are also state-owned'. Many SOEs view bank credit as gifts. They don't repay the loans even if they can, and expect that the bank will write off the debt eventually. Regardless of how banks urge them for loan repayment, some simply refuse to pay either the principal or the interest. Loss-making enterprises are not afraid of being sued: 'Feel free to press a charge against us – we just don't have the money' (Wang, 1994). Recently, as commercial banks tended to gain more independence from government intervention in making loan decisions, the general culture of nonpayment of many SOEs resulted in a significant slowing of credit extension from the banking system.

Intervention of local governments in bank operations   It has long been a tradition that local governments have a strong influence on the lending activities of the branches of specialized banks. In a case described in Wang (1994), a bank whose loan was defaulted on had no choice but to press charges against the borrowing firm, and the local court ruled in favour of the bank. However, when a top official of the municipality heard about this dispute, he blamed the bank and the court for not caring about 'stability', and forced them to stop collection of the loan. Finally, the bank did not get even one penny from the firm, and the firm ignored all further requests from the bank. In another case, the Zhenzhou Construction Bank made a loan for a tourism project. After the project was completed and turned into operation, no one came back to the bank to pay the interest. When officers of the bank visited the borrowing unit to make an inquiry, they were told that the project was already sold by the local government to another company; and that the government had made this decision because it felt that managing the project by itself would be too slow to generate profits. But it disregarded the bank – the largest creditor – in the decision-making process and did not even inform the bank of this decision afterwards.

The fact that local governments have been able to strongly influence the operation of local bank branches has to do many informal connections. Before 1994, when appointing the head of a provincial PBC branch, the PBC headquarters had to consult the province. Today, provincial governments continue to 'recommend' candidates to branches of commercial banks for filling management positions. In addition, local bank branches often rely on local governments for the supply of land for constructing office buildings, staff housing and utilities, dependent children's education and other staff benefits. For example, when a commercial bank's local branch applies to the local authority for a parcel of land for office building construction, the local government may request, in exchange for the land, that the bank branch extend credit to designated projects.[12]

Bank supervision According to the Commercial Bank Law, commercial banks are required to submit balance sheets, income statements and other reports to the PBC Bank Supervision Department on a regular basis. The PBC headquarters formulates the national bank supervision plan and conducts both off-site and on-site inspections at the national level. The regional and local branches of the PBC are responsible for supervising commercial banks and their branches at the same level. When bank regulations are violated, the PBC has the authority to impose fines, confiscate the bank's income, suspend the bank's licence, and even press criminal charges against responsible individuals. However, the current rules on loan classification and loan loss provisioning and the procedure for writing off bad loans have compromised the quality of bank supervision. They tend to distort banks' balance sheets due to the following problems. First, the risk weights assigned to different loan categories are generally lower than their counterparts in many other countries, resulting in an artificially higher ratio of capital to risk-weighted assets. Secondly, nonperforming loans are classified into three categories: over due (*yuqi*), doubtful (*daizhang*), and bad (*huaihang*). But banks are required to recognize accrued interest until these nonperforming loans are overdue for two years. This practice leads to an overstatement of banks' profits and therefore their tax liabilities. Thirdly, the limit on loan loss provisions is only 1 per cent of total loans, and inadequate provisions overstate banks' profitability and capital bases.

Conclusion

As China gradually moves towards liberalization of the banking sector by commercializing state banks and introducing more competition to the sector, it also recognizes the need to establish bank regulations that will prevent instability in the financial sector. The Commercial Bank Law introduced in 1995 was a milestone of China's bank regulation. The clauses included in this law are largely consistent with those suggested by the Basle Agreement. However, several institutional problems inherent in the Chinese system pose serious challenges to the effective implementation of the promulgated bank regulations. These problems include: (1) the large amount of nonperforming loans extended to SOEs and continued political pressure for protecting SOE employment prevents the banks from effectively reducing the share of risky assets; (2) the strong influence of local governments curtails banks' flexibility in determining the structure of their assets; and (3) problems with rules on loan classification and loan loss provisioning continue to distort banks' balance sheets and thus compromise the quality of bank supervision.

5
Development of the Stock Markets[1]

Introduction

The development of stock markets is one of the most important elements of China's reform in the financial system. Before the late 1970s, the government strictly controlled virtually all channels of investment. All investments made by enterprises were either from direct grants from the state budgetary funds or from government allocated bank credits. The whole financial system was dominated by the state-owned banks, such as the PBC, a few specialized banks and their local branches. The bureaucratic process that allocated investments across regions and sectors was often inefficient, and in many cases, caused a significant waste of resources.

Since the early 1980s, China's financial sector has experienced a number of major institutional changes. The proportion of state budgetary finances in total investments decreased rapidly as the fiscal decentralization reform evolved. Many specialized banks were created or re-established, replacing government budgetary funds as the main financial channels for enterprise investment. However, until 1997, the total credit of each bank branch was still limited by the central bank's credit plan. In addition, banks' lending and deposit rates are still controlled by the PBC, and both the central and local governments still intervene into banks' lending activities. Policy banks and, to a lesser extent, commercial banks are instructed to lend to policy-oriented projects, consequently leaving some profitable projects under-financed. In many cases, especially during recessions, a promising enterprise's borrowing from banks may involve high transaction costs. Many enterprises have found them no longer be able to rely solely on government grants or designated loans, and thus have demanded new sources of finance.

At the same time, individuals' income grew rapidly and many people began to seek investment opportunities. Due to the lack of alternative financial instruments, individuals were forced to either hold cash or deposits in the state banks where interest rates were controlled. By the end of 1997, there were Y4628 billion of household deposits in banks, accounting for 62 per cent of GDP, up from 6 per cent at the end of 1978 (State Statistical Bureau, 1992, 1998).

In 1981, the central government began to issue treasury bonds to finance budget deficits. Since then, various financial institutions and enterprises at the central and local levels have also issued their own bonds. Until 1989, the outstanding securities were dominated by bonds. As of the end of 1989, the total outstanding securities amounted to Y166 billion, of which 99 per cent were bonds (Editorial Department of Almanac of China's Finance and Banking, 1996). Although many economists had long recommended that the share-holding system be introduced as a solution to China's state enterprise reform, until the late 1980s, there had been only very limited experiments with this system. The main reason was the government's unwillingness to accept that the state-ownership is inefficient and developing shareholding companies means partial privatization.

After years of intense debate, the Shanghai Securities Exchange (SHSE) and Shenzhen Securities Exchange (SZSE) were established in 1990 and 1991, respectively. Although China's stock markets emerged only seven years ago, their growth has been phenomenal. Market capitalization at the end of 1997 reached Y1753 billion, up from Y105 billion at the end of 1992. Value traded in the market grew from Y68 billion in 1992 to Y3072 billion in 1997 (Zhong, 1998). From 1991 to 1997, the number of listed companies increased from 14 to 765. The number of individual stock investors exceeded 32 million by the end of 1997.

This chapter presents an overview of the development of the two Chinese stock markets, with the focus on their operational mechanism and regulatory framework. The second section gives a brief history of the Shanghai and Shenzhen stock markets. The third section deals with the primary market. The fourth section discusses the transaction mechanism of the secondary market. The fifth section examines the regulatory framework. The sixth section identifies several causes of the large market fluctuations in the two stock markets. The last section looks at a number of policy issues regarding future development of the stock markets.

A Brief History of China's Stock Market Development

Shanghai's securities trading emerged in 1984 and the market almost exclusively dealt with bond trading. In 1989, the volume of stock transactions only accounted for 1 per cent of the total securities turnover in the SHSE. The first two stocks issued by the Yenchung Industrial Corporation and the Feile Acoustics Corporation were traded over the counter (OTC) in 1984, with total transactions of less than Y200 000.

By the end of 1987, eight trading counters had been opened in Shanghai. Four professional securities trading corporations, which helped enterprises issue bonds and stocks, were established in 1988 and 1989. They were International Securities Corporation, Haitung Securities Corporation, Shenyin Securities Corporation, and Chenshing Securities Corporation.

The SHSE was formally established in December 1990. It adopts a corporate membership system and deals with spot transactions, not including futures. It recruits members nationwide and has served as a nationwide securities transaction center. With the establishment of the SHSE, three comprehensive legal documents were issued: the Statute of the SHSE, the Members' Management Methods of the SHSE, and the Business Regulations of the Shanghai Securities Exchange.

In a new surge of reform in 1992, the government approved a 'bolder' plan to experiment with the shareholding system in state-owned enterprises (SOEs). By the end of 1996, the number of shareholding companies at or above the county level exceeded 8000, although the shares of most of these companies were nontransferable (State Statistical Bureau, 1997a). By the end of 1997, 422 shares had been listed on the SHSE, compared to eight in 1991.[2] In 1997, the total market capitalization in the Shanghai market reached Y840 billion, up from Y3 billion in 1991.[3]

Shenzhen was the first special economic zone (SEZ) established in China. The Shenzhen Development Bank issued the first stock in Shenzhen in 1987 and raised a total of Y7.93 million. From 1989 to 1990, five corporations' stocks were issued in Shenzhen and were traded actively on the OTC market. The formal opening of the SZSE was on 3 July 1991, and the Exchange was allowed to issue 'B' shares to attract foreign funds into China. The number of shares listed on the Shenzhen market was 18 by the end of 1991, and rose to 401 by the end of 1997.[4] The total market capitalization in the Shenzhen market reached Y903 billion in 1997, 113 times that in 1991.[5]

There are many differences between the Shanghai and Shenzhen markets. Many companies listed on the SZSE are joint ventures with

Table 5.1 China's stock market: comparison with other countries (US$m, end of period)

	1991	1992	1993	1994	1995	1996	1997
Market capitalization							
China	2 208	18 255	40 567	43 521	42 055	113 755	206 366
Hong Kong	121 986	172 106	385 247	269 508	303 705	449 381	–
Taiwan, China	124 864	101 124	195 198	247 325	187 206	273 608	287 813
Thailand	35 815	58 259	130 510	131 479	141 507	99 828	23 537
US	4 099 479	4 497 833	5 223 768	5 081 810	6 857 622	8 484 433	–
China/World (%)	0.02	0.17	0.29	0.29	0.24	0.56	–
Trading value							
China	820	16 715	43 395	97 526	49 774	256 008	369 573
Hong Kong	38 607	78 598	131 550	147 158	106 888	166 419	–
Taiwan, China	365 232	240 667	346 487	711 346	383 099	470 193	1 297 474
Thailand	30 089	72 060	86 934	80 188	57 000	44 365	23 118
US	2 254 983	2 678 528	3 507 223	3 592 668	5 108 591	7 121 487	–
China/World (%)	0.02	0.31	0.59	1.01	0.49	1.88	–

Numbers of listed companies

China	14	52	183	291	323	540	764
Hong Kong	333	386	450	529	518	561	–
Taiwan, China	221	156	285	313	347	382	404
Thailand	276	305	347	389	416	454	431
US	6 742	6 699	7 246	7 692	7 671	8 479	–
China/World (%)	0.05	0.17	0.57	0.81	0.83	1.27	–

Market capitalization/GDP (%)

China	1	4	8	8	6	14	23
Hong Kong	–	–	289	311	442	–	–
Taiwan, China	68	47	87	103	71	99	–
Thailand	37	56	109	101	126	80	31
US	72	74	82	77	95	114	–
China/US (%)	1	6	9	11	6	12	–

Sources: International Finance Corporation, 1995, 1996, 1997, 1998; State Statistical Bureau, 1995, 1996, 1997a.

close relations with Hong Kong, thus giving them more international exposure. By contrast, the SHSE is dominated by SOEs and is more closely monitored by the central government. With regard to foreign invest-ment, the Shanghai system requires that all foreign investors must sub-scribe for B shares through a securities institution approved by the SHSE, while Shenzhen allows foreign investors to subscribe for B shares either directly or through an intermediary.

In the early stages of the stock markets' development, the Chinese gov-ernment attempted to control market volatility. Before the formal open-ing of the SZSE, several tentative regulations were issued. For example, on 28 May 1990, a system of readjusting price ceilings and floors was announced. The price ceiling was set at 5 per cent (5 per cent up and 5 per cent down) of the stocks' closing prices of the previous day. Similar ceilings were also imposed on the Shanghai market. These restrictions were lifted in May 1992. In December 1996, in an attempt to quell widespread speculation, the Chinese Securities Regulatory Commission (CSRC) passed a regulation that reimposed a limit on daily stock price movements to within 10 per cent of the previous day's price (Interna-tional Finance Corporation, 1997).

Although China's stock markets have grown rapidly over the past few years, they are still in a very early stage of development. As shown in Table 5.1, the size of China's stock markets (e.g. in terms of market cap-italization) relative to GDP is far smaller than those in other emerging markets, not to mention matured markets. At the end of 1996, China's market capitalization-to-GDP ratio was 14 per cent, while those of Tai-wan and the US were 99 per cent and 114 per cent, respectively.

The Primary Market

As stock markets in other countries, China's stock markets consist of the primary market, in which enterprises make their initial offerings, and the secondary market, where shareholders trade their stocks. This section discusses the primary market in China, while the next section will deal with the secondary market.

In China, an enterprise wishing to issue stocks may elect to arrange either an internal offering or a public offering. In an internal offering, an enterprise sells its stocks only to its employees. Under the current Chinese system, shares issued by a typical state-owned enterprise con-sists of three types: state shares (shares owned by the state), legal person shares (shares owned by other units with legal status), and employee shares (shares owned by the enterprise's employees). Normally, state shares and legal person shares constitute the majority of total shares. Employee shares, which are issued through internal offerings, are often sold at discount or take the form of bonus shares without any charge. The employee-shareholders are paid dividends periodically. However, the employee shares are not allowed to trade in any secondary market. By the end of 1996, about 8000 enterprises at and above the township level had conducted internal offerings (State Statistical Bureau, 1997a).

Public offering in China starts with a complicated approval procedure. Currently, the CSRC, the State Planning Committee (SPC), the State Economic System Reform Commission (SRC), and the PBC jointly determine the annual stock issuance plan, which stipulates the total number of new stocks to be listed on the exchanges and the total value of initial public offerings. For example, the annual issuance plans for 1993, 1994, 1996, and 1997 set limits of Y5 billion, Y5.5 billion, Y15 billion, and Y30 billion, respectively, on total initial public offerings (Han, 1997).[6] Beginning in 1993, each province was given a quota of new listings, and the provincial Planning Commission and System Reform Commission select the candidates. The selection at the provincial level was in principle based on industrial bureaux recommendation and the overall balance between industrial sectors. Since 1997, the emphasis of quota allocation has been to support 1000 key state-owned enterprises, 120 large enterprise groups, and 100 enterprises experimenting with the modern enterprise system, as well as selected enterprises in the agricultural, energy, and transportation sectors.

The final approval for an enterprise's public offering is made by the CSRC, based on the recommendation of the provincial government, its assessment of the enterprise's financial and management conditions, current government policies, and stock market conditions. It is required that the enterprise's financial condition be evaluated by at least two accounting firms. An investment syndicate should also be formed to make a detailed offering plan, including the terms of the new issue. The CSRC reviews all these documents and determines whether or not to list the stock on an exchange. If the stock is not allowed to be listed on an exchange, it means this public offering will be aborted because it will not be listed anywhere, not even on the OTC market. Some minimum qualifications for initial public offering include (Wang *et al.*, 1998):

1. capitalization over Y30 million;
2. at least 25 per cent of the company's shares must be for sale to the public;
3. the company must have made profit for the past three years.[7]

There are a few large Chinese investment banking firms which perform standard functions in the primary market, such as originating the securities issue and providing advice and counsel to issuing firms, underwriting, forming syndicates, and distributing securities to the public. Currently, all public offerings are assisted by investment banking firms. In 1993, Wan-Guo Securities alone distributed 69 per cent of new stocks in Shanghai. It also underwrote Shanghai Petroleum and, jointly with Merrill Lynch, helped its listing on the New York Stock Exchange (NYSE). The first Sino-US joint investment bank, China International Capital Corporation, was formed in 1996 and successfully floated the shares of China Telecom in the Hong Kong market in 1997.

Various underwiting agreements are exercised in China, including firm commitment, best-effort arrangement, and standby. However, the firm commitment mechanism is mostly widely adopted. In terms of the offering process, several arrangements have been experimented with since the inception of the stock markets. In the early 1990s, because all initial public offers were oversubscribed by a large multiple, a lottery-application system was used to determine the eligibility of investors' applications for a public offering. This system was later abolished as it had resulted in significant underpricing of new issues and generated unrealistic expectations and strong incentives for speculation. Currently, three methods – deposit lottery system, network auction, and fixed price network offer – are used. The deposit lottery system, used mainly for small share offerings, involves investors' making deposits in banks followed by a draw of lots that determines the eligible buyers. A network auction is conducted on a stock exchange, and involves the underwriter's setting a minimum price and investors' bidding for the shares. A fixed price network offer, also conducted on a stock exchange, starts with the announcement of a fixed offer price, followed by unrestricted subscriptions by investors and a lottery-based selection of eligible buyers (Wang *et al.*, 1998).

The Secondary Market

Similar to other countries' stock markets, China's secondary market is comprised of investors, market makers, organized exchanges, OTC and various brokerage firms.

Investors

Although there are few institutional investors adopting the form of close-end investment funds, the majority of investors are individual investors.

Individual investors are distinguished as general investors and prestigious investors. A general investor is similar to an individual investor in the US. A prestigious investor, however, enjoys more facilities provided by brokerage firms, including computer access to current transactions.

Brokerage Firms

Prospective SHSE members must first apply to the exchange, which checks the applicants' credentials and determines their business scope. Depending upon capitalization, the experience of their personnel and other criteria, some members are only allowed to act as brokers, while others can be dealers on their own accounts and some can be both brokers and dealers. A new member is required to place a refundable deposit with the SHSE before taking up its seat.

In China, brokerage functions are performed mainly by two types of non-bank financial institutions: securities firms and trust and investment corporations (TICs). Until recently, many securities firms were owned by state banks and TICs were owned by local governments or large state enterprises. After the promulgation of the Commercial Bank Law in 1995, banks have been required to divest themselves of their securities subsidiaries. Most securities companies and TICs with SHSH or SZSE memberships are authorized to serve as brokers as well as dealers on their own accounts. Currently, private ownership of brokerage firms is not permitted, and the securities exchanges do not accept individuals as members.

A typical brokerage firm in Shanghai may have a space of 1000 square metres, and about three-fifths of the area is used as a lobby for general investors. The rest is used by prestigious investors and brokerage employees. All transactions are assisted by networked computers, which are connected directly to the terminal of membership seats held by the brokerage firm in the stock exchanges. There is a huge screen displaying trading information simultaneously with the screen in the SHSE. Trading information on the screen normally includes closing prices from the last trading day, today's opening prices, current prices, the current highest and lowest prices, as well as the trading volume so far for all listed companies in the SHSE. There are TV screens displaying similar information in the SZSE.

A typical procedure for trading a stock is as follows. If a general investor wants to trade a stock, he/she needs to fill out a form specifying the ordering information, personal information, and the account number with the brokerage firm, and then deposits a certain amount of money. A clerk will then take the order and put it into a networked computer connected to the brokerage firm's seat in the exchange. Each order has an order number. A confirmation of the transaction will be sent to the investor when the deal is completed. An investor pays 0.35 per cent of the settlement price as service fee and a stamp tax of 0.4 per cent (Zhong, 1998). If the transaction is not successful, then the investor pays a small service fee. Telephone orders through a brokerage firm are also acceptable. In addition to the information described above, an investor who orders a deal by telephone is required to provide a code for security purposes.

The difference between the treatment toward general and prestigious investors is that the latter have direct access to a networked computer, but they are required to have a capital stock of Y100000 and must pay a monthly fee to the brokerage firm. The networked computer offers current market information from the SHSE and SZSE. Furthermore, the networked computer offers a database containing all price, volume and other information on each listed company dating back to its initial public offering. Composite stock price indices as well as categorized indices in both the Shanghai and Shenzhen markets are also listed and graphed. Software that can perform technical analysis of the stock price movements, such as K curve analysis, is also available. Although some brokerage firms also give direct computer access to general investors in order to attract more clients, the use of software and databases by general investors is very limited compared to the use by prestigious investors.

Organized Exchanges and Trading Process

On the trading floor of the SHSE, membership brokers and staff members are the only people that are seen. Membership brokers are similar to commission brokers in the US, except that the Chinese brokers are paid a salary plus a bonus by their employers (brokerage firms). They do not charge any commission on their trading activities. This is why they are not referred to as 'commission brokers'.

The operation of the SHSE is based on four principles: electronic trading, central settlement, no physical exchange of certificates and automatic transfer. A potential seller must first deposit the certificates with the SHSE. A SHSE member (e.g. a brokerage firm) can then register ask-prices on its computer, while potential buyers are entering bid-prices. As soon as a bid and ask are matched, the trade takes place. Then, after checking that the seller has deposited the certificates, the SHSE automatically transfers ownership. The SHSE balances members' accounts and any net payments are due on the next day. The system is a sophisticated modern operation, with minimized paperwork and speedy settlement.[8]

All transactions are processed by a superior, high-speed mainframe computer. The auction principle used by this computer is parallel auction. Suppose at a particular moment prices for selling a stock (unit is yuan)

are 61.3, 61.4, 61.5, 61.6, and 61.7 when prices for buying the stock are
Y61.5, 61.4 61.3, 61.2, and 61.1. The transaction with the selling price
of 61.3 and the buying price of 61.5 will be executed first for a settled
price of 61.3. The transaction with the selling price of 61.4 and the buying price of 61.4 will be settled for 61.4. The rest of the transactions will
not be executed. The price of 61.4 will be displayed immediately on the
huge screen in the stock exchange and simultaneously transmitted
through a satellite to all brokerage firms all over the country. When vol-
umes do not match between buying and selling, the next buying or selling transaction will fill in automatically. Let us look at an example in
which the first selling price is 61.3 for 1000 shares while the buying
price is 61.5 for 2000 shares; the second selling price is 61.4 for 2000
shares. After executing 1000 shares for the price of 61.3, the computer
will automatically fill in another 1000 shares for a settled price of 61.4.
Similar principles apply to the rest of the transaction.

The Regulatory Framework[9]

When the local stock exchanges were first established in Shanghai
and Shenzhen, legislation on securities came under the jurisdiction of a
number of ministries and commissions under the State Council such as
the SRC, the MOF, the PBC and the State Assets Management Bureau
(SAMB). In addition, the Shanghai and Shenzhen municipal governments
including their system reform commissions and planning commissions,
the local branches of PBC, and the local stock exchanges were also
involved in exercising the regulatory, supervisory and administrative
functions for the securities markets in Shanghai and Shenzhen. There
was not only an overlapping of legislative power but also a lack of clear
division of administrative and supervisory functions at different levels
and in different departments.

A circular issued in January 1992 by the State Council specified that
the State Council Securities Policy Committee (SCSPC) would have overall charge of the administration of the stock markets, while the CSRC is
SCSPC's executive agency responsible for supervision and regulation.
The CSRC has established a special commission for examining and approving share issues (Potter, 1993). The functions of SCSPC include:
1.   organizing and coordinating the drafting of securities regulations;
2.   determining securities-related policies;
3.   planning the development of the securities market;
4.   directing, coordinating and supervising all securities-related institu-
     tions in China, and supervision of the CSRC.

The CSRC is the regulatory arm of the SCSPC and is responsible for:
1. drafting of securities regulations;
2. supervising organizations engaged in securities business;
3. regulating the issue and trading of securities; and
4. regulating public offers of securities by Chinese companies in China and overseas.

Following the establishment of the SCSPC and the CSRC, the supervisory and administrative responsibilities of the PBC for the two securities exchanges were transferred to the CSRC and a better defined regulatory structure emerged. The PBC continues to exercise its administrative role in conjunction with the SCSPC and the CSRC in connection with the issue and listing of bonds, treasury bills, and investment funds.

On 22 April 1993, the State Council issued the 'Interim Regulations on the Issue and Trading of Shares'. These regulations have provided formal nationwide standards for stock transactions in China. The new regulations address such matters as stock issues and trading, takeovers, custody, clearance and registration of shares, information disclosure, inspection and penalties, and dispute resolution.

Disclosure Requirements

The provisional disclosure measures regarding the form and substance of prospectus require the disclosure of information on a variety of specific matters. Article 17 provides that the promoters of a company or its directors and underwriters shall assume the responsibility for the accuracy of information in a prospectus. While the penalties imposed for contravening the Provisional Regulations include fines and confiscation of profits, no relief or remedies against the directors, issuers or underwriters are provided to investors who subscribe for shares in reliance of a misleading statement.

The provisional disclosure measures also require a company with shares listed on either a domestic or foreign exchange to publish its interim report within 60 days after the end of the first six months of its accounting year and an annual report within 120 days after the end of its accounting year. There are significant differences between Chinese and international accounting practices. Financial results of companies with H shares or B shares are usually prepared in accordance with International Accounting Standards but most analysts agreed that the recent interim announcements of H share companies were too inadequate for an accurate assessment of their financial position to be made.

A listed company is also required to disclose the occurrence of any event which might have a material impact on the market prices of its shares. The provisional disclosure measures set out certain specific events which are deemed to be material events including changes to a company's articles of association, removal of auditors, mortgage or disposal of major operating assets or a writing down of the value of such assets where the amount being written down exceeds 30 per cent of their value and the merger or demerger proposal of a company.

Under the provisional share regulations, the following disclosures regarding shareholding are required to be made:

1. any legal person who holds 5 per cent or more of the issued shares of a company shall make a public announcement and a report to the company, the stock exchange and the CSRC within three business days when the holding attains the 5 per cent level and any subsequent increase or reducing of shareholding by 2 per cent or more;

2. a company listed on a local stock exchange is required to disclose in its annual report the names of every shareholder holding 5 per cent or more of its issued shares and the names of its 10 largest shareholders; and

3. the directors, supervisors and chief executives of a listed company are required to report to the CSRC, the stock exchange and their company, their shareholdings within 10 business days of a change in shareholding. The disclosure obligation continues to apply for a period of six months after their cessation of office.

Penalties for violating the provisional share regulations include fines and confiscation of profits.

Insider Dealing

On 2 September 1993, the CSRC promulgated the 'Provisional Measures on the Prohibition of Fraudulent Conduct Relating to Securities' (hereafter the Measures). The Measures prohibit, among other matters, the use of insider information to conduct the issue or trading of securities in order to make a profit or avoid a loss. Penalties for contravening the Measures include fines, confiscation of profits and suspension of listing. The measures do not provide for any criminal sanctions but the CSRC is vested with the power to require other administrative organs to prosecute violators under the applicable Chinese criminal legislation.

The Measures prescribe the following types of insider dealings:

1. insider using inside information in dealing or advising another person to deal in securities;

2. advising another person to deal in securities;

3. insider dealing insider information to another person leading to that person using such inside information to deal;

4. noninsiders obtaining insider information by improper or other means and using such information to deal or advising another person to deal; and
5. other insider trading activities.

The provisional share regulations also provide provisions on the take-over of listed companies, and on suspension and termination of listing. The details of these regulations can be found in Chan (1994).

Market Fluctuation

The two stock markets have experienced big ups and downs since their inception. For example, from December 1990 to December 1993, the composite index of the SHSE rose from 100 to 833.9; but within seven months, it dropped to 333.9. In the first few years of the market development, the most important reason for large fluctuations was that most shares were overpriced. At the end of 1992, there were only 52 A share listings. As discussed above, companies listed on the market were subject to government approval, which followed a bureaucratic process and was rather slow. The amount of shares traded on the market was also restricted. The consequence was that the stock prices were not only volatile but also often overpriced. For instance, in January 1992, the average p/e ratio in Shenzhen was about 35, while that in Shanghai was 80. One enterprise in Shanghai had a p/e ratio of more than 600 at the end of 1991.[10] Since early 1994, the two markets experienced a general downturn mainly because of a flood of new listings; e.g. A share listings on the two markets rose from 52 at the end of 1992 to 271 in August 1994. Partly as a result of the large number of new listings, the SHSE composite index declined by more than 30 per cent from the end of 1993 to the end of 1995 (International Finance Corporation, 1997).

Since the early 1996, the stock market picked up momentum as the inflationary pressure subsided and monetary policy began to show signs of relaxation. For example, the government abolished the inflation subsidies paid on interest rates for 3-, 5-, and 8-year bank deposits. This policy significantly reduced the yields on long-term deposits and diverted interests to investment in equities. From January to mid-December 1996, the SHSE index rose by about 80 per cent. However, the government's announcement in mid-December of its intention to bring speculation under control triggered a sharp decline in stock prices in the last weeks of the year (see below).

Chinese investors' lack of knowledge of stock market also helped push the market incredibly high in the early years of the stock markets.

Many people perceived that the government would not allow prices to fall. Therefore, investing in stocks became a low-risk and high-return option for many investors without realizing the inherent risks. Besides unsophisticated individual investors in the markets, mature and sophisticated institutional investors have not developed. Therefore, in the situation where stock prices increased or decreased sharply, no intermediary institutions were available to help stabilize the market. Generally, the higher the portion of individual investors in the market, the more volatile the stock market is.

In a number of cases, the government's intervention also contributed to the big ups and downs of the market. Since the stock markets are important elements of the current reform policies and a source of capital helping to drive China's economic growth, the government is keen to avoid a collapse of the market. In July 1994, the Shanghai market sank to a record low close on 29 July to finish at 328.84 points. The Shenzhen A index crashed through its 100 starting level for the second time in its four-year history, closing at a record low 95.34 points. After an emergency meeting in Beijing, on Friday, 29 July the government decided on a rescue plan. The CSRC's rescue measures, plastered on the front pages of the official press the next day, included a freeze on all new share issues held over from 1993 for the remainder of the year and the provision of more credit to major securities and investment firms. On 16 December 1996, in an attempt to control the overheated market, the *People's Daily* published an editorial stating that the authorities would take measures to curb the 'excessive speculation' at the market and the 'irrational surge' of stock prices. Within a week, the average stock market index on the two exchanges fell by more than 20 per cent.

Issues and Prospects

In less than seven years, China's stock markets have emerged from virtually nonexistence to being a major segment of the country's financial sector. It is estimated that as of 1996 more than 10 per cent of the country's productive investment was financed through the stock markets. However, these stock markets are still very primitive, and inherit many elements of the central planning system. Major issues that remain to be addressed include, among others, the nontransferability of state shares, excessive government intervention, incompleteness of regulations, and market segmentation. This section briefly discuss these issues.

State Shares

Most stock companies in China issue three types of shares: state shares (shares owned by the state); legal person shares (shares owned by other enterprises and institutions); and individual shares (shares owned by individuals). While the total number of shareholding companies exceeded 8000 by 1996, shares of only 540 companies were listed on the two stock markets. It is estimated that about 80 per cent of the total shares are state and legal person shares that are not tradable on the secondary markets; the shares traded are mainly individual shares plus a small amount of legal person shares (Zhong, 1995). An obvious consequence of the non-transferability of state shares is that it disallows the government to fully privatize the enterprises in which it retains partial ownership.

Within the policy-making circle, there are two major concerns regarding the trading of state shares: (1) it may erode the state's position of majority shareholding in many SOEs; and (2) it may lead to a crash of the market. None of these concerns is solidly grounded. First, trading state shares does not necessarily mean erosion of state ownership; it may in fact lead to growth of the value of state assets if the state chooses a wise reinvestment strategy. Secondly, a market crash can be avoided if the government chooses to sell state shares at the time of market upturns. While the cost of trading state shares can be minimized, its benefit is significant. Trading state shares provides a way to restructure the public sector: the government can sell to the public state owned shares of enterprises that produce essentially private goods, and transfer the resources to projects in which government involvement is justified on the grounds of market failure.

Government Intervention

As discussed above, the operation of China's securities markets remains subject to extensive administrative control and intervention. The most significant control imposed on the primary market is the annual stock issuance plan and the associated cumbersome approval procedures. This contrasts markedly with the US Securities Exchange Commission's mission of merely ensuring the proper registration and adequate business disclosure by companies issuing securities. In a recent administrative control measure, the CSRC imposed a moratorium on all further public issues of A shares in a bid to stimulate the depressed securities markets. The corporatization and restructuring of state-owned enterprises into joint stock companies are also subject to extensive governmental controls and require many approvals such as those of the department-in-charge, municipal or provincial government, the SAMB and CSRC.

The agencies involved in the decision-making process are too many, and their responsibilities and interrelationships are often confused.

There are a number of rationales for the government to maintain tight control over the size of the stock markets. Chief among them is that a rapid growth of the stock markets would imply a 'crowding out' of resources available for bank deposits and bond purchases. Currently, the banking system is used by the government to achieve objectives such as rescuing ailing SOEs and achieving sectoral and regional balances of development. Bonds, which are also subject to strict control by the central monetary authority, are another convenient vehicle to mobilize resources for specific purposes, including covering fiscal deficits and key development projects.[11] Another related reason for controlling the initial public offering process is the government's intention to influence the regional and sectoral distribution of resources. The process of quota distribution across regions has been rather political in nature, as reflected by the fact that different provinces have been given the same quota for the past years.

The above concerns of the government are legitimate as long as distortions in the economy prevent an efficient resource allocation (such as structural imbalances due to price distortions, regional imbalances due to the lack of labour and capital mobility) and justify directed resource allocation by the government. However, the existence of these distortions per se should not become a permanent excuse for limiting the size of the stock market and imposition of the quota system. Indeed, if the initial public offering process is liberalized, the diversion of the resources from the banking system to the stock markets may generate additional pressures for speedy reform in the state enterprise sector as well as for the bank commercialization process. In recent years, the inefficiency of the quota allocation mechanism became increasingly apparent, as some regions or ministries receiving quotas simply did not have qualified candidates for listing, and many quotas were effectively used to 'subsidize' inefficient state-owned enterprises. To ensure that the stock market contributes positively to the efficient allocation of financial resources, the current quota system should be abolished and be replaced with one that bases the approval of initial public offering on the company's financial conditions and proper disclosure of information.

Market Regulations

Despite the promulgation of the existing regulations, many important matters on the governance of stock markets are still left open, subject to policy interpretation. For example, the types of securities issued, the standards for approval of securities issuances, the forms of foreign parti-cipation, and other definitional matters have not been clearly defined. A securities law that clarifies the above issues, provides the means to protect investors, and establishes enforcement measures to prevent and deter fraud in securities transaction, is especially needed. It is hoped that the securities law, which is expected to be promulgated by the NPC, will reinforce and supplement the existing regulatory regime in such areas as:

1. the issue, listing and trading of securities;
2. disclosure of information to shareholders and the public;
3. prohibition of fraudulent activities;
4. takeovers of listed companies;
5. establishment and regulations of stock exchanges; and
6. regulation of securities institutions and securities dealers.

For foreign investors who purchase B shares, currently, China allows free repatriation of both dividends and profits earned by foreign investors. However, the current system does not provide foreign investors with the practical legal rights in the event of an enterprise's bankruptcy.

The B Share Market

Two types of shares denominated in different currencies are traded in the SHSE and SZSE. Shares sold in yuan are called A shares, and shares sold in US dollar are called B shares. A shares are available to domestic investors only, and B shares are available mainly to foreigners. The first B share was floated on the SZSE in December 1991. By the end of 1997, there were 101 B shares listed on the SHSE and SZSE (Zhong, 1998).

Although Chinese yuan has achieved current account convertibility, capital account transactions are not expected to be open in the near future. As a result, the A share and B share markets are segmented: price move-ments in the two markets have been totally uncorrelated. For example, when the A share market soared to a record high in early 1996, the B share market stagnated. This conclusion of market segmentation is shown by an econometric model in Xu and Ma (1995) using daily time series data from the SHSE and SZSE.

The market segmentation and the relatively small size of the B share market have resulted in its poor liquidity and erratic movement of prices. During its first year, the B share market experienced high volatility. For example, in May 1992, Shenzhen's B share index hit nearly 240, while by the end of November, the index was a little bit above the initial list-ing prices. In Shanghai, the index declined from 120 in May 1992 to 70 by the end of November. From the end of 1992 to the end of 1997, the IFC Investable Index, composed of mainland B shares and Hong Kong H shares, further declined by 37 per cent (International Finance Corporation, 1998). Many investors considered B shares as an intermediary product awaiting the full convertibility of the yuan.

6
State-owned Enterprise Reform

Introduction

Reforming SOEs poses a major challenge to the governments in formerly centrally planned economies. In China, while almost all other aspects of economic reform (including price management, commodity and factor markets, taxation, investment financing, trade regime, foreign exchange system, etc.) have achieved significant progress over the past 20 years, the chronic performance problem of SOEs remains the government's biggest headache. Various schemes designed to improve the incentive and performance of SOEs, such as the revenue retention system, the corporate income tax system, the contract responsibility system, and the shareholding system were experimented with and later widely adopted, but the performance of SOEs has in general continued to deteriorate relative to the non-state sector. Between 1978 and 1997, the SOEs' share in total industrial output fell from 78 per cent to 27 per cent (see Table 6.1).[1] Along with the relatively low output growth rate, the SOEs' financial performance declined steadily. In 1997, 46 per cent of SOEs were operating at a loss, and the number of employees in these enterprises accounted for 41 per cent of total SOE employees (State Statistical Bureau, 1997b).

This chapter reviews China's experience of SOE reform to date, focusing on the experiment of the shareholding system since the early 1990s and 'the modern enterprise system' proposed in the mid-1990s, and proposes a new framework for future SOE reform in China. The rest of this chapter is organized as follows. The second section presents a brief overview of the SOE reform experience from 1978 to the early 1990s. The third section discusses the problems arising in the experiment of the shareholding system and the 'modern enterprise system' over the past few years. The fourth section, the centrepiece of this chapter, argues

Table 6.1 China: industrial output of state-owned and nonstate-owned enterprises, 1978–97 (yuan bn)

	Total output*	Percentage share				
		SOEs	Non SOEs	COEs**	IOEs***	Others
1978	423.7	77.6	22.4	22.4	–	–
1980	515.4	76.0	24.0	23.5	0.0	0.5
1985	971.6	64.9	35.1	32.1	1.9	1.2
1986	1 119.4	62.3	37.7	33.5	2.8	1.4
1987	1 381.3	59.7	40.3	34.6	3.6	2.0
1988	1 822.4	56.8	43.2	36.1	4.3	2.7
1989	2 201.7	56.1	43.9	35.7	4.8	3.4
1990	2 392.4	54.6	45.4	35.6	5.4	4.4
1991	2 662.5	56.2	43.8	33.0	4.8	6.0
1992	3 459.9	51.5	48.5	35.1	5.8	7.6
1993	4 840.2	47.0	53.0	34.0	8.0	11.1
1994	7 017.6	37.3	62.7	37.7	10.1	14.8
1995	9 189.4	34.0	66.0	36.6	12.9	16.6
1996	9 959.5	28.5	71.5	39.4	15.5	16.6
1997	11 212.8	26.5	73.5	40.5	15.9	17.0

*Output measured in current prices.
**Collectively owned enterprises.
***Individually owned enterprises.
Sources: Calculated using data from State Statistical Bureau, 1997a, 1998.

Table 6.2 China: financial performance of state-owned enterprises (%), 1980–96

Year	Profit and tax per gross output value	Profit and tax per gross value of fixed assets	Percentage of loss-making firms
1980	24.3	24.9	–
1981	23.8	22.9	–
1982	23.4	22.2	–
1983	23.2	21.7	–
1984	24.2	22.3	–
1985	21.5	23.5	10.7
1986	19.9	20.7	–
1987	18.9	20.3	–
1988	17.8	20.6	12.2
1989	14.9	17.1	16.3
1990	12.0	12.4	27.6

Table 6.2   (contd.)

Year	Profit and tax per gross output value	Profit and tax per gross value of fixed assets	Percentage of loss-making firms
1991	11.6	11.8	25.8
1992	11.4	12.4	23.4
1993	11.1	12.5	28.8
1994	11.2	12.4	34.3
1995	11.0	9.3	38.0
1996	10.0	7.9	43.0

Sources: Figures in the first two columns are calculated using data from *China Statistical Yearbook* 1994, 1995, 1996, 1997a. These figures refer to SOEs with independent accounting status. Percentages of loss-making enterprises are from State Statistical Bureau, 1994 and Ma and Sun, 1996. The 1995 and 1996 figures of loss-making enterprises are the author's estimates based on State Statistical Bureau, 1997b.

that different reform strategies should be applied to different types of SOEs, depending on the nature of their products, market conditions and government objectives. It develops a new framework for China's SOE reform that involves three different sets of government–enterprise relations, corporate governance structures, and legal frameworks for government enterprises, special public legal entities, and joint stock companies with state equity participation. The last section concludes the chapter.

SOE Reform from 1978 to the Early 1990s

Before 1979, China's SOEs were typical production units in a centrally planned economy: the government determined the production plan, allocated the investment and materials supply, directed the products to designated purchasing units at planned prices, and controlled employment, wages and prices. SOEs transferred all their surplus funds to the state budget, and relied on the budget for subsidies to cover losses and grants for investment. Under this system, SOEs had extremely limited autonomy in decision-making. The inefficiency associated with this highly centralized decision-making system and the firms' lack of incentives to improve productivity seriously dampened the growth potential and technological progress of the Chinese industry.

Along with the adoption of the family responsibility system in rural areas, reforms also began in the urban industrial enterprises. On an experimental basis in 1979, a total of 84 industrial enterprises in Sichuan Province were allowed to retain a proportion of profits for their own discretionary use (World Bank, 1988). This reform was soon formalized in a state reform plan, calling for government agencies to transfer decision-making powers to SOEs in 10 major areas. As a result, SOE managers began to enjoy more autonomy in decisions related to production, pricing, materials purchasing and employment. Enterprises were also allowed to sell their above-quota output directly at negotiable or market prices. Major changes also occurred in government–enterprise revenue sharing. In 1983, mandatory profit remittances to the central government were replaced by a system in which enterprises paid income taxes and shared their profits with their supervisory authority. This system allowed the enterprises to retain a portion of their earnings for their own purposes, including new investments, worker bonuses, and welfare benefits. A clearer relationship between enterprises' financial performance and their retaining profits was thus established.

In 1983, most direct grants from the government budget to SOEs were replaced by interest-bearing loans, and the banking system became the primary channel through which the SOEs' investments were financed. After this reform, SOEs' use of external sources for investment began to carry a cost. Reforms in the financial sector have also led to the emergence of more commercial banks and nonbank financial institutions, as well the nontraditional channel of financing through the securities market for SOEs. Since 1987, as a further step for decentralizing the enterprise management system, the Contract Responsibility System was adopted by most of the SOEs. Under this system each SOE signed a contract with its supervisory agency (typically the industrial bureau), promising the remittance of a certain amount of tax revenue and profits, but retaining most of the decision-making rights in the firm's daily operation. This system granted the SOEs, at least nominally, greater management autonomy.

By the early 1990s, reforms in the urban industrial sector had touched upon almost every aspect of the government–enterprise relationship and fundamentally changed the policy environment of the state enterprises. Price liberalization, decentralization of enterprise decision-making, and the emergence of goods, materials and financial markets had provided the state enterprises with an external environment that was in many aspects similar to that of a market economy. The significance of the decentralization and marketization process could be captured by the following figures: the value of total industrial production subject to mandatory plans has declined from around 80 per cent in 1984 to 16 per cent by 1992, and the share of retail sales subject to state fixed prices dropped from 97 per cent in 1978 to 21 per cent by 1991 (World Bank, 1994a).

As numerous reform strategies (e.g. reducing government intervention, hardening budget constraints, building in profit incentives for management and workers, etc.) were tried but generally failed to produce the expected results, the diagnoses of the cause of the SOE problem by economists and government officials began to converge.[2] More and more people have come to share the belief that the problem is inherent in state ownership which, in Chinese, is 'all people' ownership. Without owning a firm's equity, workers and managers do not have the incentive to maximize the firm's value. At the same time, the state, as the owner, fails to monitor the SOE managers' behaviour through its representatives in the local governments or industrial bureaus. Central government ministries or local governments, which represent the state to manage the SOE assets, have various objectives that often contradict the goal of profit maximization. For example, local governments often desire to provide social welfare, maintain high employment and keep economic parity between firms. In addition, there are substantial problems over the monitoring of management performance. Since the owner (the state) or its representative (e.g. a ministry or bureau) does not possess complete information about the enterprise's daily operation, SOE managers can easily allocate the firm's internal resources according to their own or their employees' interests. The moral hazard problem worsens when the managers are given more managerial autonomy.

The Shareholding Experiment and Modern Enterprise System

The Experiment of the Shareholding System

With growing recognition of the limited and unsustained nature of past reforms of SOEs, the Chinese government launched the experiment of the shareholding system in the early 1990s.[3] This new system was perceived by many as the most promising direction for SOE reform. It was widely believed that by letting workers and managers own a firm's shares, their personal interests would be closely linked to the firm's performance. Therefore, they would care about the firm's long-term growth and have less incentive to request excessive wage increases or in-kind benefits. In other words, the decade-long headache of SOE 'short-term behaviour' would disappear. Unfortunately, evidence from the experimental shareholding companies suggests that various short-term behaviour problems remain and, in many cases, the problems are exacerbated since the shareholding system provides a more discretionary environment than the old system.

By the end of 1995, China had 5873 formally registered shareholding companies in the industrial sector at and above township level (State Statistical Bureau, 1996). One year later, this number increased to 8,282 (State Statistical Bureau, 1997a). Shares of most of these enterprises are not traded on the stock markets, as by the end of 1997, there were only about 750 listed companies. There are no official statistics for the number of township and village enterprises that have adopted the cooperative shareholding system, yet it was estimated to be much larger than that in the urban industrial sector. By the end of 1992 in Shenyang, 37 SOEs introduced the shareholding system in the urban area while 2450 rural firms adopted the 'cooperative shareholding system' (Du, 1993).

In most shareholding enterprises, there are three types of shares: state shares, individual shares, and legal person shares. By definition, state shares are held by the state. In most shareholding companies, the state holds the majority of shares. Individual shares are held by the enterprises' employees (who often purchase these shares at a substantial discount) and other individual investors (if the shares are traded on the stock market). Legal person shares are held by other enterprises, banks, and non-bank financial institutions. In some companies, there used to be a fourth type of share, i.e. the enterprise share or the collective share. These shares were accumulated from investment of the enterprise's retained profits. However, a recent regulation prohibited the setting up of these shares.[4]

Several preferential policies were designed to encourage the conversion from SOEs to shareholding companies. These included: a lower income tax rate than that applied to other SOEs (after 1994, however, all enterprises have been subject to the same 33 per cent income tax rate); increased management autonomy in terms of decision-making in the areas of investment, labour management, production, and marketing; and special support from government in the form of directed credits. However, during the experiment of the shareholding system, various unexpected incentive problems emerged. Although no systematic survey about stock companies' financial performance is available, many observers suggest that the performance of these companies was not significantly improved (Yu, 1992; Xu and Wang, 1997). In contrast, the state shares in many companies were discriminated against in profit division. Workers' and management's incentive for an excessive increase in wages and in-kind benefits remains strong, while the incentive for investment in long-term growth is still weak. Following is a summary of several major problems with shareholding companies.

Insiders' interests are enhanced at the expense of the state shares   In most stock companies, the state shares are not represented by persons who can effectively protect the interests of the state. The board members who represent the state shares are, in most cases, from the former industrial bureaux. They are intensely influenced by the workers and management while very few monitoring mechanisms exist to check whether they behave in the interests of the state. Moreover, since board members are not permitted to purchase shares of the firm, there is virtually no link between the board members' personal interests and that of the state.[5]

Many practices are used by experimental stock companies to benefit employees at the expense of state shares. For example, some firms offered their employees shares that were refundable at the price they were purchased. This was like a put option, but the initial price was not set accordingly high to reflect the low risks. Worker-shareholders therefore benefited if the firm made profits but did not bear any risk if the firm suffered from losses. In other cases, SOEs set up their best performing subsidiaries as experimental shareholding companies and encouraged their employees to buy shares in these new companies. Resources from other subsidiaries were transferred at zero or very low internal prices to these stock companies and, consequently, the profits in these new stock companies increased at the expense of other nonstock subsidiaries.

Wage increase becomes easier   One of the most important objectives of SOE managers is to maximize employees' welfare. But under previous systems, these firms were subject to various constraints set by the government. For example, under the contract responsibility system, the growth rate of total wages of some SOEs was limited to the growth rate of the total profits and taxes. There was also a highly punitive tax on bonuses if total bonuses exceeded four months of wages. However, under the shareholding system, which emphasizes more enterprise autonomy, many local governments no longer impose limits on total wage growth, and these firms are free to increase wages and bonuses.

Employees and other individual shareholders are still reluctant to make long-term investment   Employees are reluctant to make long-term investments in an enterprise because, in the absence of adequate legal protection of private property rights and possible hostility directed against them in a future political campaign, they worry about possible appropriation of their assets. Many employees are eager to make short-term profits from black market trading of their shares. As a response, the state ruled that employees' shares are not allowed to trade in the market within one year after their purchase.[6] Most other individual shareholders, who purchased enterprise shares from the stock market, also trade for short-term profits rather than aiming for long-term growth. According to Xu and Wang (1997), the average period of stock holding by Chinese investors is about 1 to 2 months, compared with 18 months in the United States.

The corporate governance structure does not protect the state shares The forms of corporate governance of the experimental stock companies are set arbitrarily and vary drastically from company to company. Each company adopts a structure that is a compromise of the interests of the many parties involved; e.g. a company should consider the arrangement of officials from the former supervisory bureaus. Selecting strong and capable board members who can represent the state's interests is not a priority. Some firms do not have a board of directors – they simply retain the original management structure and change the company's name to that of the stock company. Many firms grant the former directors another title – the Chairman of the Board of Directors. Some firms do not even hold shareholders' meetings. Although the state shares dominate in most stock companies, the number of board members representing the state is often less than proportional to the relative weights of the state shares.

Local governments' priority interest is to raise funds Local governments have played an important role in the design and implementation of the shareholding experiment. However, the most important objective of the local governments in their shareholding experiment is not to reform the enterprise corporate structure, but to raise funds that are not available through conventional means. By issuing shares, the localities could avoid such restrictions as credit ceilings on local branches of commercial banks.[7]

The Experiment of the 'Modern Enterprise System'[8]

Most of the enterprises authorized to experiment with the shareholding system were small or medium SOEs, due to the government's reluctance to introduce diversified ownership into large and super large SOEs. To address the problem of the entire SOE sector, in 1993, the Chinese Communist

Party's 'Decision on Issues Concerning the Establishment of a Socialist Market Economy' proposed the goal of establishing a 'modern enterprise system', namely reforming SOEs through corporatization.[9] In 1994, the Company Law was enacted, providing a legal framework for the reform. Since then, the government has adopted the strategy of 'grasping the big ones, and letting go of the small ones', that is, reforming large SOEs through corporatization without diversifying the ownership, while allowing *de facto* or *de jure* privatization of small enterprises. In 1997, the government announced, on various occasions, that it would speed up the process of SOE reform, with a focus on establishing the modern enterprise system. By the end of 1997, 100 large SOEs that were directly under the supervision of the central government had been converted into corporations, and most of them were still solely owned by the state. Several thousand large and medium-sized SOEs at the local level were also converted into corporations. In the meantime, the government also encouraged the sales, bankruptcy, merger, contracting out, and formation of joint ventures of small and medium-sized SOEs.

In 1997, several measures were used to support the introduction of the modern enterprise system to large SOEs under the government's reform programme, including the experimental enterprises at the central and local levels, as well as 120 experimental enterprise groups. These measures consisted of the following: (1) the government converted some basic construction loans made to SOEs into equity, thereby reducing the debt service burden of these enterprises. In 1997, such debt–equity swaps amounted to Y38 billion (Zhou, 1998); (2) state banks were authorized to increase the write-off of bad loans to Y30 billion; (3) the government directed most 'stock issuance quotas' (see Chapter 5) to the large SOEs under its reform plan;[10] (4) many local governments returned part of their income tax proceeds to SOEs under their reform plans; and the government continued to support major SOEs and enterprise groups through granting directed credits at preferential rates and import–export rights.

The central objective of the modern enterprise system is corporatization of SOEs. The major elements of this reform include: (1) transformation of SOEs, particularly large SOEs, into corporations with a clearly defined ownership and corporate governance structure. Under this system, the corporatized SOEs are required set up boards of directors that represent the interests of the owners; (2) creation of separate corporate entities that oversee, on behalf of the state and through a board of directors, the performance of individual enterprises (grouped geographically, sectorally or both). The managing institutions for state-owned assets (e.g. state assets holding companies) will replace existing line bureaux and ministries; (3) establishment of supervisory boards for corporatized SOEs, according to the Company Law. Its functions include ensuring that the directors and managers do not commit any illegal activities or activities that obstruct the interest of the company, and calling for additional shareholders' congresses whenever it thinks necessary. Such a board should include outside experts with knowledge of business management and of the market for the firm's products; (4) a clear separation of government administrative functions from commercial functions through the corporatization of SOEs.

The key hypothesis underlying the 'modern enterprise system' is that once their commercial functions and government functions are clearly separated, SOEs would be subject to minimum government intervention and therefore could operate efficiently in a market environment. In the meantime, once the 'owners' of the SOEs are clearly identified and their interests are represented through the representatives on the boards of directors, the managers' and workers' short-term behaviour will be effectively controlled. Unfortunately, evidence from many corporations experimenting with this system suggests that the actual implementation deviates significantly from what was expected. The main issues emerging from these experimental corporations are as follows:

(1) Among the 100 experimental enterprises at the national level (the experiments of 70 enterprises are supervised by the State Economic and Trade Commission, and the other 30 are supervised by the State Economic System Reform Commission), 80 per cent have selected the form of 'solely state-owned corporation'. At the provincial level, most experimental enterprises also elected the form of 'solely state-owned corporation'. With 100 per cent government ownership, most of these corporations continue to be burdened by enormous government and social functions, including maintaining employment, providing social services (such as education, health care, and assistance to the poor), being subject to price controls, implementing government decisions on investment projects, and supplying resources to enterprises or sectors that are considered 'priorities' by the government.

(2) In many of these corporations, the chairmen of the boards of directors are the same as the chief executive officers (or general managers), and the board members are almost identical to the members of the executive offices. Other corporations use the 'party–CEO joint committees' to substitute the boards of directors. The CEOs can exercise substantial management power without being monitored by independent

boards of directors. In other words, the 'insider control' problem is not controlled in the new corporate structure.

(3) In a number of sectors, solely state-owned holding companies were created to exercise ownership control over their daughter companies. Many of these holding companies have recentralized the management powers previously given to the subsidiaries. The boards of directors of these daughter companies exist only nominally.

(4) In many newly established corporations, the three old committees (Party Committee, Trade Union, and the Congress of Workers' Representatives) coexist with the three new committees (Shareholders' Congress, Board of Directors, and Supervisory Board); the responsibilities of these bodies and the relationships among them are poorly defined, and have led to internal conflicts and reduced efficiency of the decision-making process.

(5) Corporations experimenting with the modern enterprise system have attempted to introduce a management compensation scheme that consists of both a basic salary and a performance-based bonus. However, most SOE managers are not recruited from the managerial labour market; rather, they are appointed by the supervisory government agencies.[11] In addition, many companies still operate as monopolies. It is virtually impossible to fairly evaluate a manager's performance under such conditions.

A New Framework for SOE Reform

An important reason for the above mentioned problems is that a number of basic theoretical and legal issues regarding state enterprise reform have not been resolved in China. These issues are discussed below.

First, there is a misperception that a clear 'separation of the administrative, regulatory and social functions from the commercial functions of enterprises' can be achieved in all SOEs. In reality, SOEs are often characterized by two conflicting objectives. On the one hand, many SOEs are 'public': to varying degrees, they are controlled or supervised by the central or local governments, and their behaviour reflects the preferences of the government. These preferences may include monopoly control, job creation, balanced regional development, support for strategic industries, protection of consumer rights, equity in income distribution, etc. Government controls often take the form of mandatory production and investment planning, price controls, targeted distribution, stringent labor policy, etc. On the other hand, many SOEs are also 'commercial': they enjoy some management autonomy and have a certain degree of profit motives. Evidence from many countries' SOE reforms has shown the following: (1) there is a positive correlation between the degree of state ownership and the degree of government intervention. The ownership nature of the SOEs largely determines their level of management autonomy. Expecting all SOEs to have the same degree of autonomy as private firms is unrealistic; and (2) a firm's management autonomy is positively related to its profit motive and financial performance. Many SOEs are subject to various policy constraints and therefore unable to achieve maximum efficiency. Given the fact that many SOEs must perform certain government functions, it is again unrealistic to expect them to be fully responsible for their financial gains and losses.

Secondly, it seems to be widely accepted in China that the Company Law should be applied to all SOEs. In fact, SOEs can take many different forms, including government enterprises, public corporations (special public legal entities), and joint stock companies with equity participation of the state (see below). China's Company Law, which includes provisions on limited liability companies and limited liability stock companies, should be applied to the third category only. In contrast, in many countries, 'public corporation (or special public legal entity)' is the major form of SOEs, and laws on public corporations (which consist of many laws governing public enterprises in sectors such as railway, posts and telecommunications, utilities, etc.) provide the main legal framework for these SOEs.

This section proposes a new framework for assessing the modern enterprise system and the design of SOE reform strategy. In light of relevant international experience, it is argued that SOEs should be classified into three categories according to the types of their products and services and associated market structures: government enterprises, public corporations (special public legal entities), and joint stock companies.[12] Currently, the modern enterprise system pursued by the Chinese government in reforming the SOE sector does not distinguish these three types of SOEs. It unrealistically requires that all SOEs separate commercial and government functions, and attempts to apply the Company Law uniformly to all SOEs. A more practical reform strategy for China is to design different policies, legal frameworks, and corporate governance structures for different types of SOEs.

Three Types of SOEs

For the sake of arguments to be developed in this section, we classify SOEs into three types: government enterprises, public corporations (special public legal entities), and joint stock companies.[13] *Government enterprises* (also referred to as departmental enterprises, departmental undertakings) are non-corporate units owned by governments and directly managed by government agencies, and their objectives are non-commercial. Virtually all SOEs in pre-reform China could be classified as government enterprises. In Western countries, however, the coverage of government enterprises is much narrower, typically confined to those that supply goods and services to other units of government, and less frequently, those sell goods and services to the public on a small scale (International Monetary Fund, 1986). Government enterprises do not have an independent legal status, and as a result, they can be created or abolished at the discretion of their supervisory agencies. Examples of government enterprises in western countries include munition factories, government printing and publishing services, navy dockyards, repair and maintenance units, and business management services.

In most cases, the supply of goods and services by government enterprises (e.g. munitions) to other units of government (e.g. the military units) enables the latter to provide public goods and services (e.g. national defence). In other words, the operation of government enterprises forms part of the production process of public goods and services. The goods and services produced by government enterprises are often provided free or sold to other government units at prices that are set for public policy purposes rather than for profit maximization. As a result, no individuals or private firms are willing to supply such goods and services, and the government has to take the responsibility for their provision. It is therefore impossible for government enterprises to be fully responsible for their own profits and losses, and the separation of commercial and government functions in these enterprises is out of the question.

Public corporations (special public legal entities) are SOEs created by legislative bodies through special legislations which stipulate the special financial and regulatory relations between these corporations and the governments. In the words of Tokyo University Professor Uekusa, special legal entities must satisfy the following conditions: (1) they are owned by the central or local governments, and are established according to public law; (2) they generate revenues from their provision of goods and services; and (3) they have an independent accounting status (Uekusa, 1989). Typically these enterprises exist in monopolistic industries and industries that involve significant externalities. A key feature of public corporations in these sectors is that they have both commercial and noncommercial objectives. Examples of noncommercial objectives include price control over monopoly products and services in order to protect consumer interest, investment in sectors with extenalities or poor regions in order to provide sufficient quantities of products or services, and restrictions on worker layoffs in order to protect employment. Generally speaking, fulfilling these noncommercial objectives unavoidably reduces the profitability of the enterprises, and may even force them to operate at a loss. In the latter case, governments have to provide subsidies or other forms of assistance. Therefore, a full separation of commercial and noncommercial functions in these enterprises is also unrealistic.[14]

Holding shares in *joint stock companies*, most of which are in competitive industries, is another typical form of government ownership. Mainstream economic theories, however, suggest that there is no rationale for state ownership in competitive industries. Empirical evidence also shows that, generally, private enterprises operate more efficiently than SOEs in competitive industries (World Bank, 1995b). Indeed, over the past few decades, many countries (particularly developed countries, and more recently, transition countries) privatized a large number of SOEs in competitive sectors. Most remaining SOEs in these sectors have been or are being reformed through corporatization, and are considered to be in transition towards eventual privatization. In these cases, the rationales for the existence of SOEs in competitive sectors become: mass privatization in the short run would create massive unemployment, and/or private capital is incapable to absorb the many privatized SOEs in a short period of time. It is hoped that corporatization would help improve the efficiency of the SOEs during the transition period by offering them more management autonomy and creating a business environment that mimics that for private corporations.

Policy Environment

Many studies (e.g. World Bank, 1995b) have shown that the success of SOE reform depends on many internal and external factors. Important external factors include hardened budget constraints; increased competition in the product market, capital market, and managerial labour market; and reduced government intervention. However, these studies failed to distinguish the external (or policy) environments for different types of SOEs, and seem to suggest that the above mentioned principles apply to all SOEs. We believe that this view is overly simplistic and that different reform strategies should be considered for creating the appropriate policy environments for different types of SOEs. This subsection discusses the key features of the external environments for these SOEs in five aspects: budget constraint, product market, transferability of ownership, managerial labour market, and government intervention.

Government enterprises typically should face a soft budget constraint, since they should not be held responsible for their profits and losses. The government should provide the necessary investment and, in the event of losses, provide subsidies or other forms of assistance to ensure the continuation of the enterprises' operation. As these enterprises' main objective is to provide goods or services to other units of government, the issue of competition in the product market does not arise. Similarly, since no private sector investors attempt to engage in the production of these goods and services, the government ownership of these enterprises is nontransferable. The criteria for selecting managers for government enterprises should be different from those for commercial enterprises, as the former are required to achieve the efficient provision of goods and services rather than maximization of profits. Managers of government enterprises should therefore be appointed by the government's supervisory agencies, rather than being recruited from the managerial labour market. As the funding for government enterprises is mainly from government revenues and no profit indicators can be used to judge the enterprises' performance, the government needs to closely monitor and supervise the operations of these enterprises to ensure the proper use of these funds. In other words, the degree of government control over these enterprises should be higher than those on both public corporations and stock companies with government equity participation.

Public corporations (special public legal entities) should face a harder budget constraint than that for government enterprises, but it should be softer than that for joint stock companies. To the extent that public corporations need to fulfil some noncommercial objectives, in addition to their commercial objectives, the government should provide some initial investments and be responsible for the losses incurred to fulfil the noncommercial objectives (e.g. in the form of providing subsidies or tax reliefs). As many public corporations are providers of utility and other infrastructure services, they typically operate in a monopolistic environment where the product market involves weak competition. Theoretically, the government ownership of these enterprises is transferable, as evidenced by the privatization of many utility companies in Western Europe in recent decades, but such transfers require considerable absorptive capacities of the capital market. Managers of public corporations can be appointed by government supervisory agencies, but the best way is to recruit capable and experienced managers from the managerial labour market. Government intervention in these corporations is typically less (more) intense compared with government enterprises (joint stock companies). Government controls can take the forms of setting profit margins, price limits, production targets, distribution channels, and product standards. In recent decades, many western countries increasingly used performance contracts as a way to improve management flexibility and to encourage better financial performance of public corporations. An objective of such contracts is to distinguish commercial and noncommercial objectives, thereby facilitating a more objective evaluation of management performance.

Joint stock companies with government equity participation should face a budget constraint as hard as that for private enterprises. The government's liability should be limited to the amount of shares that it has contributed. As these companies mainly operate in competitive industries, competition in the product market provides an important incentive for innovation and productivity gain. By definition, shares owned by the government should be transferable to other investors. This constitutes another important mechanism for disciplining the management behaviour: shareholders, including government shareholders, can 'vote with their feet' by selling shares if they do not appreciate the performance of the firms. Consistent with the fact that the government has limited liabilities, it should also refrain from intervening into the firms' daily operations. The government should regulate joint stock companies with state ownership in the same way as it regulates private corporations in the same sector.

Corporate Governance

In addition to the differences in the external environment, the three types of SOEs should operate under different corporate governance structures. This subsection discusses several main elements of these corporate governance structures: owner's representative, board of directors, source of manager, and compensation of the management.

The corporate governance structure of *government enterprises* should be the same as or very similar to the government's internal governance structure. The state ownership should be represented by the enterprise's supervisory agencies, which exercise the power of appointing and dismissing the management of the enterprises. A board of directors is unnecessary, as a government enterprise is run as a subsidiary of the government agency. Compensation of the management should be in line with the pay scales applied to other civil servants. The main incentive for managers to perform well is the possible promotion within the government hierarchy.

The corporate governance structure of *public corporations* (special public legal entities) deserves some detailed discussion:

1. *Owner's representative* The owner's representative should be clearly identified and, preferably, 'personalized' in order to ensure accountability. For example, in Austria and New Zealand, representatives of state ownership in SOEs are ministers in charge of the specific sectors, and sometimes jointly with the Finance Ministers. In Japan, each special public legal entity is accountable to a designated line minister (in some cases more than one). In the United States, special legal entities (e.g. FDIC, Export–Import Bank) at the federal level report to special committees of Congress.

2. *Board of directors* If the state is the sole owner of the firm, the representative of the state appoints the board of directors. If other owners are involved, their interests should also be represented at the board. Within the scope provided by the law regarding the establishment of the special legal entity, the board is the top policy-making body supervising the operations of the firm. Among other things, the board should formulate the bylaws of the firm, determine business objectives, review and approve investment decisions, and appoint the management. Board members can be current and former senior ministry officials or other professionals with relevant management experience. An important control mechanism the government can use to influence decisions of special legal entities is the appointment of board members (including the chairman).

3. *Source of managers* Managers are appointed by the board of directors. They should be recruited from the managerial labour market whenever possible.

4. *Compensation of the management* Management compensation should be competitive in the market. That is, it should be at least comparable to those for managers of private firms in the same sector. Otherwise, special legal entities would not be able to attract the best managers. Incentive mechanisms may include performance-based bonuses and granting shares or stock options to managers. Performance contracts should attempt to distinguish commercial and noncommercial objectives in order to facilitate a fair assessment of management performance.

5. *Special investigators* The Chinese experience shows that party committees and workers' congresses are not effective mechanisms for disciplining management behaviour. Since the Ninth People's Congress, the

Chinese government has instituted a system of 'special investigators' to monitor the management of large SOEs. These special investigators would examine SOE managers' compliance with financial and accounting regulations without interfering in the daily operations of the enterprises. Our view is that there is no need to send special investigators to government enterprises, as they are run as government agencies in the first place. For joint stock companies, the stock market, managerial labour market, and market-based managerial compensation should serve as adequate disciplines, and therefore the imposition of special investigators is not justified. This system appears to be most suitable for special public legal entities where market disciplines are not strong enough.

The corporate governance structure of *joint stock companies* with state ownership should be no different from that of stock companies without state ownership. Both types of stock companies should be structured according to the Company Law. The state ownership can be represented on the board through state holding companies, or state assets management agencies at the central or local levels. In most joint stock companies, the government should not attempt to control majority shares; rather, it should maximize the benefits of free-riding on private sector participation, including by using their often better management capacity and incentive. The shareholders' meeting (including representatives of the state) should have the final authority on a number of key policies, the board of directors should decide on other major policies, and the management should be responsible for day-to-day operations. The board should recruit managers from the managerial labour market, and the government should avoid nominating former government officials who do not have the relevant experience of enterprise management. It is essential that management compensation be competitive in the market, and performance-based incentives must be incorporated into the management compensation package.

Legal Framework

Government enterprises Legally speaking, government enterprises are equivalent to government agencies, and their operations should abide by laws and regulations governing the government sector. For instance, the budget law should apply to government enterprises in their budgeting process. Laws governing special legal entities and joint stock companies do not apply to government enterprises. In particular, government enterprises are not created on the basis of special entity legislation or the Company Law, and therefore do not have an 'independent legal status'.

Public corporations (special public legal entities)   The legal framework governing special public legal entities consists of a collection of many laws. In many western countries (case studies conducted for this research include Japan, the United States, the United Kingdom, and Canada), congresses or state and local assemblies (councils) pass such laws (acts) to create SOEs in the form of special legal entities. Each of these laws applies to one special public legal entity or all public legal entities in a particular sector. In some countries, the establishment, restructuring, and major changes in business scope should all be approved by the relevant legislative body in the form of new laws or amendments of the previous laws. A typical special legal entity law should include, among other things, the following:

1. the firm's business objective, business scope, and development plan;
2. laws and regulations that the firm is subject to;
3. relationships with relevant government agencies, including the reporting procedure, financial relationship between the firm and the supervisory agency;
4. the corporate governance of the firm, including the structure of the management committee or board of directors, the selection procedure of the chief executive, and decision-making procedures; and
5. the capital structure, accounting procedures, and information disclosure rules.

Below are two typical examples of legal framework for special public legal entities in western countries.

Example 1:   Japan's 'Law on Road Corporations' consists of eight chapters and 61 articles. These articles stipulate road corporations' objectives, operating principles, and policies on business operations, personnel management, finance, management, and monitoring. In addition, 'Japan Road Corporation's Implementation Act' and 'Road Bond Act' supplement the 'Law on Road Corporation' in guiding the operations of the corporation.

Example 2:   Federal Deposit Insurance Corporation (FDIC) of the United States.

- Banking Act of 1933 (P.L. 73– 66, 48 STAT. 162). Also known as the Glass–Steagall Act. Established the FDIC as a temporary agency. Separated commercial banking from investment banking, establishing them as separate lines of commerce.
- Banking Act of 1935 (P.L. 74– 305, 49 STAT. 684). Established the FDIC as a permanent agency of the government.
- Federal Deposit Insurance Act of 1950 (P.L. 81– 797, 64 STAT. 873). Revised and consolidated earlier FDIC legislation into one act. Embodied the basic authority for the operation of the FDIC.

- International Banking Act of 1978 (P.L. 95–369, 92 STAT. 607). Brought foreign banks within the federal regulatory framework. Required deposit insurance for branches of foreign banks engaged in retail deposit taking in the US.
- Depository Institutions Deregulation and Monetary Control Act of 1980 (P.L. 96–221, 94 STAT. 132). Granted new powers to thrift institutions. Raised the deposit insurance ceiling to $100 000.
- Depository Institutions Act of 1982 (P.L. 97– 320, 96 STAT. 1469). Also known as Garn-St. Germain. Expanded FDIC powers to assist troubled banks. Established the Net Worth Certificate program. Expanded the powers of thrift institutions.
- Competitive Equality Banking Act of 1987 (P.L. 100– 86, 101 STAT. 552). Also known as CEBA. Expanded FDIC authority for open bank assistance transactions, including bridge banks.
- Financial Institutions Reform, Recovery, and Enforcement Act of 1989 (P.L. 101– 73, 103 STAT. 183). Also known as FIRREA. The FDIC was given the responsibility of insuring the deposits of thrift institutions in its place. The FDIC insurance fund created to cover thrifts was named the Savings Association Insurance Fund (SAIF), while the fund covering banks was called the Bank Insurance Fund (BIF).
- Crime Control Act of 1990 (P.L. 101– 647, 104 STAT. 4789). Increased the powers and authority of the FDIC to take enforcement actions against institutions operating in an unsafe or unsound manner, and gave regulators new procedural powers to recover assets improperly diverted from financial institutions.
- Federal Deposit Insurance Corporation Improvement Act of 1991 (P.L. 102– 242, 105 STAT. 2236). Also known as FDICIA. FDICIA greatly increased the powers and authority of the FDIC. Major provisions recapitalized the Bank Insurance Fund and allowed the FDIC to strengthen the fund by borrowing from the Treasury.

In addition to legislation, legislative bodies (or their special committees) in western countries hold regular review sessions on special legal entities' annual reports. The inquiries and commentaries on these enterprises' performance have an important impact on the enterprises' future directions, as the views of the legislative bodies often lead to new or revised regulatory policies. In the United Kingdom, Parliament holds about a dozen special sessions on SOE issues every year and questions raised by special committees can amount to a thousand.

Although both special legal entities and joint stock companies have a 'legal status', there is a fundamental distinction between them. Special legal entities are created by the legislative body through special legislation, and can be abolished by such a body through the same process. However, the legal status of a particular joint stock company established according to the Company Law is not determined by the government or the legislative body. The Chinese reform package, named the 'modern enterprise system', has ignored this difference, assuming all SOEs should operate under the Company Law.

Joint Stock Companies   China's Company Law covers two types of companies: limited liability companies and limited liability joint stock companies. As discussed above, this law should not be applied to special public legal entities. It should apply mainly to joint stock companies of either pure private ownership or with government equity participation. We suggest that the Company Law be revised in the following ways: (1) redefine the scope of the Company Law's coverage to make clear that it applies only to corporations other than government enterprises and special public legal entities; (2) remove the clause on wholly state-owned corporations from the Company Law; and (3) revise the corporate governance structure of joint stock companies and its monitoring mechanisms. Specifically, the monitoring function should be given to the board of directors, and the requirement of setting up a supervisory board should be eliminated (Yu and Ma, 1998).

Conclusions

SOEs can and should take a variety of forms, depending on government objectives, and the nature of their products and markets. However, the current strategy pursued by the Chinese government in reforming the SOE sector fails to distinguish these forms and ignores the need to design different reform packages for different types of SOEs. It unrealistically requires a full separation of commercial and government functions in all SOEs, and attempts to apply a uniform legal framework (the Company Law) to them. This chapter proposes an alternative framework for reforming China's SOE sector, taking into account the key differences in three types of SOEs' policy environments, corporate governance structures, and legal frameworks.

First, three types of SOEs should correspond to three different sectors of the economy. Specifically: (1) goods and services for government units should be provided mainly by government enterprises; (2) products and services in monopolistic industries and industries with significant externalities (water, electricity, gas, telecommunications, transportation, etc.) can be provided by special public legal entities. In most OECD countries, these enterprises account for about 3 to 7 per cent of GDP;

and (3) the government can engage in competitive sectors through holding shares in joint stock companies. Since mass and rapid privatization of large SOEs lacks political feasibility in China, most large SOEs in competitive sectors will take the form of joint stock companies in the short and medium term. We expect, however, that SOEs in competitive sectors as a percentage of GDP will decline significantly in the next 10–15 years, as the government gradually sells off its shares in many of these enterprises and concentrates on pure government functions and the first and second types of SOEs.

Secondly, given different rationales for the existence of different types of SOEs, one should not expect them to face the same policy environment. For government enterprises, their budget constraints can only be 'soft', their products are often provided free of charge rather than sold on the markets, their ownership is not transferable, their managers are typically selected by the supervisory agencies, and intervention from supervisory agencies is extensive (as government enterprises are, by design, to perform government functions). Compared with government enterprises (joint stock companies), public corporations face harder (softer) budget constraints, less (more) government intervention, more (less) competitive product markets, stronger (weaker) transferability of their ownership, and a better (worse) functioning managerial labour market. With minimum government intervention and maximum disciplines by the market, joint stock companies should operate under a similar environment as that for private enterprises.

Thirdly, different corporate governance structures should be applied to different types of SOEs: (1) government enterprises should normally be directly managed by their supervisory agencies; (2) special public legal entities should be governed by their boards of directors and the management teams appointed by the boards. The government appoints the chairmen of the boards and/or chief executive officers. Performance contracts should be used to improve management autonomy and provide incentives for the boards and the management teams. Since these enterprises often need to fulfil both commercial and government objectives at the same time, the performance contracts should attempt to reflect the impact of government objectives on enterprise profitability; and (3) for joint stock companies with government equity participation, the government's objective is to maximize the value of its shares, just as other shareholders. The government should, through its holding companies or assets management agencies, mainly use portfolio management techniques to achieve its objectives and not intervene into the daily operations of the enterprises.

Fourthly, different legal frameworks should apply to different types of SOEs: (1) government enterprises should be governed by laws and regulations applied to government agencies; (2) special public legal entities should be governed by separate 'special legal entity laws', rather than by the Company Law. A special legal entity law should clearly define, among other things, the objectives of the public corporation (in particular, its noncommercial objectives), its corporate governance structure, and its relationships with relevant government agencies (including the reporting procedure, and the financial relationship between the corporation and the supervisory agency). Accordingly, the articles regarding 'solely state-owned company' should be removed from the Company Law; and (3) Joint stock companies should be governed by the Company Law. The revised Company Law should grant the monitoring function to the board of directors, and eliminate the requirement of setting up a supervisory board.

Appendix 6.1 TVEs and a Comparison with SOEs

In contrast to SOEs, TVEs, the main part of the nonstate-owned sector, have emerged as the fastest growing sector in the economy.[15] In 1978, TVEs produced only 9 per cent of the industrial output in the country. From 1978 to 1995, TVEs' output value grew at an annual average rate of 24.7 per cent,[16] and its employment rose at an annual average rate of 9.3 per cent. In 1995, TVEs produced 56 per cent of the total industrial output,[17] far exceeding the share of SOEs in total industrial output. Currently, TVEs employ a labour force of about 130 million, more than double the size of the labour force employed by SOEs. [18]

A number of studies have suggested that collectively owned enterprises (COEs) or TVEs[19] have significantly outperformed the state-owned sector in terms of productivity growth. Using data from 324 cities in 1985 and 382 cities in 1987, Xiao (1991) finds that the total factor productivity (TFP) of the collective sector grew at an annual average rate of 4.5 per cent during 1985–7, while that of the state sector remained stagnant during the same period. Jefferson *et al.* (1992) find that TFP growth was 2.4 per cent annually in the state sector, and 4.6 per cent in the collective sector between 1978 and 1988. In Woo *et al.* (1993), the authors calculate TFP growth rates for a sample of 300 SOEs and a sample of 200 TVEs between 1985 and 1988. They find that the SOEs had only negligible growth in TFP, while the TVEs showed an annual average growth of 8 to 10 per cent under different estimation methods. A recent work by Murakami *et al.* (1994) specifically compares the performance difference between SOEs and TVEs using firm-level data from the Chinese garment industry. They conclude that TVEs are far more efficient, both technically and allocatively, than SOEs.

Unlike reforms in the state sector, the post-1978 development of TVEs is largely spontaneous. The major form of ownership varies from region to region: in Jiangsu, most TVEs are owned by township or village governments; in Guangdong, there are a large number of TVEs owned jointly by township/village governments, individuals and foreign investors; and in Wenzhou (Zhejiang), most rural enterprises are privately owned. The central and provincial governments have played a very limited role in encouraging the development of TVEs, while the township and village governments provided active promotion efforts.

Compared to SOE managers, TVEs' managers enjoy more day-to-day autonomy in management. Although some township-owned enterprises are subject to control from township governments, all TVEs are spared from direct interventions by higher level governments in such areas as production, investment, pricing, employment and wage policies. Compared to collectively owned TVEs, privately and jointly owned TVEs enjoy more managerial autonomy. In addition, most TVEs were subject to a progressive income tax and more tax concessions with an average rate significantly lower than the 55 per cent rate applied to large and medium sized SOEs until 1994.[20]

However, there are many areas in which TVEs are at a disadvantage when compared to SOEs. Since there is no government guarantee for material supply, TVEs have to purchase all materials at market prices. TVEs' external financial resources are limited to loans from the Agricultural Bank, rural credit cooperatives and personal borrowing, which operate on a small scale compared to the Bank of Construction and the Bank of Industry and Commerce that serve mainly state enterprises. Moreover, TVEs are strongly influenced by nationwide policy changes and their outputs tended to show more fluctuation than SOEs. During each period of monetary contraction, TVEs were the main victims of credit tightening. This was most apparent in the 1989–90 'rectification programme' phase when TVEs were accused of inefficient production technology, low product qualities and inadequate pollution control; the government responded with the 'shut down, stop production, merge, and transfer ownership' (Guan Ting Bin Zhuan) policy. Administrative restrictions such as pollution control were also applied to limit the growth of TVEs. During this period, about 1 million TVEs were shut down.[21]

To summarize, Table A6.1 provides a simple comparison of the advantages and disadvantages of the SOEs' and TVEs' external environments.

It is clear that the policy differentials between the SOEs and the TVEs are vast, with some favouring the former and others favouring the latter.

Table A6.1   Policy environment of SOEs and TVEs

	Advantages	*Disadvantages*
SOEs	1. tax deduction of loan repayment	1. higher average tax rate
	2. some guaranteed bank loans	2. some products are still subject to price control
	3. some material supply at planned prices	3. less managerial autonomy
	4. some guaranteed sales	4. higher labour and management costs
	5. more skilled labour and advanced equipment	
TVEs	1. lower average tax rate	1. no tax deduction of loan repayment
	2. no price control	2. no guaranteed bank loans
	3. more managerial autonomy	3. no material supply at planned price
	4. lower labour and management costs	4. no guaranteed sales
		5. less skilled labour and advanced equipment

7
Export Promotion Strategies

Introduction

It has been widely observed that the increasing openness of the Chinese economy, as measured by, say, the trade-to-GDP ratio, has been an important contributing factor to its growth performance.[1] This chapter gives an overview of China's foreign trade development, and identifies the policies that have promoted China's trade performance. These policies included mainly decentralization of the trade management system, the regional targeting policy, and the sectoral targeting policy. The targeting policies used instruments such as tax breaks, foreign exchange retention privileges, government provision of cheap materials and credits, and duty-free imports. As a part of China's regional targeting policy, the strategy of combining openness toward foreign investment with export orientation in the special economic zones (SEZs) and open coastal cities has been particularly successful. Among the targeted regions, Guangdong Province has been a model for developing a foreign investment-based and export-led development strategy.

The rest of this chapter is organized as follows. The second section first discusses China's trade performance since 1979. It then reviews the experience of the decentralization of trade management system, the regional targeting (particularly the special economic zone policy) and sectoral targeting policies. The third section takes Guangdong Province, the fastest growing region in China, as a case to analyse the role of export in economic growth and the role of foreign investment in export growth. It also looks at the applicability of Guangdong's foreign investment supported and export-led growth model to other regions in China. The last section offers some concluding remarks.

China's Trade Performance and Trade Policy

Prior to 1979, the orthodox Chinese view on the international division of labour held that China, as a socialist country, should not join the international division of labour which was dominated by the capitalist world, since such an involvement was harmful for centrally planned economies, due to both external chaotic fluctuations and dependence on foreign markets. This view also stressed that the international division of labour would lead to an unequal exchange between China and the developed countries, because with this division of labour, China and other less developed countries would be confined to producing and exporting primary products and importing manufactured goods. As a result of this mentality, foreign trade was merely a way of filling the difference between planned demand and domestic production capacity and at best performed a peripheral function in China's economic growth. To formulate a foreign trade plan, the policy-makers first estimated their necessary imports in any particular year and then drew up an export plan to earn foreign exchange to pay for the import bill. Building on this approach, there was an obvious bias in China's trade regime towards import substitution and against export promotion.

Since the launching of the reform programme in 1979, export promotion has been one of the central elements of China's efforts to modernize its economy. The policy-makers have gradually recognized that the international division of labour can provide the necessary technology and know-how and a larger market for domestic production, and in order to transform China into an industrial country, it should actively participate in world trade. The trade policies adopted since 1979 has been a remarkable success, as reflected by the increasing openness of the economy. Between 1978 and 1997, the annual average growth rate of total trade (imports + exports) reached 16 per cent. During the same period, the trade-to-GDP ratio rose from 9 per cent to 36 per cent, with exports-to-GDP ratio rising from 4 per cent to 19 per cent. Measured by the share of China's trade in total world trade, China's rank rose sharply from thirty-second in 1978 to tenth in 1997.

The rest of this section examines the main policies that contributed to China's trade performance since 1979. These policies include: (1) the decentralization of the trade management system; (2) attracting foreign investment and promoting export orientation of foreign-invested enterprises in the context of regional targeting; and (3) special policies applied to targeted export sectors. The following subsections discuss these three policies in order. The last subsection examines other policy instruments for

Table 7.1   China: imports and exports, 1978–97 (US$bn)

	Exports	Imports	Exports/GDP (%)	Trade/GDP (%)
1978	9.8	10.9	4	9
1980	18.1	20.0	6	13
1985	27.4	42.3	9	24
1990	62.1	53.4	17	31
1991	71.8	63.8	19	36
1992	85.0	80.6	20	38
1993	91.8	104.0	21	40
1994	121.0	115.7	23	41
1995	148.8	132.1	22	41
1996	151.1	138.8	18	35
1997	182.7	142.4	20	36

Note: Year-average exchange rates are used to convert Chinese GDP into US$.
Sources: State Statistical Bureau, 1993, 1995, 1996, 1997a; International Monetary Fund, 1998. 1997 figures are from Chen, 1998. The increase in exports-to-GDP ratio and trade-to-GNP ratio from 1978–1994 partly reflects the depreciation of Chinese RMB; while the decline of these two ratios since 1994 almost exclusively reflects the appreciation of Chinese RMB.

trade promotion, including tax incentives for the export sector, government provision of cheap materials and credits to the export sector, and foreign exchange policies.

Decentralization of the Trade Management System

Pre-reform China had a highly centralized trade management system to implement its export–import plan, which covered more than 90 per cent of China's total foreign trade. Before 1979, there were only 12 specialized foreign trade corporations (FTCs) at the national level, each responsible for carrying out trade in specified, non-overlapping product areas. During the 1980s, the trade management system was significantly decentralized when measured both in terms of the scope of the trade plan and the number of FTCs.

In 1984, to encourage greater competition in foreign trade, the Ministry of Foreign Economic Relations and Trade (MOFERT) authorized the creation of additional FTCs at the provincial and local levels.[2] New FTCs were created in two ways. Many specialized national FTCs saw their provincial branches spun off into separate provincial specialized FTCs. More frequently, though, so-called general FTCs were established at the provincial and municipal levels with authority to deal with a broad range of commodities. By 1988, there were about 5000 FTCs in operation. By the end of 1996, the number of FTCs in operation exceeded 7000. These are mostly state owned, each being supervised by the Ministry of Foreign Trade and Economic Cooperation (MOFTEC) at the appropriate level, whether municipal, provincial or national. In addition to FTCs, in recent years the government has granted a large number of domestically owned manufacturing firms (mainly large and medium state-owned enterprises) the trading rights for their own products and inputs. By the end of 1996, the number of manufacturing enterprises that enjoy such trading rights amounted to over 5000 (MOFTEC, 1997).[3]

Despite the creation of many FTCs and the granting of trading rights to a large number of manufacturing enterprises, most Chinese firms are still prohibited from direct trading with foreigners.[4] The motivation for the government to maintain control over enterprises' trading rights is several-fold. First, the government fears that once all enterprises are given the right to conduct foreign trade, internal competition will become overly intense, thus driving down export prices and bidding up import prices for many commodities.[5] Secondly, several foreign countries have recently charged Chinese export companies for anti-dumping cases, and the Chinese government has been under pressure to prevent such practices. Of course, one handy instrument is to control the granting of trading rights. Thirdly, government agencies that have the authority to grant trading rights naturally enjoy some 'rents' that they are reluctant to give up.

Nevertheless, the trend for further liberalization of trading rights has continued in recent years, as the government recognized that exposing more domestic enterprises directly to international competition is an effective way to promote export and enhance their competitiveness. At the end of 1996, Shenzhen, the first special economic zone, was authorized to experiment with a 'trade registration system' for exporting manufacturing enterprises (MOFTEC, 1997). That is, domestic manufacturing enterprises that meet the following conditions are automatically granted the trading rights: (1) the firm is legally registered with Shenzhen Industrial and Commerce Bureau; (2) its registered capital is above Y2 million; (3) it has regular production facilities and already started operation; and (4) it meets other relevant rules and regulations. In 1996, the MOFTEC also announced that it would authorize joint venture trading companies to operate initially in Pudong New Area.

Along with the creation of more FTCs, the planned share of foreign trade fell significantly. The number of planned export commodities fell from 3000 in the pre-reform period to less than 100 by 1988. The planned share of exports fell to 45 per cent in the same year. Since 1991, almost all mandatory export planning has been abolished, but the state still retains some control through the use of licensing (World Bank, 1994b). In 1996, 114 export commodities were subject to the licensing requirement, of which 95 were also subject to export quotas. The main commodities under quota restrictions included rice, soybean, corn, tea, coal, crude oil, and refined oil. In 1994, the MOFTEC started to organize competitive bidding for some quotas, in an attempt to enhance the economic efficiency of quota allocation and increase the transparency of the process. In 1996, quotas for 27 export commodities were allocated through competitive bidding (MOFTEC, 1997).

The scope of import planning also fell accordingly, from more than 90 per cent of total imports at the beginning of the 1980s to 40 per cent by 1988. In 1992, mandatory planned imports, including those subject to licensing and quota restrictions, were reduced to about 20 per cent of all imports (Kong, 1998). In 1996, only 36 imported goods (or 5 per cent of all imports) were subject to licensing requirement, of which 28 goods were also subject to quota restrictions. The main commodities subject to quota restrictions included automobiles and their parts, colour TVs and monitors, refrigerators, air conditioners, refined oil, wool, some chemical fibres, and sugar (MOFTEC, 1997).[6]

Attracting Foreign Investment

From 1984 to 1997, annual foreign investment rose from US$2.7 billion to US$64 billion (see Table 7.2). With the rapid growth of foreign investment in China, foreign-invested companies have become an increasingly important source of China's strong export performance. In 1996, exports by foreign-invested companies amounted to US$62 billion, or 40 per cent of China's total exports, up from 12 per cent in 1990 (State Statistical Bureau, 1997a). Foreign-invested enterprises typically have several advantages over domestic firms in exporting their products, including advanced technologies, better management and quality control, established product names, and extensive overseas marketing networks.

The rapid growth of foreign investment and their strong export orientation was a result of some deliberate policies of the Chinese government. In 1979, the government decided to experiment with limited economic opening by targeting four SEZs as export bases and foreign investment magnets. These zones included Shenzhen, Shantou, and Zhuhai in Guangdong province, and Xiamen in Fujian Province. The central government decentralized many decision-making powers, including by authorizing the SEZs to approve foreign-investment projects costing less than US$30 million and to retain all foreign exchange earnings from exports. In addition, a number of tax concessions were offered to

Table 7.2   China: actual foreign investment, 1979–97 (US$bn)

	Total	FDI
1979–83	14.4	1.8
1984	2.7	1.3
1985	4.6	1.7
1986	7.3	1.9
1987	8.5	2.3
1988	10.2	3.2
1989	10.1	3.4
1990	10.3	3.5
1991	11.6	4.4
1992	19.2	11.0
1993	39.0	27.5
1994	43.2	33.8
1995	48.1	37.5
1996	54.8	41.7
1997	64.0	45.3

Sources: State Statistical Bureau, 1997a; Chen,
1998.

foreign investors who invest in these zones. These included a 15 per
cent income tax rate and tax holidays for the first few profit-making
years.[7] To encourage exports, foreign-invested enterprises were exempt
from import duties on production inputs (see below).

The dramatic economic growth and outstanding export performance of
the SEZs prompted the central government to extend the foreign investment promotion policies to other regions. In 1984 the State Council
announced the opening of 14 coastal cities, with similar policies applied
previously to the SEZs. Subsequently, Hainan Special Economic Zone and
Pudong New Area were established by the central government, followed
by numerous smaller open zones or areas authorized by provincial and
local governments. While foreign investment surged in many coastal
areas, the problem of interregional tax competition arose when local
governments competed for foreign capital by offering unauthorized tax
concessions and exemptions. Such tax competition had a negative
impact on national revenue stability and, as a response, the central government started to control the establishment of new 'zones' in mid-1993.

While foreign investment continued to grow at a rapid pace, the
government's revenue-to-GDP ratio declined to its historical low level in
1996 (see Chapter 2). One reason identified for the government's weak

revenue performance was the generous tax exemptions and concessions offered to foreign-invested companies. In 1996, the government eliminated the exemption of import duties on equipment for foreign-invested enterprises and reduced the rebate rate on the value added tax (VAT) paid by export-oriented enterprises for locally purchased materials (see Chapter 8). Interestingly, when China's export sector was under severe pressure from the competitive currency devaluation of other Asian countries in early 1998, and given the government's firm statement that it would not devalue Chinese RMB, it re-introduced the exemption of import duties on equipment for foreign-invested companies and raised the VAT rabate rate for exporting companies to provide a new stimulus to the export sector.

Sectoral Targeting

Over the 1980s, the regional targeting policy (e.g. preferential policies for SEZs and open coastal cities) dominated China's development strategy. However, policy during this period did not completely exclude a sectoral targeting policy – which emphasizes certain industrial sectors, many of which are exporting sectors, instead of certain regions – although the term 'industrial policy' was not officially used until 1989. Among various policies promoting targeted export sectors, the important ones included favourable exchange retention policy, government sponsored export networks, and earmarked government funds for technological upgrading.

Starting from the early 1980s, the government favoured light industrial products, textiles, and machinery and electronics by raising foreign exchange retention rights on export earnings. The original retention rate – the percentage of foreign exchange earnings that an exporting enterprise is allowed to retain – for light industrial products and knitwear was 20 per cent, and that for the machinery and electronics sector was 30 per cent at a time when the average rate for other products was less than 10 per cent. In 1982, the retention rate for the machinery and electronics sector was raised to 50 per cent. In the early 1990s, preferential retention ratios were retained only for the machinery and electronics sectors which were entitled to a 70 per cent retention compared to 50 per cent for all other commodities. In January 1994, the foreign exchange retention policy was abolished when China unified its multiple exchange rates.

From 1985, the government also guaranteed firms participating in a government export network electrical power, raw materials, tax reductions on inputs, and attractive purchase prices. Several hundred factories nationwide, producing a range of products, were selected to participate in the network. Investments in the order of $100 million per annum were planned over a five-year period and the participating factories were to be accorded guaranteed supplies of raw materials, power, and packaging materials, and preferential access to transportation and tax reductions. In 1990, about Y1.7 billion was invested in construction projects in support of exporting enterprises in the textile, light industry and machinery and electronics sectors. In addition to favourable exchange retention and export network policy, the MOFERT also earmarked special investment funds for the technological upgrading of selected enterprises, many of which were channelled to various exporting enterprises, including more than a thousand enterprises in the machinery and electronics sector (World Bank, 1994b).

Other Policy Instruments for Trade Promotion

Other than policy instruments such as tax incentives, foreign exchange retention policy, and government-sponsored networks that were mainly used to promote exports in specific regions or sectors, China has also applied a number of policy instruments to promote exports in general. These instruments include incentives for foreign-invested exporting enterprises, exemption of customs duties for exporting enterprises, export credits, and exchange rate policy.

Incentives for foreign-invested exporting enterprises   In 1986, the State Council issued a set of new regulations, later known as 'twenty-two regulations', designed mainly to provide additional incentives to foreign-invested enterprises engaged in exports. According to these regulations, joint ventures receive additional preferential treatment if they are categorized as either export-oriented or technologically advanced projects. These preferential policies include the following major items: (1) profits remitted abroad by exporting enterprises will be exempted from the income tax; (2) enterprises that export 70 per cent or more in value of their products may reduce the income tax payable by half after tax reduction or exemption; (3) exporting enterprises in the SEZs and the Economic and Technological Development Zones of the open coastal cities that have been paying tax at a rate of 15 per cent, upon satisfaction of certain conditions, will pay enterprise income tax at a rate of 10 per cent; and (4) foreign investors who reinvest their earnings in China to establish or expand exporting enterprises for an operational period of not less than five years, upon application to and approval by the tax authorities, will be refunded the total amount of enterprise income tax already paid on the reinvested profits.

Exemption of customs duties for exporting enterprises Exemption of customs duties has also been used as incentives for export promotion. Two schemes designed to promote exports (based on processing or assembly type activity) were adopted in 1984. These schemes are known as 'processing with supplied materials' and 'processing with imported materials', respectively. The former entitles a local enterprise to import free of duty all raw materials provided to it by overseas suppliers to help the firm meet an export contract. The latter exempts a local firm from import duties on all raw materials that it uses to manufacture its exports. These policies have contributed in a major way to the marked rise in manufactured exports based on assembly type operations using cheap yet skilled labour. Exports based on processing of imported materials accounted for 23 per cent of total exports in 1988. Since then they have almost doubled their share by 1991, accounting for 45 per cent of all exports or 64 per cent of all of China's manufactured exports.

Export credits The Bank of China offered trade credits to exporting enterprises in domestic currency. The volume of such credits has been rising very rapidly. The total volume of trade loans outstanding at the end of 1991 reached Y181 billion, more than three times the level at the end of 1985. Most of these loans went to FTCs, and about 90 per cent of the trade loans extended to FTCs were used to finance exports. The Bank of China also offers two other types of trade loans. Export sellers' credits have been offered since 1978 to Chinese enterprises selling electronic and machinery equipment in the international market. The State Council in 1992 also approved the creation of a new system of credits to be extended to buyers of Chinese exports. These loans, made in foreign currencies, are used to finance the sale of complete sets of machinery and electronic equipment valued at a minimum of US$1 million per transaction.

Exchange rate policy Between 1986 and 1993, the Chinese foreign exchange system was two-tiered, with an official exchange rate which was typically held constant for extended periods and a secondary market rate which was determined by supply and demand factors in legal secondary markets called Foreign Exchange Adjustment Centres (FEACs). Before 1989, China's official exchange rate was significantly overvalued since the secondary market rate exceeded the official rate by a significant margin. This implied a substantial implicit tax burden on Chinese exporters. According to calculations by the World Bank, the implied rate of export tax was estimated at around a third in 1988 and 1989 (World Bank, 1994b). Since 1989, the margin between the official and the secondary market exchange rates have been substantially reduced by several devaluations of the official exchange rate – from 1989 to 1994, the annual average official rate depreciated from Y3.8 per US dollar to Y8.6 per US dollar – and a related appreciation of the secondary market exchange rate beginning in the fourth quarter of 1989. This policy reduced the implied export tax rate and thus increased the competitiveness of Chinese exporting firms.[8]

On 1 January 1994, China unified its dual exchange rates. It also established an interbank foreign exchange system in April 1994 to replace the swap centres. From 1994 to 1997, due to persistent large capital inflow and trade surplus, the Chinese RMB was under upward pressures and appreciated by about 4 per cent. As a result, exchange rate devaluation no longer provided new stimulus to the export sector during this period. At the end of 1996, China achieved current account convertibility of the RMB, that is, enterprises and individuals with valid documentations for importing goods and services could purchase foreign exchange from designated banks without prior approval from the government. This reform simplifed the procedure for importing enterprises to obtain foreign exchange, and represented a major progress in China's foreign exchange reform towards international practice.

The Case of Guangdong: The Fastest Growing Region in China

While China as a whole has successfully achieved a high growth rate over the past 20 years, its development has been rather uneven across regions. The coastal regions have, in general, grown faster than the inland regions. Among the coastal regions, Guangdong Province represents the fastest growing region in China. This section looks at Guangdong as a case for analysing the role of a foreign-investment based and export-led development strategy and the conditions that ensures the success of this strategy. It is argued that being the hometown of three out of four SEZs established in the late 1970s and the Pearl River Delta Open Economic

Table 7.3   Selected indicators: Guangdong and China as a whole (%), 1978–96

	Guangdong	China
Annual average GDP growth	14.2	9.7
Exports/GDP ratio, 1996	76	19
Foreign investment/total investment in fixed assets, 1996	46	20

Sources: State Statistical Bureau, 1997a; Guangdong Statistical Bureau, 1997.

Area approved in the mid-1980s has been a critical factor contributing to Guangdong's top performance among the Chinese provinces. We will also discuss whether and to what extent Guangdong's experience can be replicated by other regions in China.

Role of Exports

Guangdong, a province in Southern China, covers an area of 180 000 square kilometres and is inhabited by 63 million people. In 1992, when Deng Xiaoping visited Guangdong, he was impressed by the province's performance and asked whether China could develop several more regions like Guangdong. This question was based on the fact that Guangdong has been growing faster than most other regions in China. In 1978, Guangdong's per capita income was Y313, close to the national average of Y315 and ranked tenth among the 29 provinces, autonomous regions and municipalities (hereafter 'provinces'). In 1991, Guangdong's per capita national income rose to Y2134 in 1991 and ranked fifth in the country. During 1978–96, its annual average GDP growth rate reached 14.2 per cent – compared with the national average of 9.7 per cent – and ranked the top of among China's 30 provinces (see Table 7.3).

By comparing Guangdong's export sector performance with that of China as a whole, one can see that Guangdong's export boom has been a more important source of growth than in other regions. From 1978 to 1996, Guangdong's exports grew at an annual average rate of 23 per cent, compared with the national average of 16 per cent. During the same period, Guangdong's exports-to-GDP ratio jumped from 13 per cent to 76 per cent, far exceeding the national average of 19 per cent in 1996. In 1996, exports from Guangdong reached US$60 billion, accounting for 40 per cent of the country's total. Clearly, Guangdong has been following an export-led development strategy. The trade surplus in Guangdong reached about 30 per cent of the value of exports during most years of the 1980s. This figure includes consignment processing by Hong Kong companies, but despite this, the trade structure remained in surplus. Furthermore, Guangdong's trade surplus has accounted for 7–10 per cent of GDP every year except 1985.

Foreign Investment and SEZs

The strong growth of Guangdong's export sector has been supported by the massive use of foreign investment. In 1996, among the US$60 billion exports from Guangdong, foreign-invested enterprises accounted for over 50 per cent (State Statistical Bureau, 1997a). Although no data about the share of foreign-invested enterprises engaged in export business is available, it is a common observation that most of these enterprises in Guangdong are export-oriented. Many regulations provide preferential treatment to foreign-invested enterprises in the export sector. These policies include more favourable provisions of tax holidays and exemption of custom duties than those applied to other foreign-invested enterprises.

Between 1978 and 1996, foreign investment in Guangdong increased rapidly. In 1996, actual foreign investment reached Y13.3 billion, 56 times higher than that in 1980. The ratio of actual foreign investment to total fixed assets investment reached 46 per cent in 1996. Compared with the national average ratio of 20 per cent, Guangdong clearly obtained an important exogenous engine for its growth through foreign investment. Throughout the 1980s and the first half of 1990s, it accounted for about 30 per cent of the total foreign investment in China, more than any other province in China.

An obvious reason for Guangdong's success is that it is the hometown of three out of four SEZs established in the late 1970s. Special policies for attracting foreign investment and promoting international trade applied to these zones were not made available in other parts of China until 1984, when 14 coastal cities were opened. The cross-regional policy differentials created considerable comparative advantage for Guangdong in terms of the local governments' decision-making power, administrative efficiency, and tax incentives to foreign investors. After 1984, the SEZs' advantage tended to weaken owing to the opening of more cites in the coastal areas. Nevertheless, the establishment of the Pearl River Delta Economic Development Zone greatly enlarged the open area in Guangdong and provided foreign investors with more choices of location. This partly offset the weakening of the SEZs' special position and enabled Guangdong to maintain its lead performance in the second half of the 1980s. In 1991, the Pearl Delta Area, with only 27 per cent of the total area and 25 per cent of the total population in Guangdong, attracted 40 per cent of the province's total foreign investment.

Among the three SEZs located in Guangdong, Shenzhen borders Hong Kong, and the other two are also close to Hong Kong or Macao. The Pearl Delta River Open Area surrounds the three SEZs. Owing to geographical proximity and cultural and linguistic similarities, the largest source of foreign investment in Guangdong is from Hong Kong and Macao. During most years over the past two decades, actual foreign investment from Hong Kong and Macao made up about two-thirds of Guangdong's total actual foreign investment. Compared to the relationships between other regions in China and their foreign investment partners, this reflected an extremely strong investment linkage between Guangdong and both Hong Kong and Macao.

In addition, Hong Kong and Macao are the primary channels that connect Guangdong's domestic enterprises with the international markets. Besides direct foreign investment, other forms of economic integration between Guangdong and Hong Kong and Macao, including compensatory trade, leasing, and processing and assembling, have also been extensively developed. A large number of domestic enterprises have been involved in exporting products through cooperation with Hong Kong. A division of labour has emerged with production shifting from Hong Kong to the Pearl River Delta region while the marketing remains in Hong Kong. It is estimated that over 4 million people in Guangdong are now working directly or indirectly for Hong Kong-based business. Without such natural partners as Hong Kong and Macao, Guangdong could not have developed as fast as it has.

Can Guangdong's Growth Model be Replicated in Other Regions?

Having recognized the role of the export boom and foreign capital in Guangdong's growth performance, the question of whether its development approach can be replicated in other regions of China is largely an issue of creating more foreign investment-supported export-led economies.

Coastal Provinces

As indicated above, Guangdong's export boom and massive use of foreign capital was mainly supported by its economic integration with Hong Kong and Macao. For most coastal provinces, the existence of natural partners with both geographic proximity and mutual comparative advantages would also strongly affect their growth performance. The Fujian Delta area is the ancestral home of many Taiwanese, and its dialect is commonly spoken in Taiwan. Only one hundred miles across the Taiwan Strait, Fujian and Taiwan have geographical proximity similar to that between Guangdong and Hong Kong and Macao. Taiwan's well-developed light manufacturing sector is now confronting skyrocketing labour and land costs, while Fujian's unit cost of labour is still significantly lower than that of the Pearl River Delta area. Therefore economic integration is an attractive policy to both Taiwan and Fujian. Although indirect trade between mainland China and Taiwan has grown dramatically over the past two decades, direct trade has not been permitted for political reasons. Once direct trade is opened, a further increase in trade and direct investment will be inevitable.

It has been proposed by both China and Japan that Northeast Asia, including Northeast China, Shandong, Russia, the Republic of Korea (South Korea), the Democratic People's Republic of Korea (North Korea), and Japan, should form a closely integrated economic community by reducing bilateral trade protection and encouraging direct investment. Among the potential 'members' of this community, Japan and South Korea are apparently the net exporters of capital and capital-intensive products, while Liaoning and Shandong in China are the most promising partners of these two countries. Liaoning is the most important heavy industry base in Northeast China and Shandong is one of the fastest growing provinces. These two provinces are famous for their petroleum, metallurgy, coal, chemical, and building materials industries. Japan and South Korea, however, are known to be well developed in manufacturing but lacking in resources and markets. The bilateral trade and investment should thus take advantage of endowments on both sides of the Yellow Sea. Since the late 1980s, the normalization of diplomatic relations between China and South Korea has offered a great opportunity for both sides to expand their trade and investment relations.

The Yangtze River Delta is the home of China's most advanced industrial city, Shanghai, and two provinces with highly market-oriented economies, Jiangsu and Zhejiang. Without a comparable external growth source such as Hong Kong for Guangdong, Jiangsu and Zhejiang still grew at similar rates to that of Guangdong over the past two decades. This indicates their considerable potential once foreign investment and trade start to play a more significant role. With the opening of Pudong New Area, not only had Shanghai accelerated its growth, but Zhejiang and Jiangsu have also benefited. Although the Yangtze River Delta does not have a designated international partner, the technological level and capital intensity of foreign investment in this area show advantages over other open areas. Zou *et al.* (1990) predicts that in the 1990s China's comparative advantage in skilled labour-intensive and technology-intensive exports will exhibit increasing importance. The Yangtze River Delta, where China's most advanced technologies and skilled labour are located, will therefore become the most promising area in China's international trade. As indicated by the recent trend, this area will find increasing opportunities in cooperating with technologically advanced countries such as Japan, the United States and some West European countries.

Border Provinces

China has seven provinces located along its inland border line.[9] Most of these provinces have the advantages similar to those of the coastal provinces in international trade and economic cooperation with neigh-bouring countries. The border prefectures and counties in Yunnan prov-ince, where exports accounted for more than 30 per cent of China's total border exports in the late 1980s, are among the fastest growing regions in China's border area. Northern China, including Heilongjiang, Xinjiang, and Inner Mongolia, are actively promoting trade with Russia and other former Soviet Republics that are experiencing shortages of consumer goods. Formerly closed border trade between Tibet and India and between Guangxi and Vietnam have also increased as bilateral rela-tions improved.

Unlike coastal provinces, whose major trade partners are developed countries, the border provinces are generally trading with poor neigh-bouring countries. Compared with these neighbours, industries of China's border area exhibit significant comparative advantage in technology and productivity. The export demand could induce further expansion of the manufacturing sector in the border provinces. In this light the border areas, once fully utilizing their potential markets in the neighbouring countries, will obtain an exogenous growth engine.

Inland Provinces

For most of the inland regions, except some border provinces, the answer to the question is likely to be no. There is slim hope for most inland provinces to follow the export-oriented strategy and develop the regional economy on massive foreign capital inflow. Reasons include the lack of natural trade and investment partners, poor infrastructure, inadequate managerial skill and well-trained labour force. These factors will dominate even if the tax incentives for foreign investment, the trade promotion policy, and the investment approval rights are unified across regions.

New sources for growth need to be identified for the inland provinces. Among other things, domestic market integration and technological cooperation between the inland and coastal provinces will play an important role. Once the price system can accurately reflect the oppor-tunity costs of productions and various administrative inter-regional trade barriers are removed, regional comparative advantages will be brought out. The beneficiaries of international trade will not only include the coastal provinces, but also the inland provinces which sup-ply materials, energy, and labour force to the coastal export enterprises.

While borrowing the export-led growth approach is difficult in the inland provinces, many reforms that have been experimented with in Guangdong seem to be widely applicable. For example, efforts made to encourage non-state enterprises, to reduce government size and government interventions, to liberalize prices, and to develop new financial instruments (e.g. stocks and bonds), can provide more incentives to enterprises and additional momentum for growth.

Concluding Remarks

Shifting from import substitution to export promotion has been a major success of China's development strategy since the late 1970s, as manifested by the spectacular growth of the exports-to-GDP ratio and the increasing competitiveness of many Chinese industrial products in the international market. Among various policies adopted to promote exports, those applied to target export-oriented regions and sectors have been the most important ones. However, these policies are not without controversy.

Granting favourable policies to special economic zones and other open areas has obviously contributed to these regions' high export and growth performance. But to what extent growth in these regions has been at the expense of other regions that were discriminated against is still a question under debate. Some critics argue that a large amount of the investment in the SEZs have come from other regions of the country, simply due to the distorted price signals created by the tax policy differentials across regions. Others contend that the high growth performance of the targeted regions has benefited from the central government's favourable revenue-sharing arrangements. For example, Guangdong has been required to remit less revenues to the central government than other regions with similar tax capacity. Partly responding to these criticisms, the recent tax reforms have attempted to unify tax policies across domestic and foreign-invested enterprises and across regions.

The costs and benefits of sectoral targeting policies are equally controversial. While it is relatively clear that the exports of the textile industry and some consumer electronics industries have been a success due to their growing export volume, the performance of other export sectors under promotion, such as the machinery industry, is more difficult to judge. Despite the targeted support from the government, the machinery sector has been repeatedly identified as one of largest concentrations of loss-making enterprises. Many factories in the machinery sector have been making losses on their exports; the increase in export volume was to fulfil the targets set by the government (World Bank, 1994b). In addition, it seems that the selection of the targeted sectors has been based on mixed criteria of infant industry promotion and the consideration of foreign exchange earnings, which were not necessarily consistent with each other.

Despite various possible side-effects of the regional and sectoral targeting polices, one can still safely conclude that, given China's size and diversity in economic development levels, a uniform strategy applied to all the regions and sectors is inconceivable. Considering the comparative advantage – particularly the dynamic comparative advantage – of each region and sector should be the base of the national development strategy. Therefore, certain types of policy differentials across regions and sectors will be inevitable. Moreover, the merit of the strategy of experimenting with special policies in selected regions and then extending the successful ones to other regions should not be underscored. China's open door policy, which emerged from the four SEZs in the late 1970s, represents the most successful story of the regional experimentation strategy. Such a strategy has significantly reduced the risks associated new policies and avoided strong opposition from politicians with central planning mentalities.

8
Regional Policy under the Strategy of Economic Opening

Introduction: Regional Policy in China

Among numerous policies adopted during China's 20 years of reform, regional policy marked one of the most significant changes in China's development strategy and macro-management approach. Interestingly, it is also one of the most controversial policy packages in terms of its objectives, tools and effects.

Before 1980, the fundamental characteristics of China's regional policy can be summarized as having a centralized and unified relationship between the central and provincial governments, as well as a strong politically motivated regional development strategy. The economic management system operated under a 'vertical setup', using state ministries and commissions, as well as national banks and their local branches as the main body to control various economic activities of the localities. As for the regional layout and investment distribution, strategies were notably related to national defence considerations – e.g. the large-scale westward shift of production layout in 1960s and 1970s – rather than criteria of regional comparative advantage and economic efficiency.

Since 1980, China's regional policy underwent a gradual change. These changes were a part of the overall reform package which emphasized the objective of economic efficiency, instead of political ones, through decentralization and opening the economy to the rest of the world. In contrast to the previous regional policies, the new regional policy was marked by two characteristics: cross-regional policy differentials and decentralization. The first characteristic was associated with the open door policy. Coastal regions with favourable access to international trade and foreign investment were given various preferential policies in terms of tax incentives for foreign investment, investment project approval rights, foreign exchange retention, and revenue-sharing with the central government. These policies, which were referred to as the regional-tilt policies, provided strong momentum to most coastal provinces, but also caused criticism from inland provinces against the unfairness.

The second characteristic, decentralization, involved relaxing the central government's control over economic decision-making at provincial and local levels, thus giving the provincial and local governments greater autonomy in handling regional economic affairs. This policy was embodied mainly in the reform of the fiscal relations between the central and provincial governments, as well as other parallel reforms in the areas of investment approval, credit allocation, production planing, price setting and foreign trade management since 1980.

A tendency of reversing the decentralization reform was observed during the rectification programme of 1989–90. The policies adopted included: increasing the central government's administrative power to control and regulate various sources of funding; restricting the provincial governments in influencing local bank branches over the state credit plan; attempting to increase both the ratio of the central government's revenue to total government revenue and the ratio of government revenue to national income (increase two ratios); and restoring the central government's monopoly power over the prices of important materials such as steel, concrete and tobacco. However, this reversing trend did not last long, nor did it fundamentally changed the decentralized setup. The centre's efforts to restore some of its decision-making power and to 'raise two ratios' have also experienced strong resistance from the provincial governments. Some provinces, particularly those benefiting greatly from the decentralization, have reportedly challenged the central government during various negotiations between the centre and the localities.

Since 1992, China has experienced a new upsurge in deepening reform and in further opening of its economy to the outside world. The most significant moves have been the opening up of inland areas to foreign investment and the granting of permission to a wider range of enterprises to engage in international trade. The preferential policies that have prevailed in the SEZs and the 14 coastal open cities have rapidly spread to formerly closed regions. A new round of decentralization reform – both from the centre to provinces and from provinces to local governments – took place. Cross-province policy differentials in terms of administrative power and special policies to foreign investment and international trade have since been gradually reduced.

The impact of China's regional policy has long been controversial. Advocates of the regional policy in the 1980s and early 1990s argue that it has allowed the rapid growth of the coastal regions – Guangdong is the best example (see Chapter 7) – and enhanced the efficiency of resource allocation. Counter-arguments cite the intensification of regional disparity, the distortion of price signals for resource allocation across regions, the instability of central–provincial fiscal relations, and the reduced ability of the central government in conducting macroeconomic control.

This chapter analyses the effects of China's regional policy during the past 20 years and draws implications of the recent development. The regions discussed include the four SEZs opened in the late 1970s, Hainan, 14 open coastal cities, Pudong, and inland provinces. The pros and cons of the regional policy are also discussed. Chapter 9 will examine the effect of various aspects of the decentralization process on provinces' performance.

SEZs

Four SEZs were established in 1979 in the two coastal provinces of Guangdong and Fujian. Among the four zones, Shenzhen, Shekou, and Zhuhai are located in Guangdong Province, which is geographically adjacent to Hong Kong and Macao. In 1978, Guangdong's stage of development was about average of the country.[1] The other SEZ, Xiamen, is located in Fujian Province, one of the poorest provinces in China before reform.[2] As a laboratory for economic reform, the two provinces were chosen by the central government partly because they were of relatively little financial importance to the centre.

The basic motivation for establishing the SEZs was to promote inflows of foreign investment, technology, and managerial techniques. The government's plan was that foreign- and private-invested firms would dominate in the SEZs and a market-based management system would be established. More importantly, the SEZs were expected to provide experience for other regions' reform and development.

The preferential policies applied to SEZs were twofold. Domestically the policies involved an administrative decentralization: some major decision-making powers were surrendered from the central government to the zones. Most significant was that the SEZs have no real upper limit for foreign investment project approval, although a limit of $30 million was officially given. The power of price control over most commodities was also given to the SEZs' authorities. By the end of 1988, the value of retail sales at market prices accounted for 97.4 per cent of the total retail sales in Shenzhen.[3] Foreign exchange earnings were allowed to be fully retained by exporting enterprises in the SEZs, as opposed to other areas in China in which foreign exchange retention was not permitted in the early 1980s. The SEZs were also authorized to determine the fees for land use.

Another important aspect of the special policy involved tax incentives for foreign investors in the SEZs. The 1980 regulation offered a 15 per cent rate of income tax to foreign-invested enterprises in the SEZs.[4] This rate was kept in line with the prevalent rate in neighbouring Hong Kong. There were also lower rates applicable to investments of US$5 million and above, and projects with advanced technologies. These incentives compared most favourably with the standard rate of 33 per cent for the equity joint venture and the progressive-marginal rates scheme for contractual joint ventures and wholly foreign-owned ventures in other parts of China.[5] Tax holidays were also offered in the SEZs. Income tax on foreign-invested enterprises was exempt for the first profit-making year (in 1984, the period of exemption was extended to two years), plus a 50 per cent reduction for the second and third years (in 1984, the two-year 50 per cent reduction was extended to three years after the expiration of exemption) for equity joint ventures with a scheduled duration of over 10 years. Besides, policies allowed exemption of import duties for production inputs and exemption of income tax on profits for reinvestment.

From 1979 to 1984, the initial stage of the open door policy, the four SEZs enjoyed dramatic growth. Originally a small border town, Shenzhen was changed into a modern city. With an average annual growth rate of over 80 per cent, Shenzhen's industrial output increased sharply from about Y60 million in 1979 to Y700 million in 1983, half of which had been realized by using foreign capital (Wei, 1985). By the end of 1988, actual foreign investment in the four SEZs reached US$3.1 billion, accounting for 27 per cent of the country's total. Since the mid-1980s, when other coastal areas were opened, the SEZs began to face increasing competition in attacting foreign investment and their share of foreign investment in China's total gradually declined. However, these SEZs still maintained a higher rate of economic growth than the national average. In 1996, per capita GDP in these four SEZs reached Y25458, 4.5 times that of the national average (see Table 8.1).

International trade is the dominant sector in the SEZs. In 1997, the total imports and exports of the four SEZs reached US$38 billion, accounting for about 12 per cent of the nation's total (Xinhua News Agency, 1998). In most years of the 1990s, about half of the SEZs' exports were produced by foreign-invested enterprises. So far, the higher level of foreign investment and the resulting export growth have been the primary engine leading the SEZs' high GDP growth.

Table 8.1   China: selected indicators of SEZs and open coastal cities, 1996

	Open coastal cities	SEZs	China
Population (m)	90.0	7.0	1 223.9
Population as percentage of China's total	7.4	0.6	100.0
GDP (yuan bn)	1 124.5	178.0	6 859.4
GDP as percentage of China's total	16.4	2.6	100.0
GDP per capita (yuan)	12 489	25 458	5 605
Total fixed assets investment (yuan bn)	267.6	39.4	2 297.4
Actual foreign Investment (US$bn)	17.1	5.3	54.8
Actual foreign investment as per cent of China's total	31.2	9.7	100.0
Actual foreign investment/total fixed investment	53.0	111.6	19.8

Source: State Statistical Bureau, 1997a.

The environment that conduited the massive capital inflow in the four SEZs was that they were China's only regions opened to the outside world before 1984, and until the early 1990s, continued to enjoy more preferential treatments than other open areas. It is natural to argue that if more areas were opened in the early 1980s, the four SEZs might not have received as much foreign investment as they had, and might not have grown as fast as they actually have. In this sense, the policy differentials between the SEZs and other regions created the difference in growth performance.

Beside the investments from foreign countries, a bulk of investment in the SEZs was from other provinces which found attractive business opportunities and investment incentives in the SEZs. Not only coastal provinces but also many inland provinces such as Sichuang and Shaanxi established a large number of enterprises, many of which are joint ventures, in the SEZs. For these provinces, establishing a joint venture in the SEZs could enjoy more favourable tax rates than in their own territories. As a consequence, these provinces, many of which were not rich, experienced net capital outflows to the SEZs.

14 Open Coastal Cities

In 1984, the State Council announced the opening of 14 coastal cities. Mirroring the special policies in the SEZs, certain decision-making powers were extended to these newly opened cities. According to the policy introduced in 1984, the 14 cities were empowered to approve investment projects costing less than US$5 million. Dalian was authorized to approved projects costing less than US$10 million, while Tianjin and Shanghai were authorized to approve projects costing less than US$30 million. These cities were authorized to approve non-productive projects that could promise a foreign exchange surplus regardless of total investment. The cities were also given the right to approve matters such as equipment imports, and to send delegations abroad for businesses related to foreign investment projects (Wei, 1985).

Most of the tax incentives used in SEZs were also extended to these coastal cities. The 14 coastal cities consist of the economic and technological development zones (ETDZ) and other parts of the cities. The ETDZs basically enjoyed same tax preferential policy as the SEZs, while in other parts of the coastal cities tax concessions were relatively limited. According to the 1984 regulation,[6] the income tax rate was reduced to 15 per cent for all foreign-invested enterprises in the ETDZs and for technology intensive enterprises with foreign capital of US$30 million or more in other parts of the cities. Tax holidays similar to those in the SEZs were also applied to the ETDZs. In other parts of the cities, tax holidays were relatively limited. In addition, the 10 per cent profit remittance tax was exempt in ETDZs, but not in other parts of the cities.

The economic performance of the 14 cities varied significantly. Between 1984 and 1990, the annual average growth rate of industrial output ranged from 7 per cent in Shanghai to 36 per cent in Beihai. Eight of the 14 cities grew at rates higher than the national average of 14.5 per cent, while the rates of the other cities were below the country's average. Because Shanghai and Tianjin, the two largest industrial cities, grew at relatively low rates – 7 per cent and 9 per cent, respectively – the overall growth rate of the 14 cities was only 10 per cent. Since 1992, Shanghai's economic growth accelerated, thanks to the establishment of the Pudong New Area. Between 1992 and 1997, Shanghai's annual average GDP growth rate reached 14 per cent, consistently above the national average.

In the external sector, the 14 cities as a whole performed well. Before 1984, foreign capital inflows were mainly channeled to the four SEZs.[7] In 1996, however, the 14 coastal cities utilized about one-third of the country's foreign investment and exported about half of the country's total exports. Their exports-to-GDP ratio was about five times the national average.

Hainan Special Economic Zone

Hainan was one of the poorest regions in China until the mid-1980s. In 1983, agriculture still dominated the prefecture's economy, with an output share of 69 per cent in the total of industrial and agricultural output, compared with the national average of 30 per cent. Although the island was opened as a special prefecture in 1983, owing to lack of infrastructure and a lower level of overall development, its speed of utilizing foreign capital and rate of industrial growth was far behind the four SEZs during 1983–8.

As labour costs in Guangdong rose quickly, Hainan remained as one of the cheapest labour suppliers in the south. In addition, Hainan offered abundant land and natural resources. This provided Hainan with some advantages in attracting external investment in labour-intensive sectors. A major breakthrough in Hainan's development occurred in 1988 when it was declared a province and the country's largest special economic zone.

As a province, Hainan enjoyed fiscal and administrative powers similar to Guangdong. The right to approve investment projects in Hainan was substantially extended. In its 1988–93 fiscal contract with the central government, Hainan was also given a net transfer of fixed Y1.4 billion from the centre. The new provincial government was organized according to the guideline of 'small government, big society' which, in Chinese, refers to less government intervention and greater emphasis on the market. The number of provincial level government agencies was reduced from 47 to 26 and the number of provincial government employees was reduced by 725 in the late 1980s.

According to the 1988 regulation that outlined Hainan's special policies, the basic enterprise income tax and tax holidays in Hainan are the same as those applied to other SEZs and ETDZs in the 14 coastal cities. In addition, Hainan provides more aggressive tax concessions. For investment in certain fields in infrastructure (such as seaports, docks, airports, roads, railways, power plants, and coal mines) more favourable treatments in income tax were offered. Export-oriented enterprises (i.e. exports account for at least 70 per cent of the total output value) or enterprises using high-technology were allowed to deduct 10 per cent from the income tax after the three-year tax reduction. Apart from investing in enterprises, foreigners were allowed to purchase or lease state-owned and collective enterprises. The business scope for foreign investment is also expanded to real estate and excavation of natural resources. In 1992, Yangpu Port was approved by the State Council for tract development.[8] Foreign capital was involved, among others, in land development, in heavy chemical and building materials industries.

In 1988, the first year of the province's establishment and the new investment policy, foreign investment poured in dramatically. A total of 446 joint ventures, including investment from Thailand, Japan, Hong Kong, the United Kingdom, and the United States were established in Hainan. The total pledged amount of foreign investment reached US$382 million in 1988, 27.1 times higher than the previous year. The actual foreign investment reached US$117 million, 11.5 times that of 1987. However, the pledged foreign investment increased only moderately in 1989 and decreased in 1990, partly due to the downturn of the macroeconomic situation. Since 1991, the pace of foreign capital inflow picked up quickly. Between 1990 and 1994, the annual average growth rate of actual foreign investment reached 48 per cent (Table 8.2). Between 1987 and 1994, Hainan's export sector also developed at a very high pace, with exports growing continually from US$116 million to US$952 million. But the major exports continued to be agricultural and mineral products, suggesting a limited growth potential in the long term unless the export structure shifts significantly toward manufactured goods. Moreover, the export sector is yet to become the leading sector in Hainan.

Hainan's 14 per cent annual average GDP growth during 1988–94 was impressive although not as dramatic as those in the initial stages of the other SEZs. Like the other four SEZs, the higher growth rate in Hainan was supported mainly by investment, a large part of which is the net inflow from abroad and other provinces. In 1995 and 1996, however, Hainan's GDP growth slowed signficantly to an annual average rate of less than 5 per cent, together with a sluggish performance in the external sector. Several factors were responsible for the slow growth of Hainan

Table 8.2   China: performance of Hainan's external sector, 1987–96 (US$m)

	Annual GDP growth (%)	*Actual foreign investment*	*Exports**
1987	12.5	9	116
1988	10.1	117	281
1989	5.4	95	361
1990	9.5	117	471
1991	12.4	212	–
1992	23.3	515	897
1993	23.3	748	919
1994	11.9	936	952
1995	4.3	1 184	923
1996	4.8	897	658

*Trade data are from statistics of trade companies, not customs statistics.
Sources: Development Research Centre of the State Council, 1991; State Statistical Bureau, 1993, 1995, 1997a.

in recent years: (1) a large number of investments in the real estate sector during the speculative wave in 1992–3 were located in Hainan, and most of them turned out to be unprofitable as the central government tightened macroeconomic control since 1994; (2) competition from other newly established open areas, specially Pudong New Area, made Hainan's preferential policies less attractive than they were in the early stage; and (3) compared with other SEZs and open areas, Hainan continues to lack a well developed infrastructure and a skilled labour force.

Pudong New Area

Pudong, a relatively underdeveloped area in east Shanghai, was opened in early 1990. This area was expected to become an international financial centre, as well as a high-technology base in east China, and to lead the development of the Yangtze River Delta. With essentially the same, in some areas more aggressive, tax incentives for foreign investment, Pudong was designed to rely mainly on foreign investment for its modernization.

The 1990 regulation that outlined the preferential policies for Pudong provided income tax rates and tax holidays for foreign-invested enterprises that were similar to those applied in SEZs. In addition to the regular provisions, the policy encouraged export-oriented foreign-invested enterprises (i.e. enterprises that export at least 70 per cent of their output value) and foreign-invested enterprises using high technology by allowing them to deduct another 10 per cent from the income tax after the three-year tax reduction. The sectors open to foreign investment were wider than in the other coastal cities. Investments in airports, roads, railways, and power plants were allowed and enjoyed more tax exemptions and reductions than investments in other sectors. Foreign investment in the service sector such as retail and banking – which was until recently still prohibited elsewhere in China – was also permitted in Pudong on a trial basis. In 1992, the central government issued further preferential policies for the Pudong New Area. The new policies consisted of five points: (1) approval of the establishment of free trade zones; (2) authorization for the Shanghai municipality to approve enterprises' import and export rights; (3) permission for the Shanghai municipality to approve non-productive investment projects of any scale; and (4) permission for the Shanghai municipality to approve productive projects costing under Y200 million (or US$37 million).[9]

To promote the development of the Pudong New Area, the central government also allowed full retention of the incremental part of government revenues in Pudong. This helped Pudong in mobilizing the needed funds for large-scale infrastructure investment, in addition to its effort to obtain resources from selling land use rights and attracting foreign investments. At the same time, large amounts of domestic investment from west Shanghai were poured into the Pudong New Area, as domestic enterprises in Pudong were also subject to certain tax concessions if they comply with the industrial policy.

These policies, together with the completion of many major infrastructure projects, a well educated labour force, strong technology capabilities, and improved government efficiency, made Pudong the most attractive place for foreign investment in China in the 1990s. By the end of 1997, Pudong attracted 4,900 foreign-invested projects and a similar number of domestic projects, with total foreign investment reaching US$7 billion. Many of the foreign investors were world-wide major conglomerates: out of Fortune 500 firms, 78 had invested 120 projects in Pudong (Xinhua News Agency, 1998). From 1991 to 1997, the annual average GDP growth rate in Pudong was about 20 per cent, significantly higher than that of Shanghai as whole. Unlike other SEZs' development strategies which focus on manufacturing, the policy-makers in Shanghai made it clear that Pudong's objective was to become the future financial and trade centre of China. Over the past few years, Pudong attracted a large number of foreign banks, investment funds, insurance companies, and brokerage firms to set up their branches. In 1997, more than 50 domestic and foreign financial institutions were operational in Pudong. Recently, the central bank authorized a number of foreign banks to engage in banking business in Chinese RMB. In addition, Pudong has developed a number of free trade zones and export processing zones that offered good infrastructure and additional incentives to trading companies and export-oriented firms.[10]

Inland Provinces[11]

Foreign investors practically ignored most Chinese inland provinces during the first few years of the open door policy. Very few joint ventures were set up in these provinces and their sizes were small. Although foreign investment in inland provinces did increase since the second half of 1980s, it accounted for less than 20 per cent of the country's total actual foreign investment from 1986 to 1996 (see Table 8.3). In 1996, among the 18 inland provinces, 11 provinces in the middle region received about 15 per cent of the country's total foreign investment, and 9 provinces in the western region received only 4 per cent.

Table 8.3   China: comparison of inland and coastal regions, 1996

	Population (m)	GDP (Ybn)	Exports (US$m)	Exports-to-GDP ratio (%)	Foreign Investment* (US$m)
All China	1224	6859	151 066	18.3	48240
Coastal region	487	3811	128 323	27.9	38950
(%)	39.8	55.6	84.9	–	80.7
Inland region	737	3048	22 743	6.2	9291
(%)	60.2	44.4	15.1	–	19.3

*Figure for all China is the sum of regional figures. It does not include foreign investments attracted by entities under ministries.
Source: calculated using data from State Statistical Bureau, 1997a.

The import and export sectors in the inland provinces have developed relatively faster than their foreign investment, but still lagged far behind the coastal provinces, particularly the coastal cities. In 1996, total exports from the inland provinces accounted for 15 per cent of the national total and total imports accounted for 18 per cent of the national total. In the same year, the exports-to-GDP ratio in the inland provinces was only 6 per cent, while the coastal provinces have reached 27 per cent. This ratio of the inland provinces is close to China's national average in the early 1980s. In other words, the inland provinces as a whole is about 15 years behind the coastal provinces in terms of openness to trade.

One reason for the lack of foreign investment in inland provinces is that they were placed in a disadvantageous position in terms of tax policy until the early 1990s. According to the Foreign Enterprise Law promulgated in 1980, the income tax on net profits of equity joint ventures was 30 per cent plus a local surtax, making a total of 33 per cent. This rate was twice that in SEZs and ETDZs, as well as the rates for targeted projects in other parts of the 14 coastal open cities. The income taxes levied on contractual joint ventures and wholly foreign-owned ventures were progressive, with the rates ranging from 20 per cent to 40 per cent according to total income.[12] These rates were also much higher than those in open areas. Other factors that discouraged foreign investment in inland provinces include: (1) local governments' lack of power to approve investment projects. Unlike many coastal provinces and cities where the project approval limit was US$30 million, the inland provinces were subject to the project approval limit of US$5 million;[13] (2) weak infrastructure facilities, such as transportation and communication; and (3) inadequate research and development capability, managerial expertise, and skilled labour force.

Owing to an unfavourable external sector, the inland provinces' growth was mainly supported by domestic investment. Nevertheless, between 1978 and 1996, the annual growth rate of GDP in the inland provinces as a whole still reached 9.5 per cent, about 1 percentage point lower than the coastal region.[14] One of the factors contributing to the inland provinces' growth was the improved terms of trade of the inland provinces relative to the coastal provinces. In the early and mid-1990s, the prices of energy and raw materials were continually adjusted upward and the speed of adjustment exceeded the price increase in manufactured goods. This benefited the inland provinces, most of which were net exporters of primary products.

Industrial-tilt Policy versus Regional-tilt Policy

The cross-regional policy differentials in the external sector, together with the central–local fiscal relations in favour of certain regions, are often referred to as the regional-tilt policy. Prior to the mid-1990s, the regional-tilt policy dominated China's development strategy. However, policy during this period did not completely exclude the role of the industrial-tilt policy – which emphasized certain industrial sectors instead of certain regions – although the term 'industrial policy' was not officially used until 1989.

In the late 1970s, the central government adopted the policy of 'six priorities', emphasizing the light industry and agriculture in an attempt to correct the over-development of the heavy industry before 1979. As the open door policy was initiated, the export-oriented and technologically advanced industries were accorded priority in various regulations. In October 1986, the State Council issued a set of new regulations, later known as 'twenty-two regulations', designed to provide additional incentives to foreign investors. According to these regulations, joint ventures could receive additional preferential treatment if they were categorized as either export-oriented or technologically advanced projects.

The debate over the regional-tilt policy intensified during the 1988–90 fiscal contract period as many warned that regional disparity in both income level as well as in growth performance has widened. The increasing interregional trade barriers and other forms of monopolistic practices in the late 1980s also contributed to the view that the regional-tilt policy distorted market signals and resource allocation. In 1989, an industrial policy containing a detailed list of encouraged and restricted sectors was, for the first time, formally promulgated by the State Council.[15] In 1991, as an important measure to implement the industrial policy, the

State Council replaced the construction tax with the investment direction adjustment tax.[16] Previously investments in basic construction were subject to a unified construction tax rate; after the reform, differential rates applied to projects with different priorities. Specialized banks were also instructed to offer low interest rates to priority projects. In early 1995, a new version of the industrial policy, which provided an updated list of encouraged, discouraged, and prohibited sectors, was promulgated by the State Council. In July 1995, the government also issued the *Guidelines and Industrial Catalog for Foreign Investment*, which made explicit for the first time the sectors where the country would encourage, restrict or prohibit foreign investment.[17]

Although indirect measures, such as interest and tax rate differentials, were proposed to be the means to undertake the industrial policies, the most frequently used measures involved administrative restrictions through investment approval procedures and the credit plan. Priority projects were typically given easy approval, access to credits from designated banks, and even budgetary resources. In addition to the central government's industrial policy, various line ministries and local authorities issued more detailed guidelines on the direction of investment, including lists of encouraged/restricted sectors and products.

After nine years since the first industrial policy was formally announced, this policy seems to have only a limited impact on the industrial structure. The evolution of the industrial structure over the past decade was more of a result of changing demands of consumers and technological progress, than a result of the guidance from the central authorities. In addition, after two decades of decentralization, the central government no longer has adequate fiscal resources and regulatory capacities to effectively implement industrial-tilt policies. When the industrial policy was implemented in the late 1980s and early 1990s, a number of new regional-tilt policies, such as the preferential policies applied in Hainan and Pudong, were also announced. The inconsistency between different sets of policies reflected top policy-makers' lack of a clear objective and the inadequate coordination between different decision-making bodies.

Extending Open Door Policy to Inland Areas

As a significant step of the open door policy after the establishment of the Pudong New Area in 1990, the State Council declared the opening of 10 major cities along the Yangtze River in June 1992. These ten cities, including Nanjing (Jiangsu), Zhenjiang (Jiangsu), Wuhu (Anhui), Tonglin (Anhui), Anqing (Anhui), Maanshang (Anhui), Jiujiang (Jiangxi), Yueyan

(Hunan), Wuhan (Hubei), and Chongqing (Sichuang), were offered the same preferential policies applied to the 14 coastal open cities (Gao and Lu, 1993). Moreover, several comprehensive development zones, each with its own special policies for certain sectors, were established along the Yangtze River.

The central government also actively promoted the opening up of the inland border areas. In 1992, it gave permission to border cities in Northeast China and Inner Mongolia such as Heihe, Suifenhe, Hunchun, and Manzhouli to develop board trade zones. Trade and other economic cooperations between China's border provinces and Russia, Mongolia, Myanmar, India, and Vietnam were encouraged and many administrative restrictions were eliminated. Many provinces also announced their own decisions of opening border cities and towns.

In addition to policies announced by the State Council, many provinces formulated preferential policies for foreign investment in their affiliated cities and development zones. All 30 provinces and thousands of counties and townships launched their own opening up programmes by establishing various 'zones'. By mid-1993, there were 1800 zones (including SEZs, economic development zones, ETDZs, high- and new-tech zone, special zones for Taiwanese investors, special zones for Singaporean investors, border trade zones, etc.) at and above the county level. Most of these zones were set up by provincial or county authorities. There were no official statistics about 'zones' lower than the country level, but the number was believed to be surprisingly large.[18] Most of these zones offered preferential tax policies that previously applied in the SEZs, that is, a 15 per cent flat rate on corporate income, a two-year tax exemption from the first profit-making year and a three-year 50 per cent tax reduction afterwards. Some zones offered even more aggressive tax reliefs, a standard form being five-year tax exemption and five-year tax reduction by half. While tax relief policies in many of these zones were offered only to foreign investors, there were many other zones, especially those at the county and township levels, that offered the same policy to domestic investors.

In addition to the tax incentives to foreign investment, many provinces also transferred substantial power to approve foreign investment projects to their affiliated areas. Most provincial level governments have rendered the US$30 million approval limit to county level governments. Many newly opened areas used land leasing as an important source for generating revenues. Tract development, which had previously been adopted only in Hainan, was also permitted in many of the newly opened cities.

Most of the tax exemptions and reductions were not approved by the central taxation authorities and were considered as illegal by the centre. Since mid-1992, the central government repeatedly claimed that unauthorized tax reliefs offered by locally approved zones must be stopped. A circular issued by the centre required each province to 'cleanse' these unapproved zones and all promises made by the localities regarding tax concession could only be fulfilled using the localities' own budgetary funds. However, not until the State Council's September 1993 adoption of a serious austerity programme to cool down the economy did these measures take effects.[19]

While the inland areas were imitating the policies of the SEZs and coastal cities, the already opened cities made efforts to maintain their dominant position in the external sector by improving administrative efficiency. Most of the coastal open cities further decentralized administrative powers to lower level governments, including districts, counties, ETDZs, and free-trade zones. For instance, Shanghai authorized its districts and counties to approve foreign investment projects costing less than US$30 million. Tianjin municipality's foreign economic commission announced that the issuance of business licences for foreign-invested enterprises would not exceed two days and that the security bureau would set up more branches to issue border trade passes.[20] Shenzhen reportedly simplified its procedures for importing goods. Joint ventures and wholly foreign-owned enterprises are exempt from applying for import approval licences except for those under state quota and licence control.[21] Hainan established a single office responsible for all the foreign investment approval procedures. This office consists of officials from the province's Planning Commission, the Construction Bureau, the Environment and Resource Bureau, the Economic Cooperation Bureau, and the Industrial and Commerce Bureau which had previously been in charge of examining and approving relevant documents separately.

An important development in tax policy for foreign investment was the adoption of the tax code 'Income Tax Law of the People's Republic of China For Foreign Enterprises' in July 1991 (Peck, 1991). This legislation replaced both the foreign enterprises and joint venture income tax laws, which had governed foreign operations in China since the early 1980s. The important changes of the new tax code include the following. (1) A flat tax rate replaced the progressive rate incorporated in the 1981 Foreign Enterprise Income Tax Law. The former distinction between equity joint ventures and other foreign enterprises was eliminated. The new 33 per cent income tax includes a 30 per cent national income tax and a 3 per cent local surcharge. (2) There is no more tax withholding on profit remittance for all foreign-invested enterprises. (3) Tax holidays are applied to more firms. Previously, tax holidays were applied only to equity joint ventures located in designated areas or operating in specific sectors. Under the new law, all foreign investments are qualified for income tax holidays including exemption in the first and second profit-making years and a 50 per cent reduction in the third to fifth years. (4) All foreign-invested enterprises can get tax refunds for reinvestment. These changes, in general, were progresses towards eliminating policy differentials across regions and types of foreign-invested enterprises.

Levelling the Playing Field: Policy Changes since 1996

Since 1994, a number of negative effects of the regional-tilt policies have been widely debated within the policy circle and among academics. Leaders of many inland areas have strongly argued that the special policies applied to the coastal areas should be held responsible for increasing regional disparities. Some even contended that since the inland areas lack the geographical and economic advantages as the coastal areas have, the former should be given more favourable policies than the latter in order to achieve equitable development. Adding to this voice were the concerns of the Ministry of Finance (MOF) over the revenue consequences of the tax incentives to foreign investments, most of which were located in the coastal areas. It was estimated by the World Bank that the tax incentives to foreign investment in China cost about 1.6 per cent of the national GDP (Boardman, 1996). While this estimate ignored the possible revenue-enhancing aspects of the tax incentives, it indicated that eliminating tax concessions for foreign investment might be an attractive way to address the issue of fiscal deficit.

In April 1996, the government announced several major policy changes in an attempt to level the playing field for different regions (Li, 1996). While acknowledging that the SEZs had made great contributions to the country's reform and development over the past 17 years, Premium Li Peng argued that many special policies should be 'adjusted' as the situation changed. In 1996, the major policy changes that affected SEZs or foreign investment in general included the following:

1. The 100 per cent revenue retention policy for SEZs was abolished. Since the SEZs had accumulated substantial fiscal capacities, the new tax assignment system, which applies to every region in China, were also applied to SEZs, replacing the 100 per cent retention policy. Under the new system, the central government collects central taxes (which

mainly include the VAT, consumption tax, customs duties, etc.) from the SEZs, and the local tax services collect local taxes.

2. The exemption of import duties on imported materials and equipment was eliminated. In most development zones, this policy was abolished in April 1996. The five SEZs, Pudong New Area and Suzhou-Singapore Industrial Zone would continue to enjoy some preferential treatment in import duties, but they would be phased out by 2000 (SEZ Office, 1996).[22]

3. The rebate on the VAT paid by exporting enterprises for locally purchased materials was reduced. Originally, exporting companies could receive 17 per cent VAT rebate when they exported their products. From January 1996, this rebate was cut down to 9 per cent.[23] This applied to firms in all regions; but as most exporting firms were located in the coastal regions, they were hit especially heavily. One obvious reason for this policy change was the shortfall of the centre's revenue: the MOF announced in late October 1995 that it had run out of money to pay $6 billion in rebates it already owed.[24]

4. Investment project approval rights across regions were equalized. Before 1996, inland provinces were only authorized to approve projects under US$10 million, as opposed to the US$30 million limit for coastal provinces and special economic zones. In August 1996, the central government announced that all provincial level governments, relevant ministries, and centrally owned corporations directly under the State Council would have the right to approve foreign-invested projects costing less than US$30 million.[25] This decision removed a major policy differential between coastal and inland provinces.

Concluding Remarks

As the windows opening to the outside world, the SEZs have succeeded in improving China's trade status and greatly increased China's use of foreign investment and technology. Over the last two decades, many special policies adopted in the SEZs were extended to hundreds of cities and many rural areas. More importantly, the gradually developed market-oriented ownership structure and indirect macroeconomic management system in the SEZs have proved to be efficient and have also been replicated elsewhere in China. The influence of the SEZs on the nation's overall reform and development far exceeds their own growth record.

As the open door policy was extended to inland provinces, the regional policy differentials in terms of tax incentives for foreign investment were reduced. However, this does not imply that the overall investment environment has been equalized across regions. The role of tax incentives in the newly opened areas appears to be less important than that for the SEZs in the early 1980s. Once more areas offer similar tax concessions and tax holidays, the relative attractiveness of an area to foreign investment relies more on other factors, such as infrastructure, labour costs, quality of labour force, and administrative efficiency.

9
Decentralization and Provinces' Growth Performance

Introduction

Before 1979, the provinces' development patterns and their growth performances largely depended on the central government's arrangement and were strongly influenced by the centre's politically driven strategy. Since the late 1970s, the process of decentralization – i.e. the centre's granting of substantial fiscal power and decision-making powers in investment, production, and trade to the local governments and enterprises – created a situation in which each province's development was more directly linked with the province's own resource endowment and economic policy than a result of nationwide policies. Under the decentralized system, a province's development strategy, its attitude toward and capability to use reform policies, together with its relationship with the centre, jointly determine its economic performance.

This chapter attempts to identify the main factors that have influenced the provinces' growth performances during the decentralization process. This process is illustrated by the changes in the provinces' fiscal relations with the central government, ownership structure of the industrial sector, openness to trade, and utilization of foreign investment. Based on a descriptive analysis of the decentralized economic structure, this chapter develops a simple regression model to quantify the importance of various institutional determinants of the provinces' growth performances.

Fiscal Decentralization

An overview of China's central–local fiscal relations was presented in Chapter 2. This section will focus on the impact of central–local revenue-sharing arrangements on provinces' revenue retention. By 'provinces' or 'provincial governments', I refer to provincial level governments including provinces, cities directly under the State Council, and autonomous regions.

As discussed in Chapter 2, China adopted a 'fiscal contract system' between 1980 and 1993. Under this system, each province signed a contract with the central government to share the locally collected revenues or to receive transfers from the centre. Generally speaking, a province with a fiscal surplus would be required to remit a certain percentage or a fixed amount of revenue to the centre, while a province that was unable to balance its budget with its own resources would be given a contracted amount of subsidy from the centre. The method to determine the amount of revenue remittance to the centre or subsidy from the centre changed several times during 1980–93. Two major changes occurred in 1985 and 1988. From 1988 to 1993, six types of contract systems were applied to 30 provincial level governments and 10 cities with independent planning status. In 1994, the fiscal contract system was replaced by the tax assignment system (see Chapter 2). Although the tax assignment system introduced more stability and transparency into the central–local fiscal relations, it was still heavily influenced by the initial division of revenue sources between the centre and each of the provinces under the contract system.

Table 9.1 shows the effective remittance ratios of 28 provinces in 1983, 1991, and 1996. It is easy to see that the various provinces were treated very differently under the fiscal contract system. In 1983, while Guangdong received more subsidies than its revenue remittance to the centre, Shanghai was required to remit a net of 88 per cent of its revenue. While the different policies applied to Guangdong and Shanghai might partially reflect the centre's intention to equalize fiscal capacities across regions, this argument could not explain the different retention policies applied to provinces with similar development levels. For example, in 1983, the net remittance ratios of Jiangsu, Zhejiang and Shandong were 57 per cent, 47 per cent, and 37 per cent respectively, compared with Guangdong's –4 per cent. Leaders from many provinces argued that Guangdong's high growth performance was due, to a large extent, to its favourable fiscal relation with the centre, which was unavailable to most other provinces.

An important feature of the fiscal contract system is that a fiscal contract was determined based on a one-to-one negotiation between the province and the central government. There was no uniform formula by which the revenue-sharing method was determined. Thus each province's fiscal relation with the centre could not be explained by any straightforward

Table 9.1 China: revenue and expenditure by provinces, 1983–96 (Yuan bn)

	Revenue			Expenditure			Remittance ratio (%)		
	1983	1991	1996	1983	1991	1996	1983	1991	1996
Beijing	3.98	8.98	15.09	1.96	8.07	18.74	0.51	0.10	-0.24
Tianjing	3.87	5.81	7.90	2.05	4.75	11.33	0.47	0.18	-0.43
Hebei	3.64	9.93	15.18	2.83	9.73	23.19	0.22	0.02	-0.53
Shanxi	2.42	7.28	8.42	2.40	7.69	13.32	0.01	-0.06	-0.58
Inner Mongolia	0.70	3.94	5.73	2.28	6.66	12.64	-2.27	-0.69	-1.21
Liaoning	6.79	16.15	21.17	3.42	15.15	31.48	0.50	0.06	-0.49
Jilin	1.41	6.25	7.64	1.94	7.91	14.55	-0.37	-0.27	-0.90
Heilongjiang	2.16	9.47	12.69	3.07	11.01	20.89	-0.42	-0.16	-0.65
Shanghai	15.37	19.19	28.05	1.90	10.15	33.32	0.88	0.47	-0.19
Jiangsu	7.46	14.33	22.32	3.23	12.82	31.09	0.57	0.11	-0.39
Zhejiang	4.18	12.13	13.96	2.19	9.73	21.37	0.47	0.20	-0.53
Anhui	2.24	5.42	11.46	2.04	8.50	17.87	0.09	-0.57	-0.56
Fujian	1.24	6.97	14.21	1.76	7.81	20.03	-0.42	-0.12	-0.41
Jiangxi	1.35	5.06	7.71	1.73	6.47	13.18	-0.28	-0.28	-0.71

Shangdong	5.13	14.30	21.47	3.24	14.20	35.90	0.37	0.01	-0.67
Henan	3.65	10.47	16.21	3.01	10.83	25.53	0.18	-0.03	-0.58
Hubei	4.04	9.51	12.45	2.83	9.95	19.74	0.30	-0.05	-0.59
Hunan	2.93	9.61	13.04	2.53	10.18	21.77	0.14	-0.06	-0.67
Guangdong	3.63	19.21	47.95	3.77	18.25	60.12	-0.04	0.05	-0.25
Guangxi	1.39	6.15	9.05	1.88	7.59	15.70	-0.36	-0.23	-0.73
Sichuang	4.14	14.84	20.90	3.66	16.29	32.67	0.11	-0.10	-0.56
Guizhou	0.83	4.56	4.95	1.56	5.59	9.96	-0.88	-0.22	-1.01
Yunnan	1.72	9.98	13.00	2.40	11.08	27.04	-0.40	-0.11	-1.08
Shaanxi	1.45	5.42	6.76	1.88	6.73	12.18	-0.29	-0.24	-0.80
Gansu	1.09	4.00	4.34	1.55	5.13	9.10	-0.42	-0.28	-1.10
Qinghai	0.15	0.88	0.96	0.74	1.82	3.27	-3.80	-1.07	-2.41
Ningxia	0.18	0.83	1.27	0.70	1.72	2.95	-2.90	-1.07	-1.33
Xinjiang	0.56	2.65	4.83	1.86	5.25	11.49	-2.31	-0.98	-1.38

Note: Revenue refers to the total revenue collected by the localities before tax sharing.
Sources: Development Research Center of the State Council, 1991; State Statistical Bureau, 1997a.

rationales. Important variables affecting the favourableness of a province's fiscal retention policy included at least the following: the province's base year performance, the centre's expectation of the province's 'extraordinary' responsibilities, the personal relationship between provincial leaders and the central government's decision-makers, and the centre's consideration of regional equalization. The roles of these factors are explained below.

1. Base year figures plus uniform growth rates were often used to deter pressures from most provinces for increase in retention ratios or subsidies. Although the centre might be able to control the intensity of disputes with provinces using this method, it often reduced the provinces' incentive to collect revenues.

2. 'Extraordinary' responsibilities were often used by the centre to justify special treatments of a small number of provinces. For example, in the late 1970s, Guangdong and Fujian were selected as the testing grounds for market-oriented reforms and open door policies (particularly, these two provinces were selected as the homes of the four special economic zones). To support their experiments, an important policy offered by the centre was to let Guangdong remit a small amount of revenue without an increase in quota, and to grant Fujian 100 per cent revenue retention and a fixed amount of annual subsidy.

3. Personal connections may have played a significant role in a number of cases, but there is no way to quantify its importance. Speculations suggest that Shanghai's success in winning favourable central government policies since the early 1990s has to do with President Jiang Zeming's personal ties with Shanghai (he was formerly Shanghai's Mayor and Party Chief).

4. Theoretically, equalization consideration should play a dominant role in central–local fiscal relations. However, this has not been the case in China. Ma (1997b) presents a regression on the relationship between per capita income level and per capita net fiscal transfer from the centre using 1994 provincial data, and concludes that the two variables had no statistically significant relation.

Evolution of Ownership Structure

Since decentralization has proceeded along with the change in ownership structure, the latter is a significant indicator of a region's progress toward reform. During the early years of decentralization, many centrally owned SOEs – and more importantly areas of economic activity – were transferred to the jurisdiction of the provinces. Given the more decentralized system, each province acquired greater potential to determine its own priorities and policies and thereby to influence its own performance, including the extent to which it promoted collectives (especially the dynamic TVEs) and private enterprises.

Nevertheless, the central government still influences ownership structure in the provinces in at least two ways. First, many SOEs are still directly under central control, and thus reform can proceed only at the pace permitted by the centre. Second, some provinces continue to have a high concentration of SOEs either because of their endowments of raw materials or because they have traditionally been centres of heavy industry.

Although there has clearly been a reduction in state ownership during the reform era, the pace at which the ownership structure has changed has differed significantly across provinces. For instance, between 1981 and 1996, the share of state-owned industry in total industrial output fell in Zhejiang from 58 per cent to 11 per cent, while in Qinghai it declined only slightly from 83 per cent to 77 per cent. This growing diversity is reflected in a statistical measure of the share of SOEs in total industrial output: the coefficient of variation[1] rose from only 0.10 in 1981 – reflecting a highly uniform ownership structure – to 0.45 in 1996 (see Table 9.2).

The fastest growing provinces – including Zhejiang, Jiangsu, Guangdong, Fujian, and Shandong – are those in which the share of state-owned industry has fallen most sharply. By 1996, the share of the SOEs in each of these five provinces had fallen by more than 50 percentage points, creating a structure dominated by the nonstate sector. By contrast, the remote (mainly western) provinces experienced a much lower pace of change. For instance, Qinghai, Ningxia, Xinjiang, Yunnan, and Guizhou, all saw a decline of less than 30 percentage points, with the share of SOEs in industrial output staying at or above 60 per cent.

The growth of the nonstate sector took on slightly different forms in various provinces: TVEs (e.g. Jiangsu and Zhejiang), foreign-invested enterprises (e.g. Guangdong), and privage enterprises (e.g. Zhejiang). Among these, the most significant development was the growth of the TVEs mainly in the coastal provinces. From 1978 to 1995, the nationwide output by TVEs grew at an annual average rate of 25 per cent, 17 percentage points higher than that of the state-owned industrial enterprises. In 1995, more than 60 per cent of the total sales revenue of TVEs came from the 11 coastal provinces and municipalities, with only 10 per cent from the nine western provinces and autonomous regions. In the same year, the industrial output of private enterprises in the 11 coastal provinces and municipalities accounted for 60 per cent of the country's total, while the nine western provinces and autonomous regions accounted for only 10 per cent.

Table 9.2   China: industrial output produced by state and nonstate-owned enterprises, 1981 and 1996 (Yuan bn)

	1981			1996		
	Total	Share of SOEs (%)	Share of NSOEs (%)	Total	Share of SOEs (%)	Share of NSOEs (%)
All China	517.8	78.3	21.7	9 959.5	29.9	70.1
Beijing	21.7	81.5	18.5	185.3	47.9	52.1
Tianjing	19.9	83.1	16.9	238.6	24.6	75.4
Hebei	21.8	80.5	19.5	505.4	26.6	73.4
Shanxi	11.9	81.1	18.9	205.5	36.5	63.5
Inner Mongolia	6.0	83.1	16.9	93.9	48.2	51.8
Liaoning	45.1	80.6	19.4	560.2	34.8	65.2
Jilin	13.4	80.7	19.3	153.8	56.6	43.4
Heilongjiang	25.1	85.0	15.0	237.4	58.4	41.6
Shanghai	60.9	87.2	12.8	506.7	33.1	66.9
Jiangsu	46.6	61.2	38.8	1 155.6	19.4	80.6
Zhejiang	21.4	58.4	41.6	882.1	10.7	89.3
Anhui	13.0	82.2	17.8	361.8	26.4	73.6
Fujian	8.2	76.3	23.7	320.7	14.0	86.0
Jiangxi	9.2	81.8	18.2	133.6	46.7	53.3
Shangdong	34.4	71.0	29.0	912.7	26.6	73.4
Henan	20.4	81.9	18.1	527.5	29.6	70.4
Hubei	24.7	80.3	19.7	483.6	29.5	70.5
Hunan	17.6	78.0	22.0	328.1	29.3	70.7
Guangdong	25.0	68.0	32.0	1 053.1	14.7	85.3
Guangxi	8.2	82.0	18.0	173.4	33.4	66.6
Sichuang	27.5	79.9	20.1	416.9	37.7	62.3
Guizhou	4.4	85.1	14.9	62.9	59.8	40.2
Yunnan	7.1	85.3	14.7	129.1	62.1	37.9
Shaanxi	10.5	86.4	13.6	123.9	54.2	45.8
Gansu	7.4	93.5	6.5	83.7	58.1	41.9
Qinghai	1.2	83.2	16.8	13.9	76.7	23.3
Ningxia	1.2	86.4	13.6	20.2	62.4	37.6
Xinjiang	4.1	92.0	8.0	68.0	76.2	23.8
Hainan				21.6	33.0	67.0
Mean		80.6	19.4		40.5	59.5
SD		7.7	7.7		18.1	18.1
COV		0.10	0.39		0.45	0.30

Note: Mean, SD, and COV calculations do not include Tibet and Hainan.
Sources: State Statistical Bureau, 1981, 1997a.

The growth rate of the non-state owned industries best reflects the difference in the speed of market-oriented reform in different regions. In the SEZs, where many reform measures were initiated, the framework of free enterprises and indirect macro-management system was established in the early 1980s; in coastal provinces, many local governments provided support to while attempting to reduce intervention in the TVEs; in the open coastal cities and the three Delta areas attractive incentives for foreign investment were offered. In contrast, many inland areas, especially those in western provinces, still lack the policy environment for TVEs, foreign-invested enterprises and private enterprises. In these areas, local governments are accustomed to intervening in enterprises' daily operations. Moreover, the traditional management styles which prevailed in state-owned enterprises are often applied to collective enterprises, including TVEs, in the western regions.

Trade and Foreign Investment

Foreign Trade

Similar to the central–provincial fiscal relations, China's trade management system also experienced significant decentralization since the late 1980s. Until 1978, China's trade was conducted through 12 state level FTCs. These corporations procured and traded the quantities determined by the central plan and all the profits and losses were absorbed by the state budget. In turn, enterprises, which had no direct access to foreign markets, were given production targets under the plan for supply to the FTCs. The highly centralized system encountered two obvious problems: first, localities did not benefit from and thus lacked incentives to promote trade; secondly, there was only an indirect connection between manufacturing enterprises and international markets. The supply response to international market signals tended to be very inefficient.

Under the reforms since 1978, the trade management system evolved toward greater autonomy for both the localities and enterprises. By 1989, most provincial and local branches of national FTCs had become independent entities responsible for their financial results, and the number of FTCs rose to about 4000. During the same period, thousands of manufacturing enterprises were also granted the right of direct foreign trade without going through FTCs. By the end of 1996, the number of FTCs exceeded 7000, and the number of manufacturing enterprises enjoying direct trading rights exceeded 5000.

Another policy related to provinces' trade performance involved the retention of foreign exchange (see Chapter 7). With enough foreign exchange retention, an exporting enterprise was able to import necessary inputs, thus facilitating exports. Before 1991, the foreign exchange retention policy was, to a large extent, formulated on a regional basis.

The policy stipulated a 100 per cent retention in the SEZs and a relatively high share of foreign exchange retention for export-oriented enterprises in other coastal areas. These retention ratios were unified across regions in early 1991. The 1991 reform increased the transparency of the exchange retention policy and had a positive impact on the competitiveness of exporting enterprises in the inland areas. In 1994, as the two exchange rates (official and swap market rates) were unified, the exchange retention system was abolished. Since then, enterprises that need to import goods can directly buy foreign exchange from designated banks.

Table 9.3 shows that the coastal region has dominated both the country's imports and exports. In 1996, exports from the coastal region accounted for 85 per cent of the national total, and imports to the coastal region accounted for 83 per cent of the national total. In the same year, the middle region exported 12 per cent of the national total, and imported only 13 per cent of the national total. In the western region, neither imports nor exports were significant. In 1996, the western region's shares of exports and imports in the national total were only three per cent and four per cent, respectively.

Table 9.3   China: imports and exports by province, 1996 (US$bn)

	Exports	Imports	GDP (Ybn)	Exports/GDP (%)	Total trade/GDP (%)
All China	151.1	138.8	6 756.0	19	36
Coastal	128.3	114.6	3 811.1	28	53
share (%)	85	83	56		
Middle	17.6	18.4	2 080.5	7	14
share (%)	12	13	30		
Western	4.7	5.8	967.0	4	9
share (%)	3	4	14		
Beijing	5.1	9.9	161.6	26	77
Tianjing	4.7	5.5	110.2	35	76
Hebei	2.4	1.8	345.3	6	10
Shanxi	1.7	0.4	130.6	11	14
Inner Mongolia	0.5	0.5	98.5	4	8
Liaoning	7.3	6.3	315.8	19	36
Jilin	1.1	1.4	133.7	7	15
Heilongjiang	3.0	1.3	240.5	10	15
Shanghai	13.1	14.8	290.2	38	80
Jiangsu	12.0	10.3	600.4	17	31
Zhejiang	8.7	5.8	414.6	17	29
Anhui	1.3	1.1	233.9	5	8
Fujian	8.5	7.4	260.7	27	51
Jiangxi	0.8	0.4	151.7	4	7

Shangdong	10.0	8.1	596.0	14	25
Henan	1.4	1.1	368.3	3	6
Hubei	1.4	1.7	297.0	4	9
Hunan	1.3	0.7	264.7	4	6
Guangdong	60.0	52.0	651.9	76	142
Guangxi	1.4	1.0	187.0	6	11
Hainan	0.4	1.6	39.0	9	42
Sichuang	1.8	2.1	421.5	4	8
Guizhou	0.4	0.2	72.0	4	7
Yunnan	1.0	1.2	149.2	6	12
Tibet	0.0	0.1	6.5	–	–
Shaanxi	1.0	0.8	117.5	7	13
Gansu	0.3	0.3	71.4	3	7
Qinghai	0.1	0.1	18.4	5	9
Ningxia	0.2	0.1	19.4	7	10
Xinjiang	0.4	0.8	91.2	3	11

Note: The sums of provincial data may differ slightly from the national totals.
Source: Calculated using data from State Statistical Bureau, 1998.

The three regions' openness to trade can also be viewed from their trade-to-GDP ratios. In 1996, these ratios were 53 per cent, 14 per cent, and 9 per cent for the coastal, middle and west regions, respectively. It is apparent that, in addition to the decentralized trade system and the regionally based foreign exchange retention policy, export performance was also a function of a region's natural endowment as well as its level of industrial development. Guangdong, well known for its outward oriented development strategy, ranked first in terms of trade-to-GDP ratio, thanks to its proximity to Hong Kong and large inflows of foreign investment to its export sector. Industrial cities with the most developed technologies and skilled labour force, such as Shanghai, Beijing, and Tianjin, also had relatively high trade-to-GDP ratios.

Foreign Investment

The regional allocation of foreign investment has been strongly affected by the central government's regional preferential policies (see details in Chapter 8). Among these policies, the preferential investment incentives applied in the SEZs, 14 open coastal cities, Hainan, and Pudong were the most significant ones.

Data on regional allocation of foreign investment present a similar picture as that of foreign trade. In the early years of the open door policy, the coastal region, particularly the four SEZs, dominated the country's use of foreign investment. In 1983, the pledged foreign investment in the coastal region was 94 per cent of the national total, of which Guangdong, where three SEZs were located, used 71 per cent. This highly

Table 9.4 China: actual foreign investment by province, 1986–96 (US$m)

	1986	1987	1988	1989	1990	1991	1992	1993	1994	1995	1996
All China	7258	8452	10226	10059	10289	11554	19202	38960	43213	48133	54804
Coastal	2274.5	2681.9	4296.5	4566.1	4472.5	5617.4	11647.4	24488.3	29769.5	32865.9	38949.9
share (%)	82.0	83.5	76.6	78.1	81.4	83.4	89.2	84.5	83.5	82.7	80.7
Middle	367.2	355.7	917.2	886.8	834.7	811.9	1147.1	3459.1	4252.1	5353.2	7309.1
share (%)	13.2	11.1	16.3	15.2	15.2	12.0	8.8	11.9	11.9	13.5	15.2
Western	133.6	173.6	396.3	395.3	186.6	309.9	264.8	1025.8	1638.2	1501.7	1982.2
share (%)	4.8	5.4	7.1	6.8	3.4	4.6	2.0	3.5	4.6	3.8	4.1
Beijing	162.8	161.7	583.9	477.0	392.0	299.6	361.6	817.3	1379.1	1106.5	1721.1
Tianjin	134.8	223.4	242.7	167.8	98.6	260.9	262.6	623.7	1161.8	1586.9	2236.5
Hebei	19.0	10.3	28.5	92.9	97.8	96.3	113.1	396.5	529.8	613.3	917.1
Shanxi	4.5	4.9	8.3	9.8	7.8	30.8	53.8	86.4	52.6	93.6	198.9
Inner Mongolia	9.8	7.1	10.5	4.5	10.6	2.4	8.3	85.3	48.5	88.6	230.0
Liaoning	64.5	174.7	292.5	388.1	727.4	645.2	680.1	136.9	1514.7	1568.4	1892.0
Jilin	31.0	29.3	13.5	15.0	30.9	54.5	75.3	275.3	244.2	481.9	617.2
Heilongjiang	35.4	27.0	70.1	76.8	47.0	29.5	72.7	232.3	348.4	624.9	842.8
Shanghai	281.2	575.6	440.5	466.5	321.0	330.3	899.3	3178.0	2582.2	3005.4	4838.2
Jiangsu	45.6	143.1	156.7	161.2	247.7	314.7	1463.2	2843.7	3785.7	5325.8	5489.2
Zhejiang	29.5	106.9	130.6	125.5	127.8	143.8	276.6	1031.8	1156.5	1289.7	1634.0

Anhui	53.3	35.5	70.2	26.4	42.3	25.1	54.7	257.6	412.1	516.4	736.4
Fujian	165.5	142.4	294.0	387.9	426.8	570.5	1 465.6	2 906.0	3 723.3	4 149.1	4 135.6
Jiangxi	11.8	11.4	33.8	22.0	35.9	50.7	121.8	228.2	296.4	345.1	323.8
Shandong	75.9	93.8	112.3	208.3	230.5	373.1	1 026.9	1 882.7	2 601.4	2 765.0	2 871.6
Henan	12.0	21.5	67.7	59.5	34.1	75.4	53.2	304.9	461.8	649.1	783.2
Hubei	18.3	53.6	45.6	65.4	93.9	141.1	210.6	554.7	667.9	886.9	1 098.9
Hunan	28.5	3.7	13.6	130.4	140.3	102.7	135.2	617.2	341.1	560.1	756.9
Guangdong	1 404.1	1 166.6	2 414.8	2 390.3	2 015.4	2 583.8	4 746.4	9 843.1	10 927.6	10 669.7	13 258.1
Guangxi	54.4	45.1	66.7	82.7	62.6	86.5	198.8	897.6	850.5	708.4	780.9
Hainan	0.0	0.0	117.4	95.0	117.0	212.4	514.8	748.3	936.1	1 184.3	896.8
Sichuan	32.8	65.2	191.2	255.2	63.2	154.4	112.1	571.4	956.5	619.4	631.2
Guizhou	12.2	0.0	13.8	13.9	11.1	16.3	19.8	42.9	63.6	90.2	342.5
Yunnan	5.8	8.3	9.0	10.1	12.2	21.4	28.8	97.0	68.6	119.6	75.3
Tibet	0.0	0.0	0.0	0.0	0.0	0.0	0.0	0.0	0.0	0.0	2.4
Shaanxi	64.8	80.1	141.9	105.0	73.6	35.7	45.5	234.3	246.5	392.4	367.2
Gansu	1.3	0.2	17.8	1.1	1.2	4.8	0.4	12.0	95.0	82.7	221.0
Qinghai	0.0	0.0	2.7	0.0	0.0	0.0	0.7	3.2	2.4	2.2	10.3
Ningxia	0.1	2.0	3.1	0.0	0.3	3.0	3.5	11.9	9.3	6.3	49.8
Xinjiang	16.8	17.7	16.6	10.1	25.0	74.2	54.0	53.0	196.3	188.9	282.5

Sources: State Statistical Bureau, 1987, 1988, 1991, 1992, 1993, 1994, 1995, 1996, 1997a.

concentrated distribution changed gradually after the opening up of 14 coastal cities in 1984. In 1987, the coastal region still hosted 88 per cent of the country's total foreign investment, but Guangdong's share in the national total declined to 36 per cent, while Shanghai, Liaoning, Tianjin, Jiangsu, and Fujian emerged as large recipients of foreign capital. The total actual foreign investment in these provinces and municipalities made up 47 per cent of the coastal total in 1987. From 1987 to 1996, the share of foreign investment in the coastal region in the national total was basically unchanged, that is, there was no identifiable trend of diversification of foreign investment from the coastal to the inland regions. Table 9.4 presents a detailed regional distribution of actual foreign investment in China from 1986 to 1996.

Over the past few years, many scholars and officials from the inland regions have pointed out that the special policies applied in the coastal region have exacerbated regional disparity.[2] In 1996, in an effort to stimulate growth in the inland regions, the central government decided to decentralize the investment project approval right in these provinces. The provincial governments in the inland provinces can now approve foreign invested projects costing less than US$30 million, the same threshold applied in coastal open areas. In the same year, a number of preferential tax policies applied to the SEZs and open coastal cities were abolished (see Chapter 8).

Determinants of Provinces' Growth Performance[3]

The divergence in provinces' performance has been noted as a main feature of China's decentralization process over the past two decades. Between 1978 and 1996, the fastest-growing province, Guangdong, enjoyed an annual average GDP growth rate of 14 per cent, while several western provinces grew at an annual average growth rate of 7–9 per cent. Despite the high growth rate of the nation as a whole, increased disparity of provinces' growth performance could lead to potentially serious economic, social and political tensions among regions. Nevertheless, very few formal analyses have been done to explain the institutional reasons behind the difference in growth performance among the regions.

Much attention, both from the government and academia, has been focused on the outstanding growth performance of a number of coastal provinces, particularly Guangdong Province. In early 1992, Deng Xiaoping even raised the question of 'whether we can produce several more Guangdongs'. Explanations of Guangdong's performance are many. Some argue that Guangdong benefited substantially from its favourable revenue-sharing arrangement with the central government over the 1980s. If this is a major factor determining Guangdong's performance, it implies that Guangdong's high growth is at the expense of other regions, and the applicability of Guangdong's experience to other parts of China is therefore questionable. However, others contend that Guangdong's extraordinary growth was led primarily by its fast growth export sector: the growth rate of its exports was 8 percentage points higher than the national average in the 1980s. Still others argue that Guangdong's growth was the result of the vast foreign capital inflow: it hosted more than 30 per cent of total foreign capital inflow to China. It has also been suggested that Guangdong's performance is attributable to its more radical reform strategy, particularly in the government's efforts to promote the nonstate sector.

Without a quantitative analysis, it is difficult to ascertain which factor has played what role in generating the performance difference among regions. This section attempts to identify the major factors that affect the growth performance of 28 provinces, autonomous regions and municipalities (hereafter provinces), and quantify the relative importance of the factors to each province's growth, by presenting some statistical evidence bearing on a set of economic hypotheses. The first subsection lists this set of hypotheses. The second subsection presents the statistical model and test results. The last subsection concludes with the implication of decentralization on provinces' growth.

The Hypotheses

The hypotheses to be investigated are:

1. The share of state ownership in industrial production is negatively related to the growth performance.

2. The degree of government intervention, such as control through production planning, price setting, and sales restrictions, are negatively correlated with provinces' performance.

3. Provinces with revenue-sharing schedules that mandate only small remittances to the centre show stronger growth.

4. The degree of openness of a provincial economy, measured by the intensity of foreign capital utilization or trade-to-GDP ratio, positively affects its growth.

5. The 'catch-up' hypothesis: economies with lower initial levels of development should grow faster than those with higher initial levels.

6. The role of geography: regions along the east coast have a natural advantage in its development.

A simple theoretical base for the following regression analyses is to view a province's output as determined by the reduced form of a production function with capital and labour as inputs and a productivity factor. It is straightforward that the central–local fiscal arrangement, or more specifically, the share of revenue retention, affects the availability of investment resources in the province. Foreign capital inflow is also part of the capital investment. The share of state ownership in the enterprise sector affects the management's and the employees' incentive to raise productivity. The degree of government intervention affects the enterprises' management autonomy in resource allocation and is also a determinant of the production function's productivity factor. Locational factor has to do with access to market, skilled labour force, and technology. Clearly the coastal provinces have an advantage in these regards, as they generally are close to larger markets, and endowed with a more skilled labour force and R&D capacity.

The Models and Regression Results

I tried a number of regression equations in order to identify the most important factors determining provinces' growth performance, while at the same time to avoid the multicolinearity problem. The first equation (Regression 1) estimated is the simplest version of the catch-up model:

$$GR = 33.832 - 7.154\log(PNI) \tag{1}$$
$$(7.842) \quad (-4.187)$$

$$\text{Adjusted } R^2 = 0.379, N = 28, DF = 26$$

where N is the number of observations, and DF is the degree of freedom. Numbers in parentheses are t ratios of the estimated coefficients. In the regression, the annual average growth rate of per capita national income during 1980–91 is chosen as the dependent variable, GR. PNI is the per capita national income level of the initial year, 1980. I use log(PNI) rather than PNI as the explanatory variable because the former yields a higher adjusted R^2. The result shows that a region's initial development level is significantly and negatively related to its growth rate, which confirms the catch-up hypothesis.

While the catch-up hypothesis explains some of the variations of growth performance among regions, the adjusted R^2 of the first regression is only 0.379. A large part of the variation among regions' growth rates is still unexplained. To identify the contribution of the geographical advantage of coastal regions to their growth, I ran a second regression by adding a coastal dummy variable, DM, to Regression 1:

$$GR = 37.847 + 2.934DM - 9.125\log(PNI) \qquad (2)$$
$$(10.181)\ (3.656) \qquad (-6.058)$$

Adjusted $R^2 = 0.579$, N = 28, DF = 25

where DM equals one for coastal provinces, and zero for other provinces. The coefficient on DM is significantly positive and the adjusted R^2 is higher than the first regression, implying that the coastal provinces do show significant comparative advantages in growth rates over the inland provinces.

Due to the impression that coastal provinces are often more advanced in reform and more open to the outside world, I suspect that the geographical factor may coincide with many other institutional factors. In other words, the significance of the coefficient on DM may actually reflect, at least partially, the coastal regions' efforts in reform and opening up. In Regression 3, I add the ownership characteristic to the model. The regression is as follows:

$$GR = 43.057 - 10.621ONS + 1.206DM - 7.937\log(PNI) \qquad (3)$$
$$(11.340)\ (-2.776) \qquad (1.274) \qquad (-5.652)$$

Adjusted $R^2 = 0.668$, N = 28, DF = 24

where ONS is the share of state-owned industrial output in total industrial output. It is calculated by averaging the numbers for 1980 and 1991. The coefficient on ONS is statistically significant and has a negative sign, meaning that a higher share of state ownership has a negative impact on growth. With ONS in the regression, the adjusted R^2 has improved from 0.579 to 0.668. However, the coastal dummy now becomes insignificant at a 10 per cent confidence level. It is obvious that ONS is taking over most of the explanatory power ONS had in the previous regression.

The insignificance of DM in Regression 3 suggests the exclusion of this variable from the model. Interestingly, after eliminating DM from the equation, the explanatory power of the regression is nearly unaffected:

$$GR = 43.696 - 13.827ONS - 7.119\log(PNI) \qquad (4)$$
$$(11.468)\ (-4.471) \qquad (-5.630)$$

Adjusted $R^2 = 0.660$, N = 28, DF = 25

The adjusted R^2 drops only slightly from 0.668 to 0.660. This suggests that DM should not serve as a separate explanatory variable if ONS is included in the regression.

Following the same approach, I add a few more institutional variables into equation (4) to see whether they can improve the explanatory power of the regression. By incorporating LTI, the share of light industry's output in total industrial output, into Regression 4, I obtain the following equation:

$$GR = 36.019 - 8.699ONS + 7.991LIT - 7.026\log(PNI) \qquad (5)$$
$$(7.692) \quad (-2.416) \quad (2.175) \quad (-5.953)$$

Adjusted $R^2 = 0.705$, N = 28, DF = 24

where LIT is calculated by averaging the shares of light industry in total industrial output in 1980 and 1991. With LIT in the regression, the adjusted R^2 rises from 0.660 in the previous regression to 0.705, confirming the validity of adding this variable. In addition, the coefficient on LTI is positive and significant, which supports the hypothesis that less government intervention leads to a higher growth rate. This interpretation is consistent with the fact that heavy industries (such as steel, concrete, coal mining, and electricity), which grew at a relatively slow rate, have been subject to tighter control of production planning, price setting, and investment approval than light industries.

To test the hypothesis regarding the role of central–local fiscal relations, I add SRR, the share of retained revenue in total revenue collection, to Regression 5. The result is as follows:

$$GR = 34.176 - 12.502ONS + 8.745LIT + 1.113SRR - 5.913\log(PNI)$$
$$(7.226) \quad (-3.312) \quad (2.549) \quad (2.188) \quad (-4.890) \qquad (6)$$

Adjusted $R^2 = 0.745$, N = 28, DF = 23

where SRR is defined as (revenue – expenditure)/revenue. The data used in the regression are averages of SRR in 1983 and 1991. The coefficient on SRR is significantly negative, supporting the hypothesis that provinces with more autonomy in managing locally collected revenue have a higher growth potential. The adjusted R^2 improves from 0.705 to 0.745 when SRR is incorporated, confirming the additional explanatory power of SRR.

The last institutional factor I look at is the openness of the provincial economies. Although there are two aspects of an economy's openness – the openness to foreign trade and to foreign investment – I will use only one of them in the regression. This is because if both the export-to-GDP ratio and the intensity of foreign capital utilization are included in the model, multicolinearity problem will arise and it will lead to the

Table 9.5 Regression results: explaining provinces' growth performance

	Regression 1	Regression 2	Regression 3	Regression 4	Regression 5	Regression 6	Regression 7
Constant	33.832	37.847	43.057	43.696	36.019	34.176	35.551
	(7.842)	(10.181)	(11.340)	(11.468)	(7.692)	(7.226)	(7.800)
ONS			-10.621	13.829	-8.699	-12.502	-11.246
			(-2.776)	(4.471)	(-2.416)	(-3.312)	(-3.082)
LIT					7.991	8.745	6.418
					(2.175)	(2.549)	(1.836)
SRR						1.113	0.998
						(2.188)	(2.047)
FCR							13.875
							(1.855)
Dummy		2.934	1.206				
		(3.656)	(1.274)				
Log(PNI)	-7.154	-9.125	-7.937	-7.119	-7.026	-5.913	-6.482
	(-4.187)	(-6.058)	(-5.652)	(-5.630)	(-5.953)	(-4.890)	(-5.448)
Adjusted R^2	0.379	0.579	0.668	0.660	0.705	0.745	0.769
R^2	0.402	0.610	0.705	0.686	0.737	0.783	0.814
F Value	17.531	19.622	19.162	27.250	22.458	20.70	19.007

Source: Calculated from data in Table A9.1.

insignificance of both coefficients. The correlation coefficient between the two variables is as high as 0.77. After a number of trials, I choose to retain FCR, the ratio of foreign capital to total fixed investment, in the following equation:

$$GR = 35.551 - 11.246ONS + 6.418LIT + 0.998SRR + 13.875FCR$$
$$\quad\;\; (7.800) \quad (-3.082) \qquad (1.836) \qquad (2.047) \qquad (1.855)$$
$$-6.482\log(PNI) \qquad\qquad\qquad\qquad\qquad\qquad\qquad (7)$$
$$\;(-5.448)$$

Adjusted $R^2 = 0.769$, N = 28, DF = 22

where FCR is calculated by averaging the ratios of foreign investment to total fixed investment in 1983 and 1991. The result shows that the coefficient on FCR is significantly positive. This confirms the hypothesis that a higher degree of openness to foreign investment facilitates economic growth. Incorporating FCR into the model improves adjusted R^2 from 0.745 to 0.769. The unadjusted R^2 reaches 0.814, implying a surprisingly high explanatory power compared with many cross-section studies on growth.

Table 9.5 summarizes the results of the seven regressions.

Decentralization and Growth

The institutional variables used in the regressions largely reflect the extent to which provinces have taken advantage of the decentralized system. The change of ownership structure, for example, is an important indicator of how liberal a region's policy is toward non-state owned enterprises, particularly the TVEs. The rapid growth of the TVEs in many coastal regions, such as Jiangsu, Zhejiang and Shandong, is not in any way an outcome of a centrally designed reform. In contrast, the greater autonomy of provincial and local governments has played a predominant role. In these provinces, where TVEs' output far exceeds that of the state-owned industry, local governments have provided the TVEs with extensive support in the forms of credit supply, technological transfer, as well as marketing and managerial consultation.

The share of light industry in total industrial output has to do with the degree to which regions are subject to central government control. Nearly all enterprises of the light industry are locally owned state enterprises or non-state enterprises, and are subject to less control in terms of production planning, credit allocation, price and wage setting, etc. while many large and medium-sized enterprises in the heavy industries are owned by the centre and are subject to strict planning control from the centre.[4]

Increasing regions' fiscal autonomy is another major aspect of the decentralization process. While overall the share of revenue remittance from the provinces to the centre has declined significantly over the past 20 years, the distribution of fiscal burden across regions has been extremely uneven. Provinces whose fiscal resources have been tightly controlled by the centre have generally grown at relatively low rates. For example, Shanghai submitted, on average, about two-thirds of its locally collected revenues to the centre during the 1980s. A simulation based on equation (7) shows that the unfavourable revenue-sharing relations with the centre reduced Shanghai's annual growth rate by nearly 1 percentage point between 1980 and 1991.

The large foreign capital inflow to the coastal provinces partly reflects their geographical advantage. For example, two-thirds of the foreign investment in Guangdong has been from Hong Kong. At the same time, however, various favourable policies granted by the central government to the coastal regions have played important roles. These policies included the delegation of approval rights of large investment projects to the provinces and open coastal areas, and the granting of preferential tax policies to foreign investment in these regions. In contrast, inland provinces suffered from poor physical infrastructures and lacked the same autonomy in approving investment projects and the flexibility in granting tax exemptions and/or reductions. As a result, the 20 inland provinces have received less than 20 per cent of the total foreign capital over the past 20 years.

In sum, the four institutional variables – the share of state ownership, the share of light industry in total industrial output, the share of retained revenue in locally-collected revenue, and the share of foreign investment in total fixed investment – reflect different aspects of China's administrative and economic decentralization, either initiated by the centre or advanced by the provinces themselves. Comparing the results of Regression 1 and Regression 7, one can see that the introduction of these four factors has improved the adjusted R^2 from 0.379 to 0.769. This result suggests that, when the difference in the initial development level is controlled, these four factors explain nearly 40 per cent of the variations of growth performance among provinces.

Conclusions

China's cross-regional differences find expression in many aspects. The fundamental one is the ladder-type development and reform process.

From the coastal region to the western region – excluding some exceptional areas – an economy's degree of openness, the dominance of the state sector, and the degree of government intervention decline in order. The decentralization reform and open door policy, the two most important changes supporting the past two decades' growth, have shown decreasing effectiveness from the coast to the west.

A simple regression shows the determinants of regional growth performance. According to the regression results, the institutional factors that facilitated growth include ownership structure transformation from a state-dominated to a mixed economy, the reduction in government intervention in the production sector, openness to trade and foreign investment, and favourable central–provincial fiscal relations. The 'catch up' theory is also supported by the statistical results, implying that a lower initial level of development is generally associated with a higher growth rate.

Appendix Table A9.1   Data used in regressions

	GR	ONS	LIT	SRR	FCR	log(PNI)	DM
Beijing	13.49	0.71	0.454	0.696	0.046	3.02	0.0
Tianjin	11.44	0.71	0.535	0.673	0.054	3.02	1.0
Hebei	14.99	0.65	0.477	0.878	0.011	2.50	0.0
Shanxi	14.94	0.70	0.286	1.025	0.006	2.45	0.0
Inner Mongolia	16.72	0.80	0.428	2.478	0.002	2.41	0.0
Liaoning	13.58	0.71	0.335	0.720	0.058	2.79	1.0
Jilin	15.75	0.76	0.412	1.321	0.013	2.52	0.0
Heilongjiang	13.48	0.83	0.330	1.293	0.004	2.69	0.0
Shanghai	8.75	0.78	0.537	0.326	0.040	3.35	1.0
Jiangsu	17.66	0.48	0.572	0.664	0.019	2.56	1.0
Zhejiang	21.52	0.45	0.652	0.664	0.013	2.46	1.0
Anhui	15.51	0.70	0.534	1.239	0.005	2.32	0.0
Fujian	20.41	0.61	0.634	1.270	0.137	2.37	1.0
Jiangxi	15.32	0.74	0.477	1.278	0.015	2.39	0.0
Shangdong	19.15	0.56	0.538	0.812	0.025	2.44	1.0
Henan	16.62	0.69	0.501	0.929	0.008	2.31	0.0
Hubei	15.74	0.71	0.493	0.873	0.024	2.47	0.0
Hunan	15.56	0.71	0.452	0.962	0.017	2.39	0.0
Guangdong	21.22	0.54	0.652	0.993	0.196	2.50	1.0
Guangxi	16.30	0.77	0.589	1.295	0.033	2.29	1.0
Sichuang	16.79	0.72	0.489	0.992	0.015	2.32	0.0
Guizhou	16.57	0.81	0.422	1.553	0.008	2.19	0.0
Yunnan	17.40	0.81	0.504	1.255	0.005	2.31	0.0
Shaanxi	14.84	0.78	0.484	1.268	0.008	2.41	0.0
Gansu	12.97	0.86	0.252	1.354	0.005	2.47	0.0

Qinghai	13.44	0.84	0.351	3.436	0.000	2.52	0.0
Ningxia	14.38	0.83	0.287	2.988	0.003	2.45	0.0
Xinjiang	19.52	0.88	0.474	2.645	0.018	2.44	0.0

Notes: GR = annual average growth rate of per capita income between 1980 and 1991;
ONS = share of state-owned enterprises in total industrial output, average of 1980 and 1991;
LIT = share of light industry in total industrial output, average of 1980 and 1991;
SRR = (revenue – expenditure)/revenue, average of 1983 and 1991;
FCR = actual foreign investment/total fixed investment, average of 1983 and 1991;
PNI = per capita national income in 1980;
DM = 1 for Liaoning, Tianjin, Shandong, Jiangsu, Shanghai, Zhejiang, Fujian, Guangdong and Guangxi; DM = 0 for other provinces.
Tibet and Hainan are not included because of missing data.
Sources: State Statistical Bureau, 1992; MOF, 1988, 1992.

Notes

1 Introduction and Overview

1. Unless otherwise stated, statistics cited in this chapter are from various issues of *China Statistical Yearbook*.
2. One should note, of course, that despite its outstanding growth performance, China is still a low income country. Its per capita GDP – when converted into US$ using the annual average exchange rate – was US$620 in 1995, and ranked 116th among the 166 countries listed in the World Bank's *World Development Report 1997* (World Bank, 1997). In purchasing power parity terms, which take into account different currencies' purchasing powers on both tradable and non-tradable goods, China's per capita GDP was about US$2920 and ranked 82nd among 141 nations.
3. While I agree with some scholars that China's officially reported statistics in certain areas may be of limited quality, evidence based on measures of physical output and consumption suggests that the possible statistical errors would not significantly alter the general assessment of China's growth performance between 1978 and 1997.
4. In 1997, per capital disposable income of rural residents was Y2090 (US$252), and that of urban residents was Y5160 (US$622).
5. The officially measured poverty incidence uses a poverty line set by the Chinese government. International comparison is made difficult, if not impossible, by the fact that different countries apply different poverty lines.
6. From 1952 to 1977, the annual average growth rate of China's national income was 5.7 per cent (State Statistical Bureau, 1987).
7. In 1995, government procured grain at the contracted prices was about 20 per cent of total grain production (Rural Development Department of Development Research Center of the State Council, 1995).
8. Xiao (1993) reached a similar conclusion with an analysis on the relationship between the share of non-state sector activities and productivity growth.
9. From 1989 to 1995, the average annual inflation rate of CEE and FSU countries was 106 per cent, with some countries experiencing an average annual rate of nearly 1000 per cent (World Bank, 1996c).
10. For example, in most of 1980s, SOEs were obliged to sell certain amounts of their products to designated buyers at the official prices but were allowed to sell the above quota portions at the higher, market prices.
11. By the end of 1997, China consisted of 33 provincial level jurisdictions, including 23 provinces, 4 cities directly under the State Council, 5 autonomous regions, and Hong Kong Special Administrative Region.
12. Calculated using data from 'Compilation of Historical Statistics of Chinese Provinces, Autonomous Areas, and Municipalities 1949–1989' based on provincial yearbooks, and *China Statistical Yearbooks* (various issues). For some years, the sum of provincial real GDP data differs slightly from the national GDP figure.

13. Note that in 1994 China's total GDP was only around 2.5 per cent of the world's total GDP.

2 Fiscal Reform

1. There were four special levies on profits (Tseng *et al.*, 1994): (1) mandatory contributions to the key energy and transportation projects fund (earmarked for financing public infrastructure projects); (2) mandatory contributions to the state budget regulating fund (to compensate the government for revenue shortfalls resulting from the use of fixed-tax contracts, discretionary tax relief, and deduction of the principal repayments on loans); (3) a construction tax (designed to influence the aggregate level and allocation of investment by levying different tax rates on different forms of investment; this was replaced by the investment direction tax, applying only to SOEs, in 1991); and (4) wage adjustment and bonus tax, which applied to SOE wage and bonus increases in excess of the state-prescribed norm. All enterprises, regardless of ownership or circumstances, were subject to the first three levies.

2. Turnover taxes included the product tax, value-added tax, and business tax. These taxes were not included in the fiscal contract, and were collected regardless of whether or not the enterprises were profitable.

3. I agree with some scholars that the decline in SOEs' profitability could be partly explained by the increased competition from non-state owned enterprises, as evidenced by the fact that profitability declined in both SOEs and non-SOEs. However, the incentive problem inherent in SOEs did explain its poorer performance compared with other enterprises: according to Chen *et al.* (1996), in 37 out of 40 sectors, the percentages of SOEs operating at a loss were significantly higher than those of collectively owned enterprises in 1993.

4. This reduction did not significantly change the effective income tax rate for SOEs, however. According to one estimate, the effective income tax rate on SOEs (as implemented under the contract system) in 1993 was about 32.5 per cent due to various tax exemptions and reductions (private correspondence with staff of the MOF).

5. For a detailed discussion of China's central–provincial fiscal relations, see Ma (1997a).

6. The central–local fiscal system adopted in 1988 was named The Big (comprehensive) Fiscal Contract System. The rest of this chapter broadly refers to all variants of the decentralized fiscal system adopted since 1980 as the 'fiscal contract system'.

7. The method of determining local government revenues since 1994 is as follows. First, a local government would continue to remit/receive the contracted remittance/contracted subsidy to/from the centre as stipulated in the 1993 contract. Secondly, the centre would return the 1993 base figure (defined as the consumption tax-equivalent raised in 1993 plus 75 per cent of VAT-equivalent raised in 1993, adjusted for a number of revenue sharing items in 1993) to the local government. Thirdly, after 1994, the amount returned from the centre to a local government is to increase from the 1993 base figure by 0.3 per cent for each percentage increase in the national total of VAT and consumption tax (this formula was later changed into one relating the returned revenue to the total of a locality's VAT and consumption tax). For

a detailed description of how to calculate local revenues since 1994, see Zhang (1995).

8. In designing the 1994 reform, the centre expected that its share in total budgetary revenue would continue to increase over the next few years, as the centre would retain 70 per cent of any percentage increase in VAT proceeds.

9. With the State Council's special permission, Shanghai's basic pension fund is also invested, through Pudong Development Bank, in long-term capital projects.

10. Extra-budgetary revenues are obtained by government units using coercive power but are not included in the formal budget system. They include various surcharges, revenues from provision of services, service fees charged by government agencies, revenues of schools, income from revenue-sharing with other governments, etc. In theory, extra-budgetary revenues are collected based on regulations promulgated by the central or provincial level governments. Off-budget revenues are collected by government units, particularly township and village level governments, without the authorization from the central or provincial level governments. For a more detailed discussion on extra-budgetary and off-budgetary activities, see Arora and Norregaard (1997).

11. Estimates of Mr Fan Gang, China Academy of Social Science.

12. One can define models of intergovernmental relations in many different ways: a centralized versus a decentralized model (using indicators such as the share of local government revenue and expenditure in total government revenue and expenditure), a federal versus a unitary model (where the central government has the power to create and/or abolish subnational government units), an autonomous versus an integrated model (whether the local authorities exercise substantial autonomy in local affairs or not). The model classifications used in this chapter differ from the above. The distinctions among my three models are given in Table 2.5 and should not be confused with definitions from other sources. Although the central government has many discretionary powers in defining central–local relations, it is worth mentioning that China's fiscal system is a highly decentralized one when measured by the share of local expenditure in total government expenditure.

13. When discussing the cases of the United States and Canada, 'local governments' refer to governments at levels lower than the states or provinces. On other occasions, 'local governments' refer to subnational governments.

3   Monetary Reform

1. See Ma (1996b) for detailed discussions on localities' strategic behaviour in forcing the central bank to grant higher credit ceilings.

2. In an economy with strict foreign exchange controls (stable foreign exchange rate is achieved by restrictions on both current and capital account transactions), the central bank's control over domestic credit is sufficient to achieve its target for money supply.

3. See Chapter 4 for more discussion on commercial bank restructuring.

4. Data for 1980–93 are used and are taken from State Statistical Bureau (1993) and (1994). Government borrowings from the central bank are 'hard' deficits in the Chinese definition (see State Statistical Bureau 1994, pp. 213–14).

5. The dollar/yuan exchange rate increased moderately from 1:8.7 by the end of 1993 to 1:8.44 by the end of 1994 and 1:8.30 by the end of 1995.

6. According a recent article (*People's Daily*, 29 July 1996), the PBC would: (1) concentrate funds to support 300 key enterprises that produce marketable products, make profits, and have the ability to repay loans; (2) increase the amount of export credit to support SOE exports; and (3) support SOE restructuring and help SOEs reduce their debt–service ratio.

4 Banking Reform: From Administrative Control to a Regulatory Framework

1. Recently, foreign exchange business was allowed in many other specialized banks, such as the Agricultural Bank, the Industrial and Commercial Bank, and the Construction Bank.
2. During this period, this bank continued to operate in Hong Kong.
3. As of 1997, the rules regulating foreign banks' RMB business were very restrictive. In terms of their scope, these banks could take deposits, make loans, provide settlement services, provide guarantees, invest in government bonds and other securities, and conduct other approved businesses. But the licences generally limited the foreign banks to businesses with foreign-invested enterprises and foreign individuals residing in China for more than one year. They could, with PBC approval, engage in very limited business with SOEs. They were only allowed to deal in RMB with entities and individuals based in Shanghai, and their local currency liabilities could not exceed 35 per cent of their total foreign exchange liabilities (Chang, 1997).
4. The first private bank, China Minsheng Bank, was approved by the State Council and the PBC in 1995. This bank is a nationwide shareholding bank, with all its shareholders being members of the All-China Federation of Industry and Commerce. The main objective of this bank is to alleviate the shortage of funds facing private enterprises. See 'State Council Approves First Private Bank', *China Daily Report*, FBIS-China-95–1091, 25 May 1995.
5. Correspondence with Chinese officials.
6. See 'Commercial Bank Law', *China Daily Report*, FBIS-CHI-94–094, 16 May 1995.
7. Other prudential ratios imposed on commercial banks include the following: the ratio of medium-term loans to medium-term deposits should be no more than 120 per cent; a bank's excess reserves with the PBC should be at least 5 to 7 per cent of total deposits; a bank can borrow or lend no more than 4 per cent and 8 per cent, respectively, on the interbank market in relation to its total deposits; a bank's overdue loans and bad loans cannot exceed 8 per cent and 2 per cent of its total loans, respectively; a bank's external borrowing cannot exceed 100 per cent of its capital; and a bank's external lending, external capital and external remittances cannot exceed 30 per cent of its foreign assets.
8. Evidence from developed countries suggests that banking systems with high levels of concentration tend to have lower margins and operating costs as well as higher profits. Most European countries opted for universal banks on the grounds that to restrict function would put its system at a competitive disadvantage with banks from other countries that allow universal banking. Canada recently allowed its banks to enter the securities business and over a short period of time banks came to dominate the business.

9. In Japan, a single bank's holding of a single firm's shares is limited to 5 per cent. In Germany, the relationship between banks and industry is not burdened at all by regulations (Prowse, 1994).
10. The CEOs dismissed included those of the Shenzhen Development Bank and the Shanghai Branch of the Bank of Industry and Commerce (Xinhua News Agency, 1997).
11. Correspondence with Professor Yu Li, Dongbei University of Finance and Economics.
12. Correspondence with Chinese bank officials.

5   Development of the Stock Markets

1. This chapter is based on a joint paper prepared by Dr Kenneth C. Xu and myself.
2. *Shanghai Securities Daily*, 26 December 1997.
3. Taiwan Economic Journal China Database, Internet.
4. *Shanghai Securities Daily*, 26 December, 1997.
5. Taiwan Economic Journal China Database, Internet.
6. In 1995, no new quota was issued due to the bearish market.
7. See 'Forget the Fundamentals', in *China Trade Report*, February 1992.
8. Ibid.
9. This section is largely based on Chan (1994). I would like to thank the Editorial Department of *International Financial Law Review* for permission to use these materials.
10. *The Economist*, 25 January 1992, p. 82.
11. A major concern about the recent future of the stock markets is the need to finance a massive and growing budget deficit. Since 1994, the fiscal and monetary reform has disallowed direct borrowing of the MOF from the PBC to cover fiscal deficits, and all deficits should be financed by bond issuance. In 1995, China issued a record Y150 billion in treasury bonds, up from Y104 billion in 1994. The new issues nearly doubled China's cumulative treasury bonds issue. By limiting the variety of new investment alternatives such as stocks, the central government attempts to ensure the success of these treasury bond issues.

6   State-owned Enterprise Reform

1. All figures in this chapter, unless otherwise noted, are from *China Statistical Yearbook* (various issues).
2. Among the reasons suggested are (1) government intervention (into production planning, price setting, marketing, etc.); (2) government protection (soft budget constraint); (3) unfavourable tax policies and excessive charges and fees; and (4) state ownership.
3. Although initial experiments of the shareholding system started in the mid-1980s, the number of SOEs involved was very small until the early 1990s.
4. See *Provisional Regulation of State Assets Management in Enterprise Experimenting Joint Stock System*, issued by the State Assets Management Bureau and Economic System Reform Commission, 27 July 1992.
5. See Labor Department and State Economic System Reform Commission (1992).

6. Economic System Reform Commission (1992a) and (1992b).
7. It was officially reported that the plan to turn Maanshan Steel Company to a joint stock company was aimed at raising enough funds for its expansion goal of producing 6 million tons of pig iron and the same amount of steel annually by the year 2000. See FBIS, *China*, 3 June 1993.
8. The rest of the chapter is based on Yu and Ma (1998).
9. The notion of a modern enterprise system can be viewed as a continuation and extension of the shareholding experiment to the entire SOE sector in two senses. First, corporatized former SOEs will include both joint stock companies (shareholding companies) and solely state-owned corporations. Secondly, corporatization will be introduced to both large and small SOEs.
10. In 1997, total initial public offerings amounted to Y130 billion (Zhou, 1998).
11. Moreover, they must be nominated by the party committees at the same level.
12. See Yu and Ma (1998) for detailed case studies.
13. This classification could be viewed as over-simplifying compared with many countries' actual practices, but it may be necessary for crafting an analytical framework.
14. In Western Europe, the average of SOEs' share in GDP is about 5 per cent (France, Austria and Italy have higher shares). In addition to some government enterprises providing pure public goods and services, most SOEs exist in monopolistic sectors such as water, electricity, telecommunications, and transportation. A smaller proportion of SOEs exist in competitive sectors. In Japan, most public corporations also exist in infrastructure sectors with a monopolistic nature.
15. TVEs consist of collective, partnership and individually owned enterprises in the rural area.
16. Adjusted for inflation.
17. The coverage of TVEs was broadened slightly in statistics since 1984. TVE figures for 1978–83 include only township and village level enterprises; since 1984, they cover all enterprises at and below the township and village level, including privately owned enterprises and foreign-funded enterprises.
18. In 1997 and early 1998, the growth of the TVE sector slowed significantly. Duenwald (1998) argues that this is partly a correction to previous years' extraordinarily high growth rates, due to increased competition (including from reformed SOEs) and oversupply in the light industrial sectors.
19. Most TVEs are collectively owned.
20. The 55 per cent income tax rate applied to large and medium-sized SOEs was reduced to 33 per cent in 1994.
21. See UNIDO (1992).

7 Export Promotion Strategies

1. Thomas and Wang (1993) presents a cross-country econometric study that shows a positive relationship between the openness of an economy and its growth performance. China is no exception.
2. MOFERT was later renamed as Ministry of Foreign Trade and Economic Cooperation (MOFTEC).

3. Foreign-invested enterprises are automatically granted the right to export their own products and import their inputs.
4. By the end of 1997, China had 113 800 SOEs and 465 000 non-SOEs at and above the township level (State Statistical Bureau, 1997a).
5. The validity of this argument is questionable, however, given the fact that already more than 12 000 FTCs and domestic manufacturing enterprises and some 200 000 foreign-invested enterprises have the right to trade and competition in most sectors is keen.
6. China's progress in trade liberalization was also reflected by the rapid reduction in import tarrifs in recent years. In December 1992, China's average tarrif rate was reduced from 53 per cent to 40 per cent. It was further reduced to 36 per cent in December 1993, 23 per cent in April 1996, and 17 per cent in early 1998 (Chinese News Agency, 1998). The government announced that China's average tariff rate would be reduced to 15 per cent by 2000 and 10 per cent by 2005.
7. See Chapter 8 for details on these policies.
8. One should not overestimate the impact of RMB devaluation at the end of 1993 as about 80 per cent of transactions were already carried out at the more depreciated market rate before the exchange rate unification.
9. The seven border provinces are: Jilin, Heilongjiang, Inner Mongolia, Xinjiang, Gansu, Tibet, Yunnan, and Guangxi.

8 Regional Policy under the Strategy of Economic Opening

1. Guangdong's per capita national income was Y313 in 1978, close to the country's average of Y315 (State Statistical Bureau, 1989).
2. In 1978, per capita national income in Fujian was only Y233. It ranked 25th among the 29 provinces and well below the country' average of Y315 (State Statistical Bureau, 1989).
3. See 'Shenzhen forms its New Price System', *China Daily*, 4 July 1992.
4. See 'Regulations on Special Economic Zones in Guangdong Province', in *Almanac of China's Economy 1981*, The Economic Research Center of the State Council, 1981.
5. Equity joint ventures (*Hezi Jingying*) are limited liability corporations in which Chinese and foreign partners invest jointly in and operate a corporation, share the profits, losses and risks. Contractual joint ventures (*Hezuo Jingying*) can involve the foreign partner providing technology, and a capital share. Foreign investors are repaid on a schedule of return negotiated beforehand. The Chinese partner usually provides land, materials, the work force, basic buildings, and services, etc. Wholly foreign-owned ventures(*Duzi Jingying*) enterprises are wholly owned and operated by the foreign investors.
6. 'Regulation Concerning Preferential Tax Policy in the SEZs and 14 Coastal Cities', in *The China Investment Guide*, 4th edn, CITIC Publishing House, 1989.
7. From 1979 to 1983 the total pledged foreign direct investment in the three SEZ, including Shenzhen, Zhuhai and Xiamen, accounted for more than 60 per cent of the national total.

8. Tract development is to lease a tract of land to foreign investors and allow them develop the land and sell the land-use rights. According to a regulation regarding tract development, the maximum length of lease is 70 years.
9. Interview with officials of Special Economic Zone Office.
10. By May 1996, these zones included Waigaoqiao Free Trade Zone, Lujiazui Finance and Trade Zone, Jinqiao Export Processing Zone, and Zhangjiang Hi-Tech Park.
11. China's 30 provincial level juridictions (including provinces, autonomous regions, and municipalties directly under the central government) are often classified into three geographical groups: coastal, middle, and western regions. The 11 coastal provinces and municipalities include Liaoning, Tianjin, Hebei, Shangdong, Jiangsu, Shanghai, Zhejiang, Fujian, Guangdong, Guangxi, and Hainan. Provinces in the middle and western regions are referred to as inland provinces.
12. In July 1991 tax policy for foreign investment was unified across types of foreign-invested enterprises.
13. The inland cities of Chongqing, Harbin, Jinan, Shenyang, Wuhan and Xi'an may also approve projects valued up to US$5 million independent of the provinces in which they are located.
14. The annual average growth rates were calculated using provincial level GDP data from provincial statistical yearbooks. The implied growth rate for China as a whole is slightly different from that based on the national GDP data from *China Statistical Yearbook*.
15. See 'The State Council's Decision Concerning the Main Points of Current Industrial Policies', *People's Daily*, 18 March 1989.
16. See 'Provisional Regulations of Fixed Investment Direction Adjustment Tax of People's Republic of China', *People's Daily*, 19 May 1991.
17. According to these guidelines, China would encourage foreign investment in agriculture, energy, communications, raw materials, advanced technology and resource utilization. Recent evidence shows that China would also further open to foreign investors the service sectors, including wholesales, retails, information services, legal and accountancy, banking and other financial services.
18. Interview with officials of the Special Economic Zone Office.
19. State Council's SEZ Office.
20. See 'Tianjin Municipality Succeed in Transforming Administration Efficiency', *People's Daily*, 30 May 1992.
21. See 'Shenzhen Simplifies Import Procedures', *People's Daily*, 30 May 1992.
22. The United States–China Business Council claims that it will raise the cost of doing business in China by 28 per cent. See 'How and Why to Survive Chinese Tax Torture', *The Economist*, 2 December 1995, pp. 63–4.
23. The abolition of the import duty exemption and the reduction of VAT rebate in 1996 was reversed in early 1998 as China's export sector and foreign capital inflow were under pressures from other Asian countries' currency devaluation.
24. See 'How and Why to Survive Chinese Tax Torture', *The Economist*, 2 December 1995, pp. 63–4.
25. State Council announcement on 'Increase the Project Approval Right for Foreign-Invested Projects in Inland Provinces, Autonomous Regions, and other State Agencies', 22 August 1996.

9   Decentralization and Provinces' Growth Performance

1. Coefficient of variation is defined as standard deviation divided by mean. It is designed to measure the extent of disparity across observations.
2. Hu Angang, as a representative of this view, has forcefully argued against the continuation of special policies for coastal regions, and proposed that equal-footing competition be essential to reducing regional disparities.
3. This section is based on a revised version of my study on the same subject, which was included in Bell *et al.* (1993) as an appendix. Another recent study (Husain, 1998) on China's provinces' growth performance reports some similar results, and also finds that the relationship between the size of the agricultural sector and overall real GDP growth has changed over time.
4. In order to capture the degree of decentralization, ideally, an indicator should be used to describe the relative importance of centrally owned enterprises versus locally owned enterprises. Unfortunately, data for constructing such an index are not available.

Bibliography

Agarwala, R. (1992) *China: Reforming Intergovernmental Fiscal Relations*, World Bank Discussion Paper No. 178 (Washington, DC: World Bank).

Alesina, A. and Summers, L. (1993) 'Central Bank Independence and Macroeconomic Performance: Some Comparative Evidence', *Journal of Money, Credit, and Banking*, vol. 25, no. 2, pp. 151–62.

Aoki, M. and Qian, Y. (1995) *Corporate Governance in Transitional Economies: Insider Control and the Role of Banks* (Beijing: China Economic Management Press).

Arora, V. and Norregaard, J. (1997) 'Intergovernmental Fiscal Relations: The Chinese System in Perspective', IMF Working Paper No. WP/97/129 (Washington, DC: International Monetary Fund).

Bell, M., Khor, H., Kochhar, K., Ma, J., N'guiamba, S. and Lau, R. (1993) *China at the Threshold of Market Economy*, Occasional Paper No. 107 (Washington, DC: International Monetary Fund).

Blanchard, O. and Fischer, S. (1989) *Lectures on Macroeconomics* (Cambridge, Massachusetts: The MIT Press).

Boardman, H. (1995) *Meeting the Challenge of Chinese Enterprise Reform*, World Bank Discussion Paper No. 283 (Washington, DC: World Bank).

Boardman, H. (1996) 'Foreign Direct Investment Policy in China', mimeo, China and Mongolia Department, World Bank.

Burgess, R. and Stern, N. (1993) 'Taxation and Development', *Journal of Economic Literatures*, no. 31, pp. 761–830.

Burke, F. (1991) 'New Business on the Bund', *The China Business Review* (May–June), pp. 22–9.

Cardoso, E. and Yusuf, E. (1994) 'Red Capitalism: Growth and Inflation in China', *Challenge* (May–June), pp. 49–56.

Chan, T (1992) 'Now It's the Peking Bourse', *China Trade Report* (December), p. 10.

Chan, G. (1994) 'China', *International Financial Law Review (Special Issue: Capital Markets Yearbook 1994)*, October, pp. 20–30.

Chang, G. (1997) 'China', *International Financial Law Review* (London) July, pp. 21–5.

Chen, J. (1998) 'Report on the Implementation of National Economic and Social Development Plan in 1997', *People's Daily* (overseas edition), 7 March, p. 4.

Chen, J. and Fleisher, B. (1995) 'Forces Impinging on Convergence and Divergence in China's Regional Economic Growth', Paper presented in the 1995 annual meeting of Association for Asian Studies, 5–9 April, Washington, DC.

Chen, L., Deaves, R. and Wang, C. (1992) 'An Analysis of Money and Output in the Industrial Sector in China', *Journal of Asian Economy*, vol. 3, no. 2, pp. 271–80.

Chen, X., Ding, N. and Zhang, J. (1996) 'A Study on External Enviroment of State Enteprise Reform', in Ma, H. and Sun, S. (eds), *China Development Studies 1996* (Beijing: China Development Press).

Chen, Y. (1991) 'New Developments in Mainland China's Securities Market', *Issues & Studies: A Journal of Chinese Studies and International Affairs (Taiwan)* no. 27 (August), pp. 82–103.

Cheng, E. (1991a) 'Share of the Action', *Far Eastern Economic Review*, 31 January, p. 34.

Cheng, E. (1991b) 'Small Leap Forward', *Far Eastern Economic Review*, 18 July, pp. 69–70.

China Economic Monitoring Center (1998) 'Major National Economic Indicators of December 1997', *Economic Daily (Jin Ji Ri Bao)*, 8 February, p. 2.

Chinese News Agency (1998) 'China Will Continue to Reduce Its Import Tariffs', *Xinmin Evening News*, 19 February, p. 1.

Chow, G. (1987) 'Money and Price Level Determination in China', *Journal of Comparative Economics*, vol. 11, pp. 319–33.

CITIC (1989) *The China Investment Guide*, 4th edn (Beijing: CITIC Publishing House).

Clemens, S. and Hichman, M. (1992) 'What Protection for Investors in Chinese B Shares?', *International Financial Law Review (UK)*, No. 11 (July), pp. 26–30.

Clifford, M. (1992) 'After Shenzhen Chaos', *Far Eastern Economic Review*, 27 August, p. 53.

Dai, X. (1998) 'Appropriately Increase Money Supply (Address at the Press Conference of the First Plenary Session of Ninth National People's Congress)', *People's Daily* (overseas edition), 9 March, p. 4.

Development Research Center of the State Council (1991) *The Almanac of China's Economy 1991* (Beijing: Economic Management Press).

Du, H. (1993) 'The Economic Development and Structural Reform of Shenyang', background report prepared for the World Bank, mimeo.

Duenwald, C. (1998) 'China's Collective Sector: Recent Developments and Future Challenges', International Monetary Fund, mimeo.

Economic Research Center of the State Council (1981) *The Almanac of China's Economy 1981* (Beijing: Economic Management Press).

Economic System Reform Commission (1992a) 'Proposed Norms of Limited Liability Stock Companies', *People's Daily*, 20 June.

Economic System Reform Commission (1992b) 'Standards for Limited Liability Stock Companies', *People's Daily*, 20 June.

Editorial Board of Fiscal Yearbook of China (1995) *Fiscal Yearbook of China 1995* (Beijing: Editorial Board of Journal of China's Public Finance).

Editorial Board of Fiscal Yearbook of China (1996) *Fiscal Yearbook of China 1996* (Beijing: Editorial Board of Journal of China's Public Finance).

Editorial Department of Almanac of China's Finance and Banking (1996) *Almanac of China's Finance and Banking 1996* (Beijing: China Financial Publishing House).

Fan, G. (1989) 'Reform, Adjustment, Growth, and Friction Inflation', *Economic Research (Jingji Yanjiu)*, no. 1, pp. 13–25.

Fan, G. (1996) 'Market-Oriented Economic Reform and Growth of "Off-Budget" Local Public Finance', Chinese Academy of Social Science, draft.

Fan, G., Zhang S. and Wang L. (1993) 'Dual-Track Transition and Dual Track Regulation and Control – A Study of the Characteristics of Economic Fluctuations in China Since the Beginning of the Reforms (Part I)', *Economic Research (Jin Ji Yan Jiu)*, no. 10 (October).

FBIS (1993) 'Bank Official Views Upcoming Monetary Reform', FBIS-CHI, *Daily Report China*, 13 December.

Feltenstein, A. and Ha, J. (1989) 'Measurement of Repressed Inflation in China: The Lack of Coordination Between Monetary Policy and Price Control', Working Paper of Department of Economics, University of Kansas.

Feltenstein, A. and Ziba, F. (1987) 'Fiscal Policy, Monetary Target, and the Price Level Determination in a Centrally Planned Economy: An Application to the Case of China', *Journal of Money, Credit, and Banking*, vol. 19, no. 2, pp. 137–56.

Gao, D. (1998) 'Banks and Enterprises: Equal Treatment and Mutually Beneficial', *Economic Daily (Jin Ji Ri Bao)*, 12 February.

Gao, F. and Lu, B. (1992) 'Ten Major Cities Along Yangtze River All Opened Up', *People's Daily*, 6 June.

Garnaut, R. and Ma, G. (1993) 'Economic Growth and Stability in China', *Journal of Asian Economics*, vol. 4 (Spring), pp. 5–24.

Guangdong Statistical Bureau (1997) *Guangdong Statistical Yearbook 1997* (Guangzhou: Guangdong Statistical Press).

Guo, W. (1988) 'The Transformation of Chinese Regional Policy', *Development Policy Review*, vol. 6, no. 1, pp. 29–50.

Han, Z. (1997) 'On Mechanisms of China's Stock Market', in Dong F., Li, Y. and Han, Z. (eds), *State Enterprises: Where Do You Go?* (Beijing: Economic Science Press).

Hong, G. (1992) 'Development of China's Securities Market', unpublished.

Hu, A. (1995) 'An Analysis on China's Regional Disparity', paper presented in the Conference on China's Economic Reform sponsored by the Washington Center for China Studies, Beijing, November 1995.

Hu, A. (1997) 'Opportunities and Challenges for China's Economic Development', *Boston Chinese News*, 26 December, 2 January 1998.

Husain, A. (1998) 'Economic Performance and Business Cycles in China's Provinces and Regions', International Monetary Fund, mimeo.

International Finance Corporation (1995) *Emerging Stock Markets Factbook 1995* (Washington, DC: International Finance Corporation).

International Finance Corporation (1996) *Emerging Stock Markets Factbook 1996* (Washington, DC: International Finance Corporation).

International Finance Corporation (1997) *Emerging Stock Markets Factbook 1997* (Washington, DC: International Finance Corporation).

International Finance Corporation (1998) *Emerging Stock Markets Factbook 1998* (Washington, DC: International Finance Corporation).

International Monetary Fund (1986) *A Manual on Government Finance Statistics* (Washington, DC: International Monetary Fund)

International Monetary Fund (1998) *International Finance Statistics: August 1998* (Washington, DC: International Monetary Fund).

Ishikawa, Y. (1989) 'Regional Economies and Government Finances', *China Newsletter*, no. 83, pp. 9–16.

Jefferson, G., Thomas, R. and Zheng, Y. (1992) 'Growth, Efficiency and Convergence in China's State and Collective Industry', *Economic Development and Cultural Change*, vol. 40, no. 2, pp. 239–66.

Jefferson, G. and Xu, W. (1994) 'Assessing Gains in Efficient Production among China's Industrial Enterprises', *Economic Development and Cultural Change*, vol. 42, no. 3, pp. 597–615.

Johnson, H. (1993) *Financial Institutions and Markets: A Global Perspective* (New York: McGraw-Hill, Inc.).

Karmel, S. (1994) 'Emerging Securities Market in China: Capitalism with Chinese Characteristics', *The China Quarterly* (UK), no. 140 (December), pp. 1105–20.

Kaye, L. (1992) 'Out of the Loop', *Far Eastern Economic Review*, 16 July, pp. 52–4.

Kong, F. (1998) 'Policy Recommendations on Implimentation of APEC Trade and Investment Liberalization and Economic and Technology Cooperation', in MOFTEC, *Trends and Hot Issues: China in the World Economy* (Beijing: China Foreign Trade and Economic Press).

Kueh, Y. (1987) 'Economic Decentralization and Foreign Trade Expansion in China', in Chai, J. and Leung, C. (eds), *China's Economic Reform* (Hong Kong: University of Hong Kong Press).

Kumar, A., Lardy, N., Albrecht, W., Chuppe, T., Selwyn, S., Perttunen, P. and Zhang, T. (1997) *China's Non-Bank Financial Insitutions*, World Bank Discussion Paper No. 358 (Washington, DC: World Bank).

Labor Department and Economic System Reform Commission (1992) 'Provisional Regulations of Labor and Wages in Trial Stock Companies', *People's Daily*, 13 July.

Lardy, N. (1994) *China in the World Economy* (Washington, DC: Institute of International Economics).

Li, B., Li, Y. and Ma, J. (1989) 'China Regional Economic Policy', State Council Development Research Center Report, mimeo.

Li, L. and Jiang, J. (1993) 'Li Lanqing Addresses Grain Procurement Meeting', *Daily Report: China*, Federal Broadcast Information Services, 28 May, pp. 35–6.

Li, P. (1996) 'Make an Effort to Further Improve the Work in the Special Economic Zones', *Economic Daily (Jin Ji Ri Bao)*, 3 April, p. 1.

Li, P. (1998) 'Report on the Work of the Government (Address at the 15th People's Congress)', *People's Daily*, 21 March, p. 1.

Li, P. and Deng, Z. (1996) 'China's Household Income Distribution and Policy Implications', in Ma, H., and Sun, S. (eds), *China Development Studies 1996* (Beijing: China Development Press).

Ling, M. (1992) 'Stock Watch', *China Trade Report* (September), p. 6.

Liu, G., Li, J. and Qiu, X. (1994) 'An Analysis and Forecast of China's Economic Situation', *Economic Research (Jin Ji Yan Jiu)*, no. 5 (May).

Liu, Y. (1996) '87.5 Million Employees Participate in the Pension System', *Xinmin Evening News*, 5 August, p. 1.

Long, A. (1993) 'Challenges of Shanghai Securities Markets', *Security Market Week*, 7 February, p. 19.

Lu, S. (1997) 'Features of Cooperative Shareholding Enterprises', *Xinmin Evening News*, 12 October, p. 18.

Lyons, T. (1990) 'Planning and Interprovincial Co-ordination in Maoist China', *The China Quarterly (UK)*, no. 121, pp. 36–60.

Ma, H. and Sun, S. (eds) (1996) *China Development Studies 1996* (Beijing: China Development Press).

Ma, J. (1989) 'Problems in Industrial Structural Change and the Direction of Reform', *Economic Theory and Economic Management (Jin Ji Li Lun Yu Jin Ji Guan Li)*, no. 1 (January).

Ma, J. (1992) 'China's Regional Policy and Its Macroeconomic Implications', Central Asian Department, International Monetary Fund, mimeo.

Ma, J. (1993) 'Reforming Corporate Governance Structure in China', Economic Development Institute, World Bank, mimeo.

Ma, J. (1994) 'Intergovernmental Fiscal Relations in Japan and Korea', paper prepared for the Senior Policy Seminar on Intergovernmental Fiscal Relations in China (12–17 September 1994, Dalian, China) jointly sponsored by Economic Development Institute of the World Bank and the Ministry of Finance, China. Also appear in Economic Development Institute Working Paper (No. 94–41), World Bank.

Ma, J. (1995a) 'Defining the Limits of Local Government Power in China', *The Journal of Contemporary China*, no. 10 (autumn), pp. 3–22.

Ma, J. (1995b) 'Modelling Central–Local Fiscal Relations in China', *China Economic Review*, vol. 6, no. 1, pp. 105–37.

Ma, J. (1995c) 'The Reform of China's Intergovernmental Fiscal Relations', *Asian Economic Journal*, vol. 9, no. 3 (November), pp. 205–32.

Ma, J. (1996a) 'Can Guangdong's Development Model be Replicated Elsewhere?' in Hu, J. *et al.* (eds) *In Search of A Chinese Road Towards Modernization – Economic and Educational Issues in China's Reform Process* (New York: Mellen University Press), pp. 89–108.

Ma, J. (1996b) 'China: Central Government Credibility and Economic Overheating', *Economic Systems*, vol. 19, no. 3 (September), pp. 237–61.

Ma, J. (1996c) 'China's Banking Sector: From Liberalization to a Regulatory Framework', *Journal of Contemporary China*, vol. 5, no. 12, pp. 155–69.

Ma, J. (1996d) 'China's Regional Policy under the Strategy of Economic Opening', *Regional Policy in the Environment of Globalization* (Brazil: Konrad-Adenauer-Stiftung and IPEA), pp. 51–73.

Ma, J. (1996e) 'Monetary Management and Intergovernmental Relations in China', *World Development*, vol. 24, no. 1 (January), pp. 145–53.

Ma, J. (1997a) *Intergovernmental Relations and Economic Management in China* (London: Macmillan Press).

Ma, J. (1997b) *Intergovernmental Fiscal Transfer in Nine Countries: Lessons for Developing Countries*, World Bank Policy Research Working Paper, No. 1822 (Washington, DC: World Bank).

Ma, J. and Chung, C. (1993) 'China's Stock Market: Challenges and Opportunities', *Asian Economies*, vol. 22, no. 3, pp. 34–50.

Ma, J. and Gang, Z. (1991b) 'Regional Comparative Advantage of Industrial Development in China', *Management World (Guan Li Shi Jie)*, no. 3, May.

Ma, J. and Li, Y. (1994) 'China's Regional Economic Policy: Effects and Alternatives', *Asian Economic Journal*, vol. 8, no. 1, pp. 39–58.

Ma, J. and Walker, D. (1993) 'China's Financial Development in a Reform Era', Georgetown University, Mimeo.

Ma, J. and Zou, G. (1991) 'On the Open Door Policy in China's Border Areas', *Economic Research (Jing Ji Yan Jiu)*, no. 3, pp. 61–70.

Mehran, H., Quintyn, M., Nordman, T. and Laurens, B. (1996) *Monetary and Exchange System Reforms in China: An Experiment of Gradualism*, IMF Occasional Paper No. 141 (Washington, DC: International Monetary Fund).

Mckinnon, R. (1993) 'China's Financial Development and Its Relevance for Transitional Economies', Stanford University Economics Department, draft.

Ministry of Finance (1988) *China Fiscal Statistics 1952–1987* (Beijing: China Fiscal Press).

Ministry of Finance (1992) *China Finance Statistics 1952–1991* (Beijing: China Fiscal Press).

Ministry of Foreign Trade and Economic Cooperation (MOFTEC) (1997) *White Paper on China's Foreign Economic and Trade Cooperation* (Beijing: China Foreign Economic and Trade Press).

Mintz, J. (1990) 'Corporate Tax Holidays and Investment', *The World Bank Economic Review*, vol. 4, no. 1, pp. 81–102.

Mooney, P. (1992) 'Irrational Rationing', *Far Eastern Economic Review*, 20 August, p. 65.

Murakami, N., Liu, D. and Otsuka, K. (1994) 'Technical and Allocative Efficiency among "Socialist" Enterprises: The Case of the Garment Industry in China', *Journal of Comparative Economies*, vol. 19, pp. 410–33.

National People's Congress (1995) 'Commercial Bank Law of the People's Republic of China', in Yuan, B. and Wang, D. (eds), *Finance and Credit* (Tianjin: Nakai University Press).

Naughton, B. (1992) 'Implications of State Monopoly Over Industry and Its Relaxation', *Modern China*, vol. 18, no. 1, pp. 14–41.

Naughton, B. (1995) 'China's Macroeconomy in Transition', *The China Quarterly*, no. 144, pp. 1083–104.

New World Times (1998), 'Zhu Rongju Says that Social Protection Must be Ensured', *New World Times* (11 September), p. 1.

Oksenberg, M. and Tong, J. (1991) 'The Evolution of Central–Provincial Fiscal Relations in China, 1971–1984: The Formal System', *The China Quarterly (UK)*, no. 125, pp. 1–32.

People's Bank of China (PBC) (1995) *China Financial Outlook 1995* (Beijing: People's Bank of China).

People's Bank of China (PBC) (1997) 'Circular on Prohibiting Bank Funds from Flowing to the Stock Market', *People's Daily* (overseas edition), 6 June.

People's Daily (1993) 'Vice Finance Minister Xiang Huicheng Speaks on Reform in Tax-Assignment System', *People's Daily* (Overseas Edition), 23 November.

People's Daily (1996) 'Ten Measures of the People's Bank of China to Support State-owned Enterprises', *People's Daily* (Overseas Edition), 29 July, p. 2.

People's Daily (1997a) 'China's Monetary Control Succeeded in 1996', *People's Daily* (Overseas Edition), 14 January, p. 1.

People's Daily (1997b) 'The Ninth Five Year Plan had a Good Start', *People's Daily* (Overseas Edition), 31 January, p. 1.

Peck, J. (1991) 'Standardizing Foreign Income Taxes', *The China Business Review* (September–October), pp. 12–15.

Perry, E. and Wong, C. (1985) *The Political Economy of Reform in Post-Mao China* (Cambridge, Massachusetts: Harvard University Press).

Polizatto, V. (1992) 'Prudential Regulation and Banking Supervision', in Vittas D. (ed.), *Financial Regulation: Changing the Rules of the Game*, EDI Development Studies (Washington, DC: World Bank)

Potter, P. (1991) 'Shanghai Securities Regulations', *East Asian Executive Reports*, 15 August, pp. 7–11.

Potter, P. (1992) 'Securities Markets Opening to Foreign Participation', 1 April, pp. 7–9.

Potter, P. (1993) 'China: PRC State Council Issues National Stock Regulations', *East Asian Executive Reports*, 15 July.

Prowse, S. (1994) 'Corporate Governance in an International Perspective: A Survey of Corporate Governance Mechanisms among Large Firms in the

United States, the United Kingdom, Japan, and Germany', *BIS Economic Review*, no. 41.

Qian, Y. (1993) 'Lessons and Relevance of the Japanese Main-Bank System for Financial System Reform in China', Department of Economics, Stanford University, mimeo.

Ross, S., Westfield, R. and Jaffe, J. (1988) *Corporate Finance* (Homewood, Illinois: Irwin).

Russell, R. (1985) 'Employee Ownership and Internal Governance', *Journal of Economic Behavior and Organization*, vol. 6. pp. 217–41.

Rural Development Department of Development Research Center of the State Council (1996) 'Recommendations on Rural Economic Reform in 1996 and the Ninth Five Year Plan,' in Ma, H. and Sun, S. (eds) *China Development Studies 1996* (Beijing: China Development Press).

Sachs, J. and Woo, W. (1994) 'Reform in China and Russia', *Economic Policy*, April, pp. 101–45.

Special Economic Zone (SEZ) Office (1996) 'Explanation on the Adjustment of Custom Duties', *People's Daily*, 1 April, p. 2.

Shale, T. (1994) 'Bulls Go Wild in China Shop', *Euromoney*, no. 306 (October).

Song, Haiyan (1998) 'Stock Returns and Volatility: An Empirical Study of Chinese Stock Markets', *International Review of Applied Economics*, vol. 12, no. 1, pp. 129–39.

Shenyang Municipal Government (1992) 'Interim Regulations of Experimenting Enterprise Shareholding System', 28 October .

Sicular, T. (1990) 'Plan, Market and Inflation: Potential Problems with China's Two-Track System', Discussion Paper No. 1501, Harvard Institute of Economic Research, Harvard University.

State Council (1992) 'Rules of Transforming Management of State Enterprises', *People's Daily*, 24 July.

State Council (1993) 'State Council's Decision Regarding the Implementation of Tax Assignment Fiscal Management System', 15 December.

State Council Special Economic Zones Office (1991) *An Introduction to China's Coastal Open Areas*, mimeo.

State Property Management Bureau, Economic System Reform Committee (1992) 'Provisional Regulations State Assets Management in Enterprises Experimenting Joint Stock System', *People's Daily*, 27 July.

State Property Management Bureau, Ministry of Finance and State Industrial and Commerce Administration Bureau (1992) 'Trial Measures of State Assets Registration', *People's Daily*, 5 July.

State Statistical Bureau (1987) *National Income Statistics, 1949–1985* (Beijing: State Statistical Press).

State Statistical Bureau (1988) *China Statistical Yearbook 1988* (Beijing: State Statistical Press).

State Statistical Bureau (1989) *Forty Years of China* (Beijing: State Statistical Press).

State Statistical Bureau (1991) *China Statistical Yearbook 1991* (Beijing: State Statistical Press).

State Statistical Bureau (1992) *A Statistical Survey of China 1992* (Beijing: State Statistical Press).

State Statistical Bureau (1993) *China Statistical Yearbook 1993* (Beijing: State Statistical Press).

State Statistical Bureau (1994) *China Statistical Yearbook 1994* (Beijing: State Statistical Press).

State Statistical Bureau (1995) *China Statistical Yearbook 1995* (Beijing: State Statistical Press).

State Statistical Bureau (1996) *China Statistical Yearbook 1996* (Beijing: China Statistical Press).

State Statistical Bureau (1997a) *China Statistical Yearbook 1997* (Beijing: China Statistical Press).

State Statistical Bureau (1997b) '13000 State-Owned Enterprises Will Go Bankrupt', *Xinmin Evening News*, 3 July, p. 1.

State Statistical Bureau (1998) *A Statistical Survey of China 1998* (Beijing: China Statistical Press).

Sven, H. (1988) 'Corporate Governance and the Role of the Board of Directors: The International Experience and Its Relevance for Enterprise Reform In China', mimeo, Industry, Trade and Finance Operation Division, China Department, World Bank.

Sze, J. (1993) 'The Allure of B Shares', *The China Business Review* (January–February), pp. 42–8.

Thomas, V. and Wang, Y. (1993) *The Lessons of East Asia: Government Policy and Productivity Growth* (Washington, DC: World Bank).

Tseng, W., Khor, H., Kochhar, K., Michaljek, D. and Burton, D. (1994) *Economic Reform in China: A New Phase* (Washington, DC: International Monetary Fund).

Tsui, K. (1991) 'China's Regional Inequality, 1952–1985', *Journal of Comparative Economics*, vol. 15, pp. 1–21.

Uekusa, M. (1989) 'The Privatization of Public Enterprises: Background and Results', in Imai, K. and Komiya, R. (eds.), *Business Enterprise in Japan: Views of Leading Japanese Economists* (Tokyo: Tokyo University Press).

United Nations Industrial Development Organization (UNIDO) (1992) *China: Towards Sustainable Industrial Growth*, Industrial Development Review Series, Blackwell Publishers.

Vittas, D. (ed.) (1992) *Financial Regulation: Changing the Rules of the Game*, EDI Development Studies (Washington, DC: World Bank).

Wang, G. (1996) 'China's Enterprise Financing and the Development of Capital Market', *Finance and Trade Economics (Cai Mao Jing Ji)*, no. 9, pp. 3–10.

Wang, Y. (1991) 'Government Reform, Fixed Capital Investment Expansion, and Inflation: A Behavior Model Based on the Chinese Experience', *China Economic Review*, vol. 2, no. 1 pp. 3–27.

Wang, Y. (1993) *Stock Market* (Shanghai: Shanghai People's Press).

Wang, Y. (1994) 'Eliminating Ignorance of Legal Knowledge; Reducing Risk Associated with Credit', *Financial Studies (Jinrong Yanjiu)*, no. 9, pp. 58–9.

Wang, L., Chen, X. and Yang, M. (1998) *Investment Banking Practices: Share Offering and Trading* (Shanghai: Lixing Accounting Press).

Wang, Z. (1998) 'How to Look At the Phasing Out of Credit Ceilings', *Economic Daily (Jin Ji Ri Bao)*, 11 February.

Wei, Y. (1985) 'Bring the Role of Coastal Cities into Full Display to Promote Economic and Technological Exchange with Foreign Counties', in MOFERT (ed.), *Guide to China's Foreign Economic Relations and Trade: Cities Newly Opened to Foreign Investors* (Hong Kong: Economic and Information Agency).

Woo, W., Fan, G., Hai, W. and Jin, Y. (1993) 'The Efficiency and Macroeconomic Consequences of Chinese Enterprise Reform', *China Economic Review*, vol. 4, no. 2, pp. 153–68.

World Bank (1988) *China: Finance and Investment* (Washington, DC: World Bank).

World Bank (1990) *China: Financial Sector Policies and Institutional Development* (Washington, DC: World Bank).

World Bank (1992) 'China: Budgetary Policy and Inter-governmental Relations', EA2CO, mimeo.

World Bank (1994a) *China: Internal Market Development and Regulations* (Washington, DC: World Bank).

World Bank (1994b) *China Foreign Trade Reform* (Washington, DC: World Bank).

World Bank (1995a) *China: The Emerging Capital Market*, China and Mongolia Department, mimeo.

World Bank (1995b) *Macroeconomic Stability in a Decentralized Economy* (Washington, DC: World Bank).

World Bank (1995c) *Bureaucrats in Business: The Economics and Politics of Government Ownership* (Oxford: Oxford University Press).

World Bank (1996a) *The Chinese Economy: Fighting Inflation, Deepening Reforms* (Washington, DC: World Bank).

World Bank (1996b) *China: Pension Reform* (Washington, DC: World Bank).

World Bank (1996c) *From Plan to Market: World Development Report 1996* (Washington, DC: World Bank).

World Bank (1997) *World Development Report 1997* (Washington, DC: World Bank).

Wu, J. and Lou, J. (1991) 'China: Inter-governmental Fiscal Relations and Macroeconomic Management', Paper for the Senior Policy Senimar on Macroeconomic Management, World Bank.

Xia, M., Lin, J. and Grub, P. (1992) *The Re-emerging Securities Market in China* (New York: Quorum Books).

Xie, P. (1995) 'Financial Services in China', United Nations Conference on Trade and Development, Working Paper No. 94.

Xiao, G. (1991) 'Managerial Autonomy, Fringe Benefits, and Ownership Structure: A Comparative Study of Chinese State and Collective Enterprises', *China Economic Review*, vol. 2, no. 1, pp. 47–74.

Xiao, G. (1993) 'Productivity Growth and Non-State Sector Development in China', mimeo, World Bank.

Xie, S. (1990) 'China's Stock Market: Problems and Future Development', *China Newsletter (Japan)*, No. 89 (November–December), pp. 18–25.

Xinhua News Agency (1997) 'Heads of Financial Institutions Penalized for Violating State Rules', *People's Daily* (overseas edition), 13 June, p. 1.

Xinhua News Agency (1998) 'China's SEZs Improve the Soft Environment for Foreign Investment', *People's Daily* (overseas edition), 1 April, p. 2.

Xu, K. and Ma, J. (1995) 'Price Behavior of China's Stock Markets', paper presented in the Ninth Annual Conference of the Chinese Economists Society, University of Michigan.

Xu, K. and Ma, J. (1996) 'How Does China's Stock Market Work?' Unpublished.

Xu, X. and Qian, Y. (1998) 'China Continues to Open its Financial Sector', *People's Daily* (overseas edition), 16 January, p. 1.

Xu, X. and Wang, Y. (1997) 'Ownership Structure, Corporate Governance, and Corporate Performance: the Case of Chinese Stock Companies', World Bank Policy Research Working Paper No. 1794.

Yan, Y. (1996) 'A New Way to Fund Social Security – Social Security Tax', *Economic Highlights*, 29 November, p. 2.

Yang, D. (1990) 'Patterns of China's Regional Development Strategy', *The China Quarterly*, no. 122, pp. 230–57.

Yang, D. (1995) 'Rural Industry and Regional Development Pattern', Paper presented in the 1995 annual meeting of Association for Asian Studies, 5–9 April, Washington, DC.

Yao, D. and Luo, Z. (1992) 'China to Open in All Directions', *People's Daily*, 5 June.

Yi, G. (1992) 'The Money Supply Mechanism and Monetary Policy in China', *Journal of Asian Economics*, vol. 3, no. 2, pp. 217–38.

Yi, G. (1994) *Money, Banking, and Financial Market in China* (Boulder, Colorado: Westview Press).

Yu, G. (1992) 'Problems with Shareholding System and the Impacts', *Economic Research (Jin Ji Yan Jiu)*, no. 9.

Yu, L. and Ma, J. (1998) 'China's SOE Reform and Corporate Governance Structure' (in Chinese), paper presented at the conference on China Economic Policy Study, sponsored by Washington Center for China Studies, Ford Foundation, and Natural Science Fundation of China (Beijing, June 1998).

Zhang, J. (1995) 'Tax Assignment System and Fiscal Reform', in Editorial Board of Finance Yearbook of China (ed.), *Finance Yearbook of China 1995* (Beijing: China Finance Journal).

Zhang, Q. (1994) 'The Technical Difficulties of Implementing Assets–Liability Ration Management System', *Financial Studies (Jin Rong Yan Jiu)*, no. 9, pp. 70–1.

Zhang, S. and Zhong, J. (1997) 'The Cumulative Effect of Reform and the Choice of Consistent Policies', *Economic Research (Jin Ji Yan Jiu)*, no. 9, pp. 3–12.

Zhang, T. (1996) 'Transitional Intergovernmental Fiscal Transfer Program', presentation at the Senior Policy Seminar on 'Intergovernmental Fiscal Transfers', sponsored by the Economic Development Institute of the World Bank and the Ministry of Finance of China, 10–12 October, Beijing.

Zhong, S. (1998) 'A Note on China's Stock Markets', Unpublished.

Zhong, W. (1995) 'The Macroeconomic Implications of Stock Markets in China', *Finance Studies (Jin Rong Yan Jiu)*, no. 10, pp. 71–5.

Zhou, L. (1998) 'China's SOE Reform Achieved New Progress', *People's Daily* (oversaes edition), 3 January, p. 1.

Zhou, Z. and Ou, Y. (1992) 'Hainan Establish Joint Office to Approve Foreign Invested Projects', *People's Daily*, 30 May.

Zou, G., Ma, J. and Wang, Z. (1990) 'China's Coastal Development Strategy and Pacific Rim Economic Integration', *Journal of East–West Studies*, no. 19, pp. 1–61.

Index